To
Stefano

OBSESSIONS
The Twisted Cruelty

Francesco Bisagni

Routledge
Taylor & Francis Group

LONDON AND NEW YORK

First published 2017 by Karnac Books Ltd.

Published 2018 by Routledge
2 Park Square, Milton Park, Abingdon, Oxon OX14 4RN
711 Third Avenue, New York, NY 10017, USA

Routledge is an imprint of the Taylor & Francis Group, an informa business

British Library Cataloguing in Publication Data

A C.I.P. for this book is available from the British Library

ISBN-13: 9781782205302 (pbk)

Cover image by Stefano Ardito

Typeset by Medlar Publishing Solutions Pvt Ltd, India

CONTENTS

PART IV
THE DEPRESSIVE THRESHOLD

ACKNOWLEDGEMENTS

All my patients and their families who inspired this book have taught me a lot over many years of my practice and deserve my gratitude. Their pain and endurance, their struggle with a paralysing sense of immobility, and their determination to engage me in an attempt to free their lives for development, have shown me a dimension of human nature that at times has had a tragic quality.

My gratitude also goes to all my colleagues and friends who have inspired and supported my efforts.

ABOUT THE AUTHOR

Francesco Bisagni, MD, a psychiatrist, was trained as a Jungian analyst in Italy and also, with the supervision of Michael Fordham and Rosemary Gordon, in London. He completed his training as a child and adolescent psychoanalytic psychotherapist according to the Tavistock Model at the Italian Association of Child Psychoanalytic Psychotherapy (AIPPI). He is currently a training analyst of the Society of Analytical Psychology (SAP) and registered at the British Psychoanalytic Council. He is a psychoanalyst of the National Association for the Advancement of Psychoanalysis (NAAP) in the United States. He is co-founder, training and supervising analyst, and currently chair of the Centre for Studies in Contemporary Psychoanalyses (CSPC) in Milan, where he lives and practises privately as a child and adult analyst and as a seminar leader. He has extensively taught and lectured internationally over the years, and he is author, co-author, and editor of many publications, including books and articles published in Italy and in the major analytic journals, including the *International Journal of Psycho-Analysis*, the *Journal of Analytical Psychology*, *Analytische Psychologie*, *Cahiers Jungiens de Psychanalyse*, *Revue de Psychologie Analytique*, and the *Journal of Child Psychotherapy*.

FOREWORD

In the treatment of rigid, controlling, severely obsessional patients, Dr Francesco Bisagni has evolved a remarkable multidimensional analytic approach. Through this text, we discover his impressive synthetic capacities as a theoretician as well as a clinician. It is evident from his case presentations that he has suffered considerably along with his patients through prolonged exposure to their symptoms, but also that he has undergone transformative experiences homologous to what they require through his masterful wrestling with countertransferential activations. The alchemical fires of these clinical encounters have rendered Dr Bisagni a true expert in the treatment of obsessional disorders; this book is the rare fruit of those efforts, offering the opportunity to learn from a master.

In the first section of the book, we are usefully introduced to the subtleties of differential diagnosis for the obsessional and compulsive disorders. Implications for clinical interventions follow from the structural understanding of the variants of these disorders such as OCD (obsessive–compulsive disorder), OCPD (obsessive–compulsive personality disorder), and ASD (autistic spectrum disorders). These in turn are distinguished from numerous other disorders that have some overlapping features, for example, body dysmorphic disorder, hoarding, trichotillomania, excoriation, and so forth. Key historical papers and pioneers of the field provide a range of theoretical frameworks, which are subsequently grounded in case studies. The author draws from the works of Sigmund Freud, Karl Abraham, Melanie Klein and the Kleinians, W. R. Bion, and C. G. Jung.

As a psychiatrist and psychoanalyst, Dr Bisagni presents a highly nuanced set of cases in which he serves in the roles of therapist/analyst, prescribing psychiatrist, and under select circumstances even combining both roles. Thus, we are provided with multipronged understandings and insights into psychosomatic as well as psychotherapeutic aspects of the treatment of severe obsessional cases. Cross comparison of the presented material helps the clinical reader obtain a well-rounded perspective on the different layers of body and mind requiring engagement for successful treatment.

In preparation for exploring the inner world of these patients, descriptions of the constraints they impose, consciously and unconsciously, upon the treatment relationship are discussed from several theoretical vertices. The modified analytic style Dr Bisagni has developed to cope with these patients is a complex blend of "rigour, flexibility, resilience, and liveliness", as he informs us. These traits are ever in flux and need to be modulated and fine-tuned to the treatment process as it goes through its gyrations. Often this entails holding on to small, almost microscopic gains in the moment, slowly stringing them together in a highly non-linear fashion to produce change over the course of long-term therapy. Attunement to slight changes in the unconscious alliances of the patient and their families provides warnings of resistance as well as pointing to directions eventually requiring exploration.

Symptoms of these disorders are known to hold psychological process in abeyance. Immobility and refusal of separateness give rise to a series of defensive mechanisms operating largely outside awareness but having a profoundly stagnating impact on any attempt at engagement. Therefore, we are necessarily taken through the ways displacement, isolation, and undoing operate in these disorders. In particular, the reader is shown how the tendency to isolate thoughts, especially from their affective roots, severs associative process, resulting in dislocated, unconnected thoughts that have a sort of amnestic feel about them. Consequently, the capacity for symbolisation is markedly impaired, and the patients are unable to employ metaphoric thinking, rather remaining stuck in the more concrete substitutions of metonymy, "based on contiguity". Analysing and working through of these thought patterns can, as shown here, gradually produce psychological transformation, for example, the capacity to productively dream and perform dream work, as discussed by Thomas Ogden (2003).

To better formulate the challenges facing the clinician, the author brings forward the innovations in understanding of transference dynamics described by Bion. The massive distortions of projective processes operating in these cases reveal how far from simple translation of historical events the re-enactments are. The difficulty penetrating such process is tied to Bion's caveat about opacity being an insidious state. The tendency to want to "do" something to make contact or link with the patient needs to be sufficiently resisted if the defences are to be successfully invited into the analysis.

The material on "Bionian and Jungian intersections" offers a pathway to connect an evolving theoretical framework with the contemporary paradigm shift being brought about by complexity studies. Recent Jungian forays into applications of complexity to Jungian thought have been quite productive, as summarised in the book. Building bridges to parallel ideas in Bion's opus, for example the link made here between the notion of mind as an emergent property (of the body, brain, environmental, linguistic, cultural field) and Bion's notion of the selected fact, show how both theorists were presciently proto-emergentists. The potential for convergence of aspects of their theories, at least to the point of a rich, dialectical engagement, is supported by the arguments offered.

Without overtly focusing on resistance to emergence, the description of the defences employed by obsessional patients described here do accurately point to anti-emergentist manoeuvres. The fear and anxiety activated by self-organising systems tending to engender emergent phenomena has rarely been discussed. The awe-inspiring features of self-organising transformations have tended to capture attention, whereas the distress and anguish caused by the thoroughly disruptive nature of such experiences has often been overlooked. The symmetry breaks required for increased complexity is a topic I have commented on briefly, including the distress this can cause those undergoing such a change (Cambray, 2009, pp. 57–67). I see the current work as offering an expanded clinical understanding of this darker, more difficult affective resistance to emergence; a development for which I am grateful.

Obsessional use of overvalued ideas that inhibit mental freedom and constrain the intersubjective space are presented in most of the cases.

Their countertransferential agonies are expressed in experiences and metaphors of asphyxiation, painful contortion, or twisted cruelty, enacted often in psychosomatic ways, with dangers of masochistic imprisonments and immobility for the unwary clinician. The willingness of the clinician to endure these rigours in seeking psychological improvement is a profoundly altruistic act, from which the reader may benefit and learn.

In moving his patients from stereotypic thoughts and action towards experiences of underlying unsaturated archetypal patterns, Dr Bisagni offers a vision of reparative reconstruction of the psyche. The potential for not only individual but cultural transformation seems implicit in these musings. The deeply emergentist view he holds, while kept quietly in the background, nevertheless moves understanding of severe obsessional disorders out of fated genetic endowment formulations into dispositional responses to the environment (internal as well as external). A measure of malleability can manifest in this view, offering cautious hope, as is exemplified by the cases presented.

The fleshing out of the primary theoretical reflections occupies the remainder of the book, Parts II, III, and IV. The pain, suffering, and degradation presented by the obsessional patients through the enactments in their therapies can be discomforting to imagine as one reads through the details. Nevertheless, the compassion, patience, and hard-won understanding, even when frustrated and inflamed, shown by Dr Bisagni through his well-timed interventions, offer supervisory solace to any clinician attempting to work with this patient population. I found reading this work to be quite impactful in my own practice.

Professor Joseph Cambray
Provost, Pacifica Graduate Institute
Carpinteria, California

INTRODUCTION

This is a collection of ordered, classified, and well-considered clinical material, and such books are rare in the Jungian tradition. Jungian analysts seldom write about the vicissitudes of work with patients, fearing that external factors might disrupt the delicate balance between conscious and unconscious in the therapeutic relationship. Writing in the Jungian tradition tends to frame the conscious and unconscious phenomena that emerge in the consulting room in terms of scientific, social, physical, metaphysical, and philosophical questions. Jung was interested in exploring the mind beyond what might be understood as the personal unconscious, searching for what he called the "collective unconscious". Recently, Jungian analysts have given much thought to attempting to reframe what we call the collective unconscious. This presents an important question: what do Jungian analysts do in the consulting room? How do they work with their patients? Where does the collective unconscious come about in their work?

This book engages the reader in thinking about defences of the mind and their vicissitudes in the consulting room. The reader is also challenged to think about the necessity of writing in general, and in particular writing about clinical material.

Why does one write? Writing is a vehicle of communication, clarification, and transformation. Writing helps to put a boundary around an experience so that, once it is contained and framed in a coherent way, it offers a platform from which the process of sharing can begin. Reading means opening up to an experience that is contained in a specific language, and if taken in, can change us profoundly. Specifically, this book is concerned with clinical work, with the relationship between two people who meet regularly in a consulting room, and how these meetings can produce profound changes in their psyches. Eventually, reading about this can change us, the readers, in a sort of parallel process.

Dr Bisagni is a psychiatrist, Jungian analyst, and Tavistock-trained child psychotherapist. His writing comes from an internal place of integration, in which many years of clinical experience have been ordered. He is also a gifted therapist who never loses his empathic stance. His writing touches upon the four functions of the mind as understood by Jung: thinking, feeling, sensation, and intuition. The reader will have to engage his whole mind with the written text to absorb the totality of the book's contents. Focused on obsessive–compulsive disorders, this is a contemporary book in which the psychoanalytic model, current developments in analytical psychology and in psychiatry are integrated in such a natural way that it will be essential for an engaged discourse about OCD in the future.

Obsessive–compulsive disorders encompass a great many symptoms, from the autistic spectrum to eating disorders to all sorts of phobias, and also including thought disorders and depression. Many people today suffer from some sort of obsessive–compulsive disorder, a complex pathology that is difficult to treat. Under the rubric "a thought is just a thought", popular psychology obscures the complexity of OCD and the suffering of people affected by it. In fact, the cases presented in this book show that the thought that provokes OCD is unconscious and remains isolated in the mind. Intrusive thoughts and their other manifestations are there to "cover" the real, secret, unknowable primitive thought that cannot become conscious. Sometimes intrusive thoughts contain in themselves a solution to the problem, but because they are taken by the thinker in a concrete way and not as a symbolic attempt of the mind to offer a solution, they can drive people to all sorts of behaviours, including suicide. Psychoanalytic psychotherapy is an effective treatment to help people suffering from OCD: it offers a space in which it is possible to gain an understanding of the unknown and haunting content that produces such thoughts. Understanding and meaning have a therapeutic and healing function. Psychoanalytic psychotherapy is a slow treatment, less and less available in the UK National Health Service, that can be costly and not easy to access. In a society in which *fast* is the primary value, this book offers a diametrically opposite stance: only with time, patience, and endurance is change possible. Mental health does not know the variable of time: it takes the time it takes. The mind needs time to know the truth about itself, to be able to investigate its contents, and if this truth is not accessible, the mind cannot grow. But what does it mean to offer understanding and meaning?

The book describes in a beautiful and moving way that, for the mind to grow, a space in which it can be thought about is needed. This space can only be in another mind. Dr Bisagni shows what is necessary for this space: the other mind has to be able to remain totally empty when receiving the patient. The capacity to create this empty space to accommodate the patient requires great humility and skill on the part of the therapist. In this space, there is no wish to do anything, it is a space in which the desire to control, heal, or change is relinquished. In this space, there is not-knowing and curiosity. And an enormous capacity for generosity, as the patient enters into the analyst's mind with all his knots, confusions, and unthinkable, unknown, hidden traumas, including his most bizarre and at times self-destructive ways of mending and coping. The analyst opens her whole entity to the patient, rejecting nothing, and begins to think her patient. This thinking creates order, fosters mental processing, gives meaning to and revitalises the patient's capacity to discover and own his mind. Once the patient discovers a mind of his own, he can begin to apprehend himself, thinking his own thoughts without being afraid of them or feeling persecuted by them.

This process can take a long time. But what is it that the analyst does when he thinks his patient? Part of the analyst's work is done unconsciously and cannot be explicitly described. It is the result of the analyst's life-long experience, which includes his own analysis, the supervision he has undergone, all the cases he has seen or heard about, the books and papers he has read or written, his whole life experience. The patient's self is put in contact with this implicit work that the analyst is doing, and the patient begins to unfold. While he is apprehended by his analyst, the patient begins to apprehend himself.

The capacity of reverie of the analyst is so vividly acute in the case material described in this book that it acquires a poetic value: it brings the reader inside the creative and transformative process. The extraordinary mind of the analyst, able to remain empty, makes something possible for the patient: he finds a space in which he can become. This has the quality of a miracle: the discovery that coming into being is possible has not only a therapeutic effect but a salvific one: the patient discovers his right to be himself and begins to be. This is happening in parallel to the analyst being engaged in discussing theory with himself, in evaluating the conscious and unconscious processes that are happening in the sessions. The mind of the patient changes. Unconscious thoughts are understood, made conscious, exchanged, talked about. The power of *logos* has a healing value; it can be described as the capacity to stay above, formulate, put into words what the mind could not apprehend, could not allow, was not ready to tolerate. The open mind of the analyst, which allows every aspect of his patient to enter in, sets in motion a "sacred" process in the mind of the patient, a salvific *miracle*. This miracle is: I have the right to exist, all my thoughts and feelings are an aspect of me, they are my experience of being in the world, I need to accept them and take responsibility for them; only so I can be and relate to the world I am in. I can be alive if I allow myself to be.

This is for me an aspect of the collective unconscious that analysis triggers, something that is inherent to us humans as the need to have a container in which we can grow. This space is the world in which we live, the womb of our mother, the mind of another who gives us permission to be. Only in such a space is creation possible. If this space is threatened by others who occupy it with their own stuff, or by our conscious or unconscious fears, we disable ourselves. The case material in this book is a gift as it describes the powerful experience of not being thought about as opposite to finding a space in which we are allowed to be, and how the persecuting thoughts are bits of the personality looking for someone to give them a place to be thought about.

Children who were not granted this space by their parents, like Giulio, are in danger of a psychological death, as their coming into being is negated by what occupies their parents' minds. In Giulio's case, his parents do not know how to see their child, they have in their mind a fantasy child, who is not Giulio. And Giulio becomes ill, afraid of letting anything out, probably unconsciously knowing that what would get out is what he is, and this would let down his parents' idea of him. This state of affairs made Giulio very ill. Marcelino too is ill because his adoptive mother sees her dead brother and her dead foetus in Marcelino, and Marcelino is afraid of being dirty, smelly, wrong. There is more.

His adoptive parents suffered as children from the same lack of capacity in their own parents, and they transmit their own trauma. Their incapacity to create a space for their child makes the whole family ill. Marcelino, not knowing how to be, ends up by identifying with his birth parents whom he is told were mentally disturbed. For mentally disturbed Marcelino, there has never been a space in anybody's mind. But in a sort of human miracle, his analyst offers him this space, and Marcelino unfolds in an unexpected way.

We get to know Marco who is persecuted by the thought of wanting to kill his mother and has a breakdown. This breakdown opens a way for Marco to begin to come into being as the person he is, not a version of his mother's idealisation of him. In working with Marco, Dr Bisagni is asked by his little patient to work as both a psychiatrist and as a psychoanalyst. He skilfully takes up the challenge by prescribing medication while working psychoanalytically. The process of weaning from the medication paves the way for Marco to find his own mind and acquire his own identity.

And there is Maria, who is obsessed by sexual thoughts, including having sex with her mother. Her long analysis resolves when she discovers separateness and can finally separate from her mother, having acquired a sense of a space inside her mind in which she can think herself. Maria grew up without a name in her mind for another. She was living in a space of un-differentiation.

In the case of Pietro, Dr Bisagni shows the challenges of working as a psychiatrist with a psychotherapist, and the thinking behind the management of the case, offering the patient an analytic couple who are not in rivalry but working together for the benefit of their patient.

The book opens up another consideration: to what extent can the mind of an analyst remain open? What are the limits of the capacity to tolerate a patient? In every patient, there is a human being who is suffering, but the suffering can bring people to adopt extremely destructive defence mechanisms to avoid pain. The story of Paolo, a young man with HIV, who was harming himself and others by participating in destructive sexual activities, confronts the reader with this question. The capacity of remaining open that Dr Bisagni shows with this case gives hope to those who have fallen into despair and remain in their personal hell, imagining that nobody would accept their cry of despair, which is beyond the hearing capacity of any god. This case material challenges the analyst who rejects the suffering of another human being because they cannot accommodate it in their mind.

Alex too was lucky to have meet Dr Bisagni's mind, which was able to withstand the patient's stubborn need to bring to his sessions his body more than his mind, insisting on its smelly and disgusting quality in which hatred and faeces were totally confused.

Dr Bisagni's mind is capable of performing both the paternal and the maternal functions for his patients, is able to remain open with affection, interest, curiosity, and to think, understand, give meaning, but he is also generous enough to accept those who suffer and their pathology.

In this book, we encounter someone who "knows" theory from inside, as theory has become part of him, integrated in his mind. In the gentle handling of Sonia, who was living hidden in phantasy inside her parents' intercourse and was therefore suffering from depression, Dr Bisagni understands the meaning of her attacking thoughts. This understanding allows her to engage with reality and to take responsibility for her own life as a separate, grown-up person. This is also the long journey that Fabio has to undergo, when, despite having lost a leg, he is able to discover gratitude.

The book confronts the reader with this important aspect of our work, the capacity to feel grateful. As much as we accept the patient and their devastating symptoms, we rely on the patient's capacity to open his mind to us, and to allow us to offer him our way of thinking and our language. It is a mutual gesture of generosity, ours and the patient's. Here, self-idealisation, envy, hatred, and omnipotence have to be understood, managed, and transformed.

In a paradigmatic way, the story of Lia represents the limit. Love, understanding, and meaning are not always acceptable, made a space for, and recognised. The patient who allows himself to enter into the mind of his analyst and to be thought by him, is also capable of generosity in the sense that he accepts being related to. Lia did not open herself to this experience, choosing to remain locked in a *folie à deux* with her son, impervious to coming into being as a separate person relating to her son who is other.

Reading Dr Bisagni's book is an act of generosity. Digesting it and responding to it will be an act of understanding, which will increase our capacity to think about our work and its challenges.

Alessandra Cavalli
SAP Training Adult and Child Analyst—London

PART I

THEORY: MODELS AND PERSPECTIVES

I used to have a morbid idea that my parents knew my thoughts; I explained this to myself by supposing that I had spoken to them out loud, without having heard myself do it.

Freud, "Notes upon a case of obsessional neurosis" (1909, p. 162)

From the material a patient produces, there emerges, like the pattern from a kaleidoscope, a configuration which seems to belong not only to the situation unfolding, but to a number of others not previously seen to be connected and which it has not been designed to connect.

Bion, Commentary, in *Second Thoughts* (1967, p. 127)

CHAPTER ONE

Psychiatric contributions: classifications and treatments

According to the *Diagnostic and Statistical Manual of Mental Disorders*, fifth edition (DSM-V, 2013), obsessive–compulsive disorder (OCD) is the fourth most common mental disorder after depression, alcohol/substance misuse, and social phobia, with a lifetime prevalence in community surveys of 1.6 per cent. The World Health Organization ranks OCD as one of the ten most handicapping conditions by lost income and decreased quality of life (Murray & Lopez, 1996). When the disorder starts in childhood or adolescence, young people may avoid socialising with peers or become unable to live independently.

After years of scientific debate and controversies, obsessive–compulsive disorder and related disorders have been classified as a separate section in the DSM-V, and this includes body dysmorphic disorder, hoarding disorder, trichotillomania (hair-pulling disorder), and excoriation (skin-picking) disorder, among other conditions. In previous editions of the DSM, OCD had been classified among the general anxiety disorders, which caused several problems, to say the least, in diagnostically identifying the many variants of the disease and the complex and multidetermined comorbid conditions. Furthermore, the previous classification made it more difficult to find common territories of exploration and clinical research for those clinicians who have a psychodynamic orientation. This difficulty has been partly overcome due to some specific elements that have been outlined in the new DSM-V classification that offer interesting indicators for a possible dialogue with the psychoanalytic approach. In particular, the new classification is more precise and allows a better comparison with other major psychiatric conditions, especially depression and thinking disorders, and in this respect it allows a more cogent interrelation with the psychoanalytic vertex.

What is an obsession?

Obsessions have the following essential features: they are recurrent and unwanted thoughts, impulses, or images that are experienced as intrusive and cause great distress; they are disproportionate worries about everyday life issues; these thoughts are recognised by the affected individual as an ego-dystonic product of his mind, although a relevant distinction is made in the DSM-V in this respect. It regards the distinction between patients respectively with *good or fair insight, poor insight,* or *absent insight/delusional beliefs,* which gives us an indication of the complexity of the so-called ego-dystonic quality of obsessional ideation, and how such ideation may turn out to be contiguous to a frank psychotic/delusional situation, in the absence, however, of other features typical of schizophrenic disorder. The first part of the book deals with clinical conditions where the diagnosis of OCD is clear, on the one hand, but on the other the quality and intensity of ideation, at least transitorily, resembles delusional thinking, and insight in moments of particular severity is quite poor.

OCD is in general a symptomatically heterogeneous condition, in which various different kinds of obsessions coexist. As appropriately outlined by Abramowitz, Taylor, and McKay (2009), certain obsessions tend to co-occur to form five main dimensions:

- obsessions about being responsible for causing or failing to prevent harm; checking compulsions and reassurance-seeking;
- symmetry obsessions, and ordering and counting rituals;
- contamination obsessions, and washing and cleaning rituals;
- repugnant obsessions concerning sex, violence, or religion;
- hoarding, that is, obsessions about acquiring and retaining objects.

What is a compulsion?

Compulsions are repetitive behaviours or mental acts that the individual feels compelled to do in response to an obsession. They commonly include behaviours like cleaning, continuous hand-washing, checking, ordering and arranging, hoarding and asking for reassurance, and various mental acts like counting, repeating words silently, ruminations, neutralising thoughts. Compulsions are aimed at preventing or reducing distress, or preventing some dreaded event. The individual usually momentarily stops compulsive behaviours when he feels that "everything is all right", the main problem being that such reassuring and controlling activity has limited effectiveness and the anxiety linked to obsessions is soon, and endlessly, reactivated. Whatever the case may be, what is most important in properly diagnosing OCD is not the simple description of a specific behaviour but the intended aim of that behaviour, namely, if it occurs in response to an obsession.

Furthermore, as appropriately described by Veale and Roberts (2014), a compulsion in OCD is not in itself pleasurable, which differentiates it from impulsive acts such as shopping, gambling, or paraphilias that are associated with immediate gratification. The term "ritual" is synonymous with compulsion but usually refers to motor acts. "Rumination" in OCD refers to mental acts repeated endlessly in response to intrusive ideas and doubts. A specific issue may regard tics. Although proper tics may be mistaken for compulsions in a strict sense, they can be differentiated by the focal uncomfortable somatic sensations that precede and are relieved by the tic. There is a wide range of behaviours in this respect, which include motor tics, and phonic or vocal tics of different complexities. The behaviour is considered a compulsion if it is performed in response to an obsession and is intended to reduce anxiety or prevent harm.

Shame and avoidance

OCD may be difficult to diagnose when the obsessions and compulsions are covert or stigmatising. The person may simply seem preoccupied or anxious. Clinicians may not be able to immediately see patients trying mentally to replace unacceptable sexual or aggressive thoughts with what they believe to be safer or more adequate thoughts, praying, or trying to reassure themselves that a particular action is safe. OCD is often hidden, and plenty of relevant mental elements are frequently disguised, as patients believe that their intrusive thoughts are liable to be criticised or misunderstood and must therefore be actively kept under strict control. Misunderstandings are not only feared but at times are actively sought, within the general attitude of taking control over the feared reaction by the interlocutor.

Avoidance, too, is an integral part of OCD. This attitude may range from simply avoiding specific actions to a general phobic position when faced with life events and potentially emotionally involving situations. Specific actions may include taking care not to touch toilet seats, door handles, or taps used by other people; hiding knives or potentially harmful objects; unrealistically avoiding sex or any kind of physical contact due to the fear of contracting AIDS or other sexually transmitted diseases; or avoiding being left alone with a child if there are fears of being a paedophile or a potential killer. Avoidance is dynamically linked to phobia, and may end up looking like a general form of emotional detachment and an overall disinvestment of meaningful relationships. This is particularly important when the content of obsessive thoughts regards aggressive impulses and feared violent actions. As Heyman, Mataix-Cols, and Fineberg appropriately observe in this regard (2006), aggressive thoughts are common in OCD and must be carefully differentiated from violent thoughts occurring in other psychiatric disorders, such as the urge to hurt people in psychopathy. Shame and self-reproach are essential features that differentiate the two clinical conditions.

Comorbidity

The issue of a clear differential diagnosis is always relevant in order to implement appropriate and focused treatments. On one level, the criteria for making a diagnosis of OCD are precise and regard the ongoing and impairing presence of a variety of ego-dystonic thoughts impinging on the subject as well as a cohort of mental and/or motor activities aimed at controlling such thoughts as much as possible. Although a clear differential diagnosis has to be made between OCD and anxiety disorders, major depressive disorders, tic disorder, and psychotic disorders, comorbid conditions are frequent. Many patients with OCD have lifetime anxiety disorders (including panic attacks and specific phobias), major depressive disorders, and tics. The most common comorbid diagnoses in surveys of people with OCD are depression (in about one-third), social phobia (in one-third), alcohol misuse (in one-quarter), specific phobias (in one-quarter), generalised anxiety disorder (in about one-tenth), and other related obsessive–compulsive disorders such as body dysmorphic disorder (in about one-tenth) (DSM-V, 2013).

What in descriptive terms is defined as comorbidity represents for a psychoanalytically oriented clinician the core issue of dealing with the inevitable complexity of the personality structures and the polymorphous symptom formations that are by definition overlapped and often fluid and interspersed with one another in each affected individual. The structure of the book reflects precisely this issue. One section of the book concerns the contiguity of OCD with thinking disorders, where the intensity and pervasiveness of the ideation temporarily diminished the patients' capacity for insight and required specific intervention. Another section of the book regards the contiguity of OCD with depression.

Obsessive–compulsive disorder and obsessive–compulsive personality disorder

Highly relevant in clinical terms is the distinction made in the DSM-V between obsessive–compulsive disorder and obsessive–compulsive personality disorder. The two clinical conditions are not seen as variants of the same psychopathological cluster but are classified in two separate sections in the DSM. It is the psychoanalytic tradition that, at times questionably, finds an overlap or a contiguity between the two. Roughly speaking, OCD proper implies the presence of impairing symptoms, while OCPD regards personality traits, such as the tendency to control, order, symmetry, and so forth, without relevant and overt symptoms. Last but not least, as outlined in the sixth edition of *The American Psychiatric Publishing Textbook of Psychiatry* (Hales et al., 2014), OCPD individuals tend to be ego-syntonic with regard to their functioning, while the obsessions in OCD are always, although to a variable degree, ego-dystonic.

Of course, the divide between the two conditions is not always as neat as one might expect in the clinical observation, considering that symptom formation presents a wide range of severity, and more particularly, individuals affected by OCD often hide their symptoms until they become utterly severe and overwhelming. Personality traits, on the other hand, may be extremely rigid even though symptoms are vague or unapparent, so the distinction between the two clinical conditions is not always easy to assess. However, this distinction is relevant with regard to the therapeutic approach. Generally speaking, OCPD, similarly to all personality disorders, can definitely benefit from psychoanalytic treatment conducted according to the classical approach. On the contrary, as shall be described in this book, when severe symptoms are present, a modified psychoanalytic approach is necessary and requires an attentive use of medication in an integrated approach, according to criteria that will be described further on.

Autism and obsessive–compulsive disorder

A peculiar aspect of the matter we are dealing with regards autism spectrum disorders and their supposed interrelatedness with obsessive–compulsive functioning, particularly the issue of sameness. At first sight and from a strictly psychiatric standpoint, the two conditions have nothing or very little in common. However, some issues deserve reflection.

First of all, there has been a classificatory revision of autism in the DSM-V. Individuals who previously met the criteria for a diagnosis of autistic disorder, Asperger's disorder, or pervasive disorder not otherwise specified according to the DSM-IV, are now given the diagnosis of autism spectrum disorder (ASD) according to the DSM-V. Manifestations of the disorder vary greatly depending on the severity of symptoms, developmental level, and chronological age; hence the term "spectrum". Autism spectrum disorder encompasses disorders previously referred to as early infantile autism, Kanner's autism, high-functioning autism, Aperger's disorder, childhood disintegrative disorder, pervasive developmental disorder, and atypical autism.

Diagnostic criteria for ASD include persistent deficits in social communication and interaction, especially in social-emotional reciprocity, in nonverbal communicative behaviours, and in developing, maintaining, and understanding relationships. Such a cluster of manifestations marks the main difference from OCD.

The second cluster of criteria for ASD regards a cohort of restricted, repetitive patterns of behaviour such as: stereotyped or repetitive motor movements, use of objects, or speech; insistence on sameness, inflexible adherence to routines or ritualised patterns of verbal and nonverbal behaviour; highly restricted, fixated, and perseverative interests that are abnormal in intensity or focus; hyper- or hypo-reactivity to sensory input or unusual interest in sensory aspects of the environment.

All these symptoms are considered diagnostically relevant if they are present in the early developmental period, and if they appear to be causing significant impairment in social, occupational, or other important areas of current functioning. Intellectual disability can frequently co-occur. Severity is classified according to the intensity of the two main clusters.

The evidence of the second cluster of symptoms, regarding repetitiveness and adherence to routines, has always engaged psychoanalytically oriented therapists in terms of the possible common territories with obsessive–compulsive functioning in general, and the issue of sameness and omnipotent control in particular. The dynamics of this particular component will be dealt with further on in this book. From a descriptive point of view, repetitive behaviours include simple motor stereotypies, such as hand flapping or finger flicking, the repetitive use of objects, such as spinning coins or lining up toys, and repetitive speech, such as echolalia, parroting of heard words, a stereotyped use of words and phrases, the use of "you" when referring to oneself, and the like. Excessive adherence to routine and restricted behaviours may manifest as distress to small changes, repetitive questioning, pacing a perimeter, or abnormality in intensity or focus on certain objects and activities. Some fascinations and routines are often related to hyper- or hyporeactivity to sensory input, manifested through intense responses to sounds or textures, smelling or touching objects, fascination with light or spinning objects, or rituals involving taste, smell, texture, and appearance of food.

Considering that adults with ASD but no intellectual or language disabilities may learn to dissimulate and suppress their repetitive behaviour in public and may look pseudo-normal in their social conducts and relations, and considering how less severe OCD individuals may also learn to hide their symptoms and behave in public in a pseudo-adjusted way, differences between the two clinical conditions may not always be so evident at first sight. The lack of socio-emotional reciprocity, the impaired capacity for empathy, and the extreme difficulty in emotionally understanding other people, which constitute the first cluster of criteria for diagnosing ASD, usually orient the diagnosis, however severely OCD patients may develop a sense of deep detachment and emotional withdrawal. The tri-dimensionality and complexity of their inner suffering is something we do not usually encounter in ASD persons, although the latter, especially if not co-affected by intellectual disabilities, may develop depressive states during adolescence and adulthood, which makes their condition more complex. It is usually the anamnesis and the history of the onset of the illness and its development over time that clarifies the diagnosis in all cases.

As will be described in a case study, typically and unquestionably autistic repetitiveness in an ASD patient was intertwined with severe obsessional functioning in the mother, so that the tendency to sameness, immobility, and control became systemic in the family group. The clinical example provided, despite the diagnosis of ASD being clear in the patient, interrogates the complex identification processes and the nature of certain repetitive behaviours over the course of time, beyond the possible genetic predisposition. The specific situation of that family was made more interesting in that the younger brother of the autistic patient developed severe OCD in his late adolescence, the two brothers seemingly expressing two modes of exerting control in order to keep the family structures steady and to virtually block development.

Psychological treatments

The only recognised empirically supported psychological treatment for obsessive–compulsive disorder is cognitive behavioural therapy (CBT), including exposure and response prevention (ERP) (Abramowitz, 2006). Exposure consists of repeated and prolonged confrontation with stimuli that provoke anxiety and the urge to perform compulsive rituals. The patient encounters actual feared stimuli and confronts anxiety-provoking obsessional images, thoughts, and doubts. Response prevention means refraining from performing compulsive rituals to reduce anxiety or seek reassurance. The aim of exposure and response prevention is to teach patients that obsessional anxiety does not persist indefinitely, and that avoidance behaviour and compulsive rituals are unnecessary to avert harm. Additional motivational interventions, beyond the possible implemented pharmacological treatments, are regarded as necessary for patients with very severe symptoms (Abramowitz et al., 2011).

Studies conducted using the Yale–Brown obsessive–compulsive scale (Y–BOCS) (Goodman et al., 1989) demonstrate that exposure and response prevention is better than other forms of psychotherapy and than placebos. Although often effective, exposure and response prevention can provoke anxiety in patients, and approximately a quarter of patients drop out of treatment (Franklin et al., 2000). The effects of this treatment is reported as lasting up to at least two years (Abramowitz, 2006). Overall, the findings from randomised controlled trials suggest that exposure and response prevention substantially improve obsessive–compulsive symptoms, and its effect is greater than that produced by pharmacotherapy (Abramowitz et al., 2009).

Guidelines published by the National Institute for Health and Clinical Excellence (NICE, 2005) state that "although the efficacy and effectiveness of CBT has been demonstrated, there are limits to its utility" (p. 104). ERP can be unpleasant and distressing to clients and may lead to discontinuation of therapy. When taking into account those who refuse or drop out of treatment and those who do not benefit immediately or relapse, researchers have estimated that the number of those treated successfully with behaviour therapy is around 55 per cent (p. 104). The guidelines report that no systematic reviews or meta-analyses of the effectiveness of psychoanalysis for OCD were found, therefore a narrative review was undertaken. A total of sixty-four papers were reviewed, dating from 1912 to 2002. None of the papers considered was a randomised controlled trial or cohort study, and so the evidence reviewed consisted of single case reports, a few case series, and theoretical reviews. Conclusions of this review were that "there is no evidence of efficacy or effectiveness for psychoanalysis in the treatment of OCD. Given the lack of evidence and the resources required for such intensive treatment, there is doubt as to whether it has a place in mental health services for OCD" (p. 104).

Updates to the NICE guidelines in 2013 indicate tele-mental health and technology interventions for OCD such as computerised or telephone CBT as initial treatment options for adults: these are reported as possibly promising, although current evidence is limited. Acceptance and commitment therapy may improve symptoms of OCD to a greater extent than progressive relaxation training. Initial treatment options for adults include medication with selective serotonin reuptake inhibitors (SSRIs), such as sertraline, or group CBT. Of these two options, both sertraline and group CBT may result in similar response rates, but more people may have clinical remission with group CBT than with sertraline. Initial treatment options for children and young people include family-based CBT, which may be associated with higher rates of response to treatment than psychoeducation plus relaxation training

(NICE, 2013). Psychoanalytically oriented treatments are not quoted in the NICE update.

Psychoanalytically oriented psychiatrists do not seem to suggest a different view. Gabbard (2001) states that parallel to the realisation that psychoanalysis does not alter the obsessive–compulsive symptoms, there has been a growing tendency within psychiatry to view the disorder as one that has a largely biologically based aetiology, considering that the evidence for biological components to the aetiology of OCD is convincing. With my complete agreement, Gabbard (2001) says that "part of the difficulty in the field stems from the disentangling of obsessive–compulsive personality disorder (OCPD), which is eminently responsive to psychoanalysis, and OCD" (p. 210).

Genetic studies have found that there is a heritable component in OCD, including concordance rates of 80 to 87 per cent in monozygotic twins and 47 to 50 per cent in dizygotic twins (van Grootheest et al., 2005). OCD tends to run in families, with a recent study finding an increased risk of OCD among relatives of probands (8.2 per cent) compared with control subjects (2.0 per cent) (Hettema et al., 2001). Gene studies have found a number of genes that may be associated with OCD, including many associated with serotonin, dopamine, and glutamate (*The American Psychiatric Publishing Textbook of Psychiatry*, 2014).

Functional neuroimaging studies have found abnormalities within all nodes of the ventral cognitive loop, which includes the orbitofrontal cortex, the caudate nucleus, and the dorsomedial thalamus. Namely, these brain regions are hyperactive at rest in patients with OCD compared with healthy volunteers; this hyperactivity is amplified during OCD symptom provocation, and the hyperactivity is attenuated with successful treatment (Dougherty et al., 2010).

Notwithstanding cogent data provided by genetic and neurobiological studies, "the psychoanalytically informed clinician still has much to contribute to a comprehensive treatment plan for such patients" (Gabbard, 2001, p. 211). My view partly differs from Gabbard's in that I do not define my clinical approach as "psychodynamic psychiatry", which is "an approach to diagnosis and treatment characterized by a way of thinking about both patient and clinician that includes unconscious conflict, deficits and distortions of intrapsychic structures, and internal object relations" (Gabbard, 1994, pp. 4–5). Rather, I consider my core approach as psychoanalytical, the psychiatric intervention being restricted to pharmacological support that is implemented according to the guidelines described in the case material to come.

With regard to the psychoanalytically oriented treatment of OCD, Esman (2001) draws the conclusion that after more than one century of psychodynamic treatments, there is no reason to be optimistic.

In the present book, eleven cases are reported. Two of them are adults, nine are children or adolescents. The majority of them have concluded their analyses or are in an advanced stage of the treatment. Only one of these patients is in the first stage of his analysis, and although relevant changes are already observable, it is not yet reasonable to speak in terms of outcome. One patient is autistic and is described in the book with regard to the issue of sameness and to the obsessional functioning in the family group. One patient interrupted the treatment due to the unmanageable symbiotic bond with his mother, and is the only unsatisfactory outcome among the cases reported. The rest of the cases, children, adolescents, or adults, were able to remarkably benefit from psychoanalytic treatment. Some of them required medication during a part of their treatment. In all cases but one, the symptomatic and structural improvements led to the termination of pharmacological support, with stable clinical conditions over time. One patient is at the time of writing making an attempt to decrease and hopefully to stop medication altogether. Certainly, the classical psychoanalytic approach and technique were maintained in their basic foundations, namely, a high frequency of sessions and the centrality of the transference and interpretative work. Flexibility of a technical approach integrated with pharmacological support, cogently taking the reverberations of the latter into account in terms of the transference, was, however, necessary. A wider view of psychoanalytic theories and models was no less important, the centrality of interpersonal, family, and group dynamics as well as the transgenerational factor being considered. With children and adolescents, the work with families was of course paramount.

Finally, the personal analytic attitude and style had to be adjusted to the specific features of such an impairing disease, the treatment of which required rigour, flexibility, resilience, and liveliness. Certainly, the number of cases discussed in the book would not be sufficient to draw conclusions with statistical evidence and support. This is surely a limitation that for a single clinician can never be overcome. In this respect, quantitative and measurable evidence will not be provided in this book. However, visible and stable changes occurred in the patients in a strictly psychoanalytic sense: above all, changes were effected in the personality structure, and these led to a better quality of life. Structural changes determined that obsessive–compulsive symptoms were no longer necessary for the expression of the internal world, and a more evident plasticity and mobilisation of mental functioning came to the fore. Basically, a transformation in apprehension of psychic pain was evident, compared to the blocking manoeuvres of the obsessional functioning. Pain became a mobile element, at the disposal of transference work. As a psychoanalyst, and apart from all difficulties and limitations, I would conclude that there is reason to be optimistic in the treatment of these patients.

CHAPTER TWO

Psychoanalyses: symptoms, structures, and contexts

When using a psychoanalytic vertex, the issue of the clinical interrelatedness between obsessions and compulsions as symptoms, described according to the complex psychoanalytic model, and obsessional defences/functioning/structures and other pathological structures, becomes relevant. In this respect, obsessions and compulsions can be specifically studied and understood in relation to depression, phobic symptoms, and character—and other forms of disinvestment and withdrawal—and to magical and delusional thinking. Both symptoms and structures are inextricably intertwined with environmental factors, which are dynamically interacting.

It is beyond the scope of this book to review all psychoanalytic models directly or indirectly implied in obsessive–compulsive functioning. Only some specific issues will be focused upon, together with an outline of the main models that background and support my clinical approach.

Apparatus for linking, symptom, and immobility

Psychoanalysis has deeply developed its metapsychological foundations and technical approaches over the years, and overcome the exclusive intra-subjective view, rooted in the Freudian first and second topography, as well as the dual inter-subjective model based on the centrality of unconscious fantasies, as developed by the original Kleinian and post-Kleinian model of object relations theory, and the narcissistic model developed by self-psychology. Contemporary psychoanalysis, which certainly faces challenges in its encounter with modern patients who do not respond to the classical methods, conceives a metapsychology of the unconscious for specifically articulating intra-subjective and inter-subjective space in terms of a third topography (Kaës, 2007), which expresses itself in the specific phenomenology of the group mind and the unconscious alliance. Inter-subjective space in this respect is a specific conjunction that *creates* the unconscious. A plural topography leads us to acknowledge that the unconscious is never fully confined to the individual's psychic space, and is not totally describable according to the first or second Freudian topography formulation. Rather, the psychic *space for linking* belongs to a different *locus* of the unconscious. Clinical experience tells us that even the slightest change in unconscious alliances and shared pacts of a family or a group challenges the unconscious structure of the individual who is part of that family or group; reciprocally, every change to the subject's structure, psychic economy, or dynamics challenges and is often strongly opposed by the forces that support the alliances within the links of which the subject is, at the same time, an active and a passive constituent.

We deal with configurations that as such do not exclusively belong to the subject, despite the subject belonging to a group in the role of a cooperating actor, and do not exclusively belong to the group, which of course would not exist without its component subjects. We could describe these configurations as elements that produce and connect the unconscious matter of inter-subjective links, and we can describe them in terms of an inter-subjective topography, economy, and dynamics. Unconscious alliances, shared dreams, and implicit dogmas become evident at the intersection of repressed relations that subjects and group develop in the inter-subjective space. So more than one topography is always implied in the symptom formation and in its migration within the system. In dynamic terms, not only do we have an intra-psychic conflict, but also an unconscious conflict between the subject and a part of the subject's mind that is placed in another person, or that is placed by the other person into the subject.

Freud (1914c) pointed out how the subject is torn between two demands: being self-oriented and being inevitably a member of an inter-subjective chain of which he is at the same time a servant, within a ring of transmission, he is both an heir and an author. Kaës (2007) described how multiple defences in the creation of unconscious alliances operate, essentially working at the service of a repressing–denying function that tends to keep the alliance unconsciously stable and self-maintained. Alliances are the result of compromises operated and maintained by subjects, and each time a repressed or denied element in one subject comes to the fore, un-denied or un-repressed elements in the other members are unveiled. Alliances work by producing symptoms and by keeping them endlessly operating, by supporting their misleading function in the interest of each component of the group and of the shared group dogmas. A subject is subjected to symptoms also in the interest of someone else and in the interest of their bond. This is what makes symptoms at times inextricable and so difficult to undo. If all symptoms work for steadiness, obsessional symptoms and structures in particular, as will be shown through case material, strongly work for immobility and un-separateness. Co-repression, co-denial, and unconscious alliances are at times particularly tenacious.

Dynamically speaking, we can observe that each link mobilises, transforms, and organises psychic energy in each member of a group. The apparatus for linking is a metapsychological organisation that manages, transforms, and shapes the individual minds. The transference, in this respect, operates in terms of diffraction and the quanta of energy migrates within the group and in the lateral transferences and countertransferences typically observable in individual therapy. This is particularly relevant when working with children and adolescents, whose subjectivity is by definition porous and physiologically inserted into the network of the parental mind with regard to children, and of the peer mind with regard to adolescents.

Intra-subjective defences and transformations

Although maintaining a binocular view that takes the inter-subjective element into account, typical intra-psychic defence operations, as described in Freud's seminal writings, are commonly observed when treating obsessional patients. Some of them are particularly relevant in terms of their reverberation on the transference, and therefore deserve further reflection. I will focus in particular on displacement and isolation.

The concept of displacement is connected with the assumption that the affect is independent of the idea. In the energetic model, as originally conceived in the "Project for a scientific psychology" (Freud, 1895), the hypothesis is that quota of energy are capable of being displaced along neural pathways in order to be discharged, according to the primary process. But what is more relevant within our perspective is that the phenomenon of displacement occurs between different ideas, which is typical of obsessional neurosis and concerns the formation of a substitute by means of displacement (Freud, 1894a). Displacement is also implied in dream work, by facilitating condensation, in so far as it leads to ideas or verbal expressions formed at the intersection of two chains of associations. Representability, as a further mechanism implied in dream work, is facilitated when displacement is operated between an abstract idea and an equivalent, leading to visualisation with a consequent increase in sensory intensity. Finally, displacement is implied in secondary elaboration by serving its specific purposes (Freud, 1900a).

The defensive nature of displacement is clear in Freud's descriptions, whether considering its role in phobia and in obsessional neurosis, or its function in dream work, and it is constantly linked to the operational role of censorship *vis-à-vis* the psychic conflict. However, dream work implies a freer movement along the associative chains where the process of symbolisation is central and remains, as it were, alive and propulsive. Symbolisation corresponds to a metaphoric dimension, which is governed by the law of association by similarity. Instead, the formation of obsessional ideas through displacement, at the intersection of two associative chains, follows the law of metonymy, in which association is based on contiguity. In addition, obsessional ideas tend to repeat themselves endlessly, while dream work is by definition mobile and renewable. Such a distinction is clinically relevant when approaching the concretism in the quality of thinking and verbal expressions of the obsessional patient, particularly with regard to the analyst's apprehension of the metonymic nature—so close to psychotic functioning—of representations and associations. One of the aims of psychoanalytic work with obsessional patients is, in this respect, to activate wake-dreaming and re-establish the movements along the associative paths through metaphoric steps as opposed to metonymic contiguity. Obsessive thoughts should be turned into dreams, and displacement given back to its plastic function of disguising and revealing psychic reality.

Linked to these mechanisms and with specific regard to the relationship and relative independence between idea and affect, in the seminal paper on the case of the Rat Man, Freud underlines the notion of false connection, which he had already described in "The neuro-psychoses of defence" (Freud, 1894a), and states:

> When there is a *mésalliance*, ... between an affect and its ideational content (in this instance, between the intensity of the self-reproach and the occasion for it), a layman will say that the affect is too great for the occasion—that it is exaggerated—and that consequently the inference following from the self-reproach (the inference that the patient is a criminal) is false. On the contrary, the [analytic] physician says: No. The affect is justified. The sense of guilt is not in itself open to further criticism. But it belongs to some other content, which is unknown (*unconscious*), and which requires to be looked for. The known ideational content has only got into its actual position owing to a false connection. We are not used to feeling strong affects without their having any ideational content, and therefore, if the content is missing, we seize as a substitute upon some other content which is in some way or other suitable, much as our police, when they cannot catch the right murderer, arrest a wrong one instead. Moreover, this fact of there being a false connection is the only way of accounting for the powerlessness of logical processes to combat the tormenting idea. I concluded by admitting that this new way of looking at the matter gave immediate rise to some hard problems; for how could he admit that his self-reproach of being a criminal towards his father was justified, when he must know that as a matter of fact he had never committed any crime against him?
>
> (Freud, 1909d, pp. 174–175)

Reformulated beyond the exclusive intra-subjective metapsychology, the notion of false connection is far more subtly relevant than one could envisage at first sight, as it implies the transference—which is a *de facto* issue—as well as the countertransference and the subsequent formation of interpretation in the analyst's mind. Obsessional patients, like few others, show a strong capacity to activate sterile, stereotyped, rationalised interpretations in the analyst, who easily feels forced to provide whatever comments, commonly oversaturated, to link elements with one another at all costs. This leads to the risk of merely substituting the patient's false connections with other psychoanalytic false connections, which is of course totally unproductive. A sophisticated capacity to play with unpredictability, as it were, and to be creative and surprising in the face of the constant manifestations of the repetitiveness of false connections, is an essential requirement for the analyst.

If one interpretation may look totally true, its exact opposite may look equally true. Both are ineffective. This is analogous to one of the main features of obsessional symptoms, as Freud points out, when reflecting upon compulsive acts typically occurring in two successive stages, of which the second neutralises the first.

> Compulsive acts of this sort are theoretically of special interest, for they show us a new type of method of constructing symptoms. What regularly occurs in hysteria is that a compromise is arrived at which enables both the opposing tendencies to find expression simultaneously—which kills two birds with one stone; whereas here each of the two opposing tendencies finds satisfaction singly, first one and then the other, though naturally an attempt is made to establish some sort of logical connection (often in defiance of all logic) between the antagonists.
>
> (Freud, 1909d, p. 192)

The quoted statement could be reformulated with regard to the interpretative work and the mutual unconscious satisfaction of patient and analyst in feeding each other with false connections, each producing its hopelessly sterile dialectic opposite.

Before moving forward to what more specifically regards the transference, I will consider the mechanism of isolation, which gives us further clues.

The term "isolation" deserves some clarification, because it is sometimes used in the psychoanalytic parlance in a quite distorted or loose way. Strictly speaking, the term describes a defence mechanism consisting in the systematic severing of the associative connections of a thought or an act with what succeeds or precedes it in time, so that the meaningful links are broken. It may be expressed, especially within the obsessive–compulsive functioning, through pausing in the train of thoughts or formulas and by inserting a hiatus in the temporal continuum of thoughts and actions. Although the concept was present since his early formulations, Freud more widely describes isolation in

Inhibitions, Symptoms and Anxiety (1926d), where he revises his earlier views on many issues, including obsessional neurosis, in the light of what is commonly known as the second theory of anxiety.

In Chapter Six of this paper, Freud explores two psychic mechanisms that are viewed as surrogates of repression: one is undoing, which means magically making an event not to have happened; the second is isolation, which is peculiar to obsessional neurosis and is interestingly put in relation to amnesia.

> When something unpleasant has happened to the subject or when he himself has done something which has a significance for his neurosis, he interpolates an interval during which nothing further must happen—during which he must perceive nothing and do nothing. This behaviour, which seems strange at first sight, is soon seen to have a relation to repression. We know that in hysteria it is possible to cause a traumatic experience to be overtaken by amnesia. In obsessional neurosis this can often not be achieved: the experience is not forgotten, but, instead, it is deprived of its affect, and its associative connections are suppressed or interrupted so that it remains as though isolated and is not reproduced in the ordinary processes of thought. The effect of this isolation is the same as the effect of repression with amnesia.
>
> (Freud, 1926d, p. 119)

A little further on Freud makes one more relevant statement, when connecting isolation to the issue of touching and being touched, physically and emotionally, in close relation to the process of free association. Freud touches upon one of the core issues of the obsessional configuration, which is of paramount clinical importance.

> We have all found by experience that it is especially difficult for an obsessional neurotic to carry out the fundamental rule of psycho-analysis. His ego is more watchful and makes sharper isolations, probably because of the high degree of tension due to conflict that exists between his super-ego and his id. While he is engaged in thinking, his ego has to keep off too much—the intrusion of unconscious phantasies and the manifestation of ambivalent trends. It must not relax, but is constantly prepared for a struggle. It fortifies this compulsion to concentrate and to

isolate by the help of the magical acts of isolation which, in the form of symptoms, grow to be so noticeable and to have so much practical importance for the patient, but which are, of course, useless in themselves and are in the nature of ceremonials.

But in thus endeavouring to prevent associations and connections of thought, the ego is obeying one of the oldest and most fundamental commands of obsessional neurosis, the taboo on touching. If we ask ourselves why the avoidance of touching, contact or contagion should play such a large part in this neurosis and should become the subject-matter of complicated systems, the answer is that touching and physical contact are the immediate aim of the aggressive as well as the loving object-cathexes. Eros desires contact because it strives to make the ego and the loved object one, to abolish all spatial barriers between them. But destructiveness, too, which (before the invention of long-range weapons) could only take effect at close quarters, must presuppose physical contact, a coming to grips.

(Freud, 1926d, pp. 120–121)

The question regards how displacement, undoing, and especially isolation, shape the transference. They seemingly impinge upon the transference–countertransference cycle much more heavily than "simple" repression.

Isolation in particular could be seen as or reduced to a specific form of attack on linking, in Bion's terms. However, I would try to consider it in the light of the model of transformations (Bion, 1965) in connection with the forms of the transference.

In general terms, Bion defines transformations as a series of changes that are experienced by the subject or by a group, where elements vary from a previous to a subsequent stage and where the existing invariants allow the recognition of the identity of the changed elements through the transformational process. A transformation is conceived as regarding the patient, the analyst (in response to the patient's change), and the relationship between patient and analyst. Transformations regard the "phenomenal part of O" (Bion, 1965, p. 40), the transformation that moves from O, the unknown, or thing-in-itself, to K, the knowledge we can have of O. Significantly, transformations are strictly influenced by emotional links (L and H, Love and Hate) that occur at different levels and in different ways in the patient and in the analyst, thus implying the similarities in the transference and in the countertransference, even though they are supposed to remain asymmetrical. In Chapters Ten and Twelve, Bion outlines what he defines as the cycles of transformations in an ideal session. A first cycle describes the patient freely associating and the analyst listening without memory and desire, at the beginning of a session: the transformational process would ideally lead to the emergence of O, in the analyst's mind. Once O is transformed into K, which is cycle number two, an interpretation is shaped in the analyst's mind and phrased. Cycle three starts once the receiving patient undergoes transformation as a result of the interpretation, and starts a new cycle by communicating his reactions to the analyst.

However, transformations are not all the same, and shape the transference in remarkably different ways.

Bion distinguishes transformations in rigid motion, projective transformations, and transformations in hallucinosis. Regarding transformations in rigid motion, which I would like to focus upon, Bion describes this as a process whereby there is very little deformation between the original object and the end product of the transformation. The invariants are rigid and more easily recognisable, O is more easily reachable, interpretation more easily shaped, and understanding relatively easily achieved. The transference as Bion affirms was described by Freud in terms of the past being transferred to the analyst with little deformation, and is an example of transformation in rigid motion. This is something totally different from projective transformations, whereby deformations of the original object are so massive that it is hardly recognisable in the end product of transformation. Interpretations in this latter case may become highly speculative.

I would not overlook the fact that Freud repeatedly describes the complexity of the transference, considered from dynamic, economic, or topographic points of view; a reductive and simplistic conception of the transference as a mere repetition of past events can be found only in his early writings. Instead, the complexity of defence mechanisms makes Freud's views on the transference highly articulated.

As Bion himself warns, opacity is an insidious state. It regards oversaturation induced by memory or desire, or by various kinds of distortions that prevent the capacity for contact with O.

If these are general statements, broadly valid for a number of clinical situations at different moments, with the obsessional patient more specific issues are recognisable in the analytic contact due to the presence of typical defences that are constantly at work. Among these, the mechanisms of displacement, undoing, and especially isolation described above, are particularly relevant in shaping transformations and the transference. The peculiar creation of false connections in displacement, magically making a psychic or real event as not having happened in undoing, and a break in time sequence and disconnection of meaning from a chain of thoughts in isolation, impinge on the availability of the patient to free associate, operate in favour of misunderstanding and support tortuousness and repetitiveness of sterile thinking, and turn the past into a succession of foggy memories. Words lose their metaphoric potential and, being imprisoned in the concreteness of metonymy, fail to be evocative.

Freud's legacy cannot in any case be overlooked, especially when considering the importance of words in connection with the body and the unconscious, no matter what importance is given to imagery and metaverbal components. When considering the function and use of words in analytic work, we have to bear in mind the fundamental distinction Freud made between *thing representation* and *word representation* (Freud, 1915e, 1917d). The intrinsic nature of words has always been understood by psychoanalysis, since its very origin, as totally intertwined with somatic processes. In this respect, perhaps it is helpful to recall that the thing representation is the result of a complex associative function. In fact, the representation re-cathects and revives the memory trace, which in itself is just the registration of an event. However, the thing representation is not to be reductively understood as just a mental correlate of the thing *per se*—the thing is not merely "copied and pasted" in the mind as a representation in a sort of one-to-one correspondence—as the thing has a place in different systems or associative complexes originating out of the inputs coming from the different sensory organs.

This way of conceiving thing representation is important, as it founds the representational process upon biological and somatic processes, including a sufficient development of brain circuits and the cortex.

It involves a primary process linked to all types of sensations coming from the peripheral sensory organs, which find a way of representing themselves as well as the outer world. It is important to underline how the basic constituents of representations come from manifold sensory-emotional paths, which gives us a clue as to the impact that the complex and multi-determined physical-emotional states of a mother have upon her baby's developing mind/brain. Such essential inter-relatedness, which has been extensively investigated by research in the psychoanalytic field as well as in developmental psychology and neuroscience over the last decades, is well grounded in the early Freudian formulations on the representational process.

The word representation is connected with the thing representation through its aural image, and in general its relation to somatic processes is rather complex and multi-layered. The associations of the auditory and phonation images in the first instance, and subsequently of the graphic signs of the eye and hand movements in the act of reading and writing, give rise to and progressively articulate the word representation in more and more complex forms.

Among many possible approaches to such a complex issue, I would like to underline how the sound component is significant at many levels: first, it is one of the multi-sensory-emotional elements that form the thing representation; second, it is one of the elements that, through an associative process, builds up the word representation; and third, it is a connecting factor between thing and word representation. However, it has to be emphasised how the associative paths that lead to word representations are more limited in number than the innumerable connections of sensorial stimuli that lead to the thing representation. Consequently, we might assume that the sensorial component has subtler and unpredictable influences on the "effects and impacts of words" compared to the symbolic, cognitively sophisticated component.

These considerations confirm—especially if we recall how and when children learn to speak—that the Freudian notion of *word as action* is strictly linked to the intentionality to communicate and to the complex series of operations involved in mastering reality, such as the regulation of the active and passive components activated in relationships, and ultimately the continuous coping with persecutory and depressive anxieties. Words are totally corporeal in their origin and never cease to have a deep impact upon the body–mind, including the speaker's. They are always experienced as forces, able to create closeness and distance, and to regulate the rhythm of the ongoing interplay between individuals. The task of making a more and more refined use of these forces is a central concern of our profession. The specific use of words in obsessional patients, the somatic and the metonymic elements, the quality of actions they convey in the transference–countertransference interplay, the replicating of immobility and distance in their sound and rhythm, before and beyond any particular content, will be made clearer in the case descriptions.

Bionian and Jungian intersections

One may consider, taking into account the post-Jungian speculations on the emergent mind, how the process of emergence can be specifically affected when obsessional functioning is massively operating.

The issue of the emergent mind is linked to research in the field of neuroscience (Cambray, 2006; Wilkinson, 2006). When exploring the phenomenology of psychic facts beyond the epistemic limits of the causality principle, the notion of the emergent mind has much in common with Bion's selected fact (Bion, 1962). This has deep implications for the definition of development as a whole, both in the conceptualisation and clinical use of interpretation, and for the role of the analyst's subjectivity.

Emergence is a concept drawn from complexity theory of dynamic systems. It refers to the interactions between agents producing results that operate at a level of organisation above that of the agents themselves. Such self-organisation arises spontaneously out of the interactions of the component parts. According to this model, the mind is conceived of as emerging from the underlying neural processes. Emergent processes operate at the edge of order and chaos, and are seen as the locus for the coming into being of psychic life. In this perspective, it is epistemologically relevant to place our analytic work beyond the restrictive concept of development, and take into account the principle of self-organising emergent qualities, with their ongoing creation of new and unexpected meanings and psychic agencies. Self-organising, however, does not mean that everything happens magically in some mystical or automatic and unshared way. Most of all, it does not mean that it works without a reciprocal dialogue and deep inter-relatedness between subject and object. Nor can it be seen as being under the dominance of conscious intentionality, but as the outcome of receptivity, engagement, and a partial suspension of memory and desire. The patient is in a place he is unaware of being in, and the analyst is partially and intentionally positioned in an intermediate state of unintentionality, in that intermediate state between mind and matter that Jung calls "true imagination" (Jung, 1912).

In a more recent article, Cambray makes a clinically relevant statement, when he affirms that:

> from the perspective of where a treatment begins there will be a feeling of enigma whenever the engagement leads to a thorough-going transformation with emergent properties; emergence is inexplicable

from the viewpoint of contributors/agents but only makes sense in terms of the whole, which can be most easily described in field terms—in therapy this need not just be dyadic, it can be intrapsychic, as when parts of the personality are reorganized into a more integrated whole. Emergence in complex systems is known to most readily occur at the edge of order and chaos; too much order leads to rigidity, while too much chaos is dissolutive. Therapeutic action designed to foster emergence would then of course be best oriented toward this edge, not as a fixed goal but as a rudder to guide the therapeutic couple. More generally, I would like to suggest the use of the phrase "the moment of complexity", to capture the orienting possibilities of the field itself.

(2011, p. 301)

The mind is continuously born out of complexity whose boundaries and features are always beyond our limited knowledge, with neither simplistic nor random causalities. Chaos may be depicted as complex and evasive—not at all pure and untouched. Chaos implies that humans are opaque and undetectable beings, with millions of traces working silently and loudly as one, or one against the other. Order is—in the first instance—the mother's wish that her baby may live with sufficient trust and joy. In essence, emergence is relational as well as highly sensitive to and dependent upon the slightest qualities of interpersonal exchanges, whether conscious or not.

Long before field theory, Bion had formulated the concept of selected fact, borrowed from Henry Poincaré's book *Science and Method* (1908). In *Learning from Experience*, Bion quotes Poincaré as follows:

If a new result is to have any value, it must unite elements long since known, but till then scattered and seemingly foreign to each other, and suddenly introduce order where the appearance of disorder reigned. Then it enables us to see at a glance each of these elements in the place it occupies in the whole. Not only is the new fact valuable on its own account, but it alone gives a value to the old facts it unites. Our mind is frail as our senses are; it would lose itself in the complexity of the world if that complexity were not harmonious; like the short-sighted, it would only see the details, and would be obliged to forget each of these details before examining the next, because it would be incapable of taking in the whole. The only facts

worthy of our attention are those which introduce order into this
complexity and so make it accessible to us.

(1962, p. 72)

And shortly after, Bion adds:

The selected fact is the name of an emotional experience, the emotional experience of a sense of discovery of coherence; its significance is therefore epistemological and the relationship of selected
facts must not be assumed to be logical.

(1962, p. 73)

Overvalued ideas, as encountered in the obsessional ideation and re-
enacted in the unconsciously demanded rigidity of interpretations,
are easily activated by the obsessional patient and strongly oppose the
basic conditions for the emergence of the selected fact. This is highly
connected with the specific tendency to over-saturate the mental space
by rigid control and pseudo-logical statements that operate through the
continuous creation of false connections. Moreover, displacement, isolation, and undoing make mental contents and their circulation in the
inter-subjective space asphyxiated, twisted, and repetitive. The resilient
disposition to the unsaturated, the firm positioning in an intermediate state of openness, the flexible balance between receptivity, focused
attention, assertiveness, and dreamy wait state, are all in some way to
be "imposed" by the analyst against the most tenacious tendency to
immobility and occlusion. More often than not, and for a long time,
there is no cooperation, conscious or unconscious, from the patient.
Resilience in the analyst has to be nourished, resilience always being at
risk of slipping into the deep ravine of masochistic imprisonment and
immobility.

Resilience can be helped in many ways: one of them is theory as a
tool for reading phenomena and giving meaning to the raw material of
the mind. A specific way, among many others, of conceiving two basic
Jungian concepts—the self and the archetype—can help support resilience and possibly create in the analyst the most favourable conditions
for the emergent to emerge.

I tend to emphasise a view of the self as the *unsaturated* potential to
become a subject within a relationship. Fordham describes the self as
without phenomena (Fordham, 1985). This state of being without phenomena, which draws close to the Kantian notion of empty thought,

can be seen as meaningful in the way it also echoes Bion's notion of preconception or, in different ways, the notion of O, the thing-in-itself, the ultimate reality. The self can be seen and experienced as a *nothingness*, so that the whole psyche-soma is a potential void without representations, an unsaturated disposition that precedes the relational coming-into-being of a possible future subject. Such a potential emptiness prepares for the inevitability of the encounter, which it is possible to postulate virtually as always existing. It is a prerequisite for seeking and being sought, in order to coagulate subjectivity. In this respect, the notion of self as an innate potential for subjectification helps support resilience and an evolutionary view of symptoms and defences in the transference–countertransference interplay.

Within the framework of models stressing inborn potentials, which certainly permeate Jungian psychology, issues can be addressed differently from a pre-formationist perspective, which posits the existence of complex representational structures already present at birth, as opposed to a pre-deterministic perspective, according to which structures develop through pre-determined stages of differentiation and elaboration, leading one to infer a disposition rather than an endowment of inherited complex representations (Urban, 2005). While using the term "archetype", I tend to qualify it with the term "unsaturated", which is closer to Fordham's pre-deterministic view, as well as to Bion's model of preconceptions.

The definition of archetype, which is no less complex than the idea of the self, is multifaceted and often contradictory in Jung's writing (Jung, 1959). Consequently, Jungians have developed radically different ways of understanding the functioning of the mind, the idea of psychic development, the idea of transference itself, and the way of conducting analytic work. On this topic, I refer to a remarkable contribution by Knox (2003, 2009), followed by other authors (Hogenson, 2009; Sinigaglia & Sparaci, 2010; Vezzoli, 2009). Even recently, because of Jung's cultural legacy in relation to the theory of the archetype, Jungian thinkers are questioning the idea of inborn patterns and of the heritability of complex forms (Goodwyn, 2010; Knox, Merchant, & Hogenson, 2010).

Among the various definitions of the archetype that Knox (2003) draws out of Jung's writing, I refer here to its definition as an abstract organisational structure in the mind, with no representational or symbolic content. According to this approach, any Lamarckian perspective which, openly or otherwise, has influenced Jung's speculative thought, appears inadmissible. This perspective suggests that the inborn contents of the infant's mind consist mainly in primary predispositions and attention biases that can activate the learning process.

My stressing the definition of archetype as unsaturated seems appropriate to the description of an element devoid of representational content. A further distinction could be made between an unsaturated archetype and a learned archetype, the latter resulting from successive introjective operations and from progressive saturation in parallel with Bion's model of preconception–realisation (Bion, 1962); I will just mention the obvious differences between this *a priori* potential and the earliest introjective sedimentations that make up what is known as "implicit memory".

Clinically speaking, and similarly to what has been stated with regard to the self, the main relevance of a postulate such as the idea of the unsaturated archetype would consist in the assumption of a potential that makes the mental apparatus open to representability and the development of tri-dimensionality. The basic function of this assumption is to support the analyst's effort to maintain resilience in spite of the constant repetition of immobilising defensive phenomena that quite effectively prevent the emergent from emerging.

Sadism and the anal position

In the Freudian speculation, obsessional neurosis has been traditionally linked to the anal phase of development and to sadism. This way of understanding was of course linked to a specific metapsychology, which as such evolved within Freud's thought in connection with other relevant theoretical developments. It is worth briefly outlining some of these elements for the purpose of theoretical clarity, and in order to point out which of these models can still be regarded as theoretically and clinically valid.

We have first of all to consider that Freud's findings on the successive early organisations of the sexual instinct developed over many years and include, among others, the *Three Essays on Sexuality* (1905d), particularly the 1915 additions; the seminal reflections on narcissism and paranoia in the case of Schreber (1911c); "The disposition to obsessional neurosis" (1913i) with regard to the anal-sadistic stage; and "The infantile genital organisation" (1923c) with regard to the phallic stage. Over such a long period of time, Freud had in parallel evolved core metapsychological elements that cannot be overlooked in the comprehension of the overall model of organisation of the libido. Namely: the original traumatic theory, with the consequent distinction between a passive participation in early trauma in hysteria and an active participation in trauma in obsessional neurosis, was repudiated (Freud, 1906a); and the distinction between libido and ego instinct (first dualism) was abandoned in favour of the distinction between the life and death instincts (second dualism) (Freud, 1920g).

It is in the framework of the early model of development and pre-genital organisation of the libido, even though the traumatic theory had already been abandoned at that time, that Freud first linked some obsessional character traits, essentially orderliness, parsimony, and obstinacy, to anal erotism (1908b). However, it is in "The disposition to obsessional neurosis" (1913i) that Freud outlines paramount theoretical points which are still, however, within the frame of the first dualism libido/ego instincts. In this paper, Freud hypothesises that in individuals who are predisposed to obsessional neurosis, the development of the libido and the development of the ego can be out of phase, the former being retarded, with the consequence that hate prevails over love, hate pre-existing love. Through fixation, hate becomes in this light the basic endowment of the ego in the obsessional individual. Freud affirms:

> I cannot tell if it may seem too rash if, on the basis of such indications as we possess, I suggest the possibility that a chronological outstripping of libidinal development by ego development should be included in the disposition to obsessional neurosis. A precocity of this kind would necessitate the choice of an object under the influence of the ego-instincts, at a time at which the sexual instincts had not yet assumed their final shape, and a fixation at the stage of the pregenital sexual organisation would thus be left. If we consider that obsessional neurotics have to develop a super-morality in order to protect their object-love from the hostility lurking behind it, we shall be inclined to regard some degree of this precocity of ego development as typical of human nature and to derive the capacity for the origin of morality from the fact that in the order of development hate is the precursor of love.
>
> (1913i, p. 325)

Whether or not we consider the primacy of hate—and I shall return to this issue—hate, in the guise of sadism, is always a protagonist on the obsessional scene, according to clinical observations. What is no longer sustainable today is the equivalence made by Freud in connection with this issue and, in the same paper (1913i), between femininity, homosexuality, and passivity, on the one hand, and masculinity, activity, and heterosexuality, on the other. These are categories that have been appropriately and definitively disentangled from one another. The issue of sadism as an active property of the ego remains nevertheless crucial, regardless of gender identity, sexual orientation, or roles.

But why is it still worth calling it *anal* sadism? The dualism retention–expulsion, the pattern of control and distancing, the cruelty and excitement that accompany such activity, to say nothing of the issues of moral and physical cleanliness, and their connection with the stimulation of the anal mucous membranes and musculature, can certainly be considered valid in metaphorical and dynamic terms, if not in genetic terms. Metaphors become more vivid when we consider how parts of the self, thoughts, emotions, relations, and other people are treated and used by the obsessional individual as excrements to be controlled and expelled, with an overall suppression of the sense of respect for otherness. The immobility of the obsessional doubt, as opposed to creative dialectic, is the ultimate description of the constipation of the mind and can be regarded as the obsessional symptom *par excellence*. The sense of excitement, triumph, and superiority linked to this functioning is not difficult to assess, especially in the transference and countertransference interplay. The phobic attitude, as a strategy to stay on the threshold of life, avoiding conflicts and limits while gazing at emotions, feelings, and losses from a safe distance, supports the omnipotent position of considering the internal as well as the external world in the same way as controllable faeces.

In his seminal paper "A short study of the development of the libido viewed in the light of mental disorders" (1924), Karl Abraham describes with theoretical acuity the interrelatedness between obsessional neurosis and melancholia, in relation to the issue of object loss. The essay is a milestone in the evolution of psychoanalytic theory with regard to the differentiation between two components within the oral phase, incorporation and oral sadism, as well as in the anal phase, expulsion and retention, and represents the foundation of Klein's elaborations on the paranoid-schizoid and depressive positions. Moreover, Abraham's observations are particularly relevant when he considers the similarities of the two clinical conditions, in particular when melancholic and obsessional patients are in a state of partial clinical remission, that is, when they are not, respectively, in a full depressive or manic state, or overwhelmed by massive obsessional symptoms. Anal sadism is described as the main feature of this intermediate state between depression and obsessional neurosis in relation to object loss.

> we have come to the conclusion that in melancholia the patient gives up his psycho-sexual relations to his object, whereas the obsessional neurotic does in the end manage to escape that fate.
>
> (Abraham, 1924, p. 423)

Abraham outlines the similarities in their character structure and the common prevalence of ambivalence, reflecting upon the issue of object loss in the light of the anal stage of development. Anal erotism is viewed as containing two opposite pleasurable tendencies, the same existing also in the field of sadistic impulses. After considering the pleasure of evacuation of the bowels as linked to the excitations of the anal zone, and the opposite pleasure of retaining the faeces, Abraham states:

> Psycho-analytic experience has shown beyond a doubt that in the middle stage of his libidinal development the individual regards the person who is the object of his desire as something over which he exercises ownership, and that he consequently treats that person in the same way as he does his earliest piece of private property, i.e. the contents of his body, his faeces. Whereas on the genital level "love" means the transference of his positive feeling on to the object and involves a psycho-sexual adaptation to the object, on the level below it means that he treats his object as though it belonged to him. And since the ambivalence of feelings still exists in full force on this inferior level, he expresses his positive attitude towards his object in the form of retaining his property and his negative attitude in the form of rejecting it. Thus when the obsessional neurotic is threatened with the loss of his object, and when the melancholiac [sic] actually does lose his, it signifies to the unconscious mind of each an expulsion of that object in the sense of a physical expulsion of faeces.
>
> (Abraham, 1924, pp. 425–426)

Also with regard to sadism, two opposing tendencies are observable: one expresses itself in the shape of dominating, and the other in the shape of destroying. The two are combined with the anal tendencies of retaining and expelling, and reinforce one another.

Before discussing how these elements come into play in melancholia, Abraham describes how they work in obsessional neurosis, and states:

> For we are able to detect in our patient's compulsive love of order [...] the cooperation of [...] sadistic impulses as well. [...] Compulsive orderliness is at the same time an expression of the patient's desire for domination. He exerts power over things. [...] As soon as something special occurs that threatens the "loss" of their object [...] neurotics react with great violence. The patient summons up the whole energy of his positive libidinal fixations to combat the danger that the current of feeling hostile to his object will grow too strong. If the conservative tendencies—those of retaining and controlling his object—are the more powerful, this conflict around the love-object will call forth phenomena of psychological compulsion. But if the opposing sadistic-anal tendencies are victorious—those which aim at destroying and expelling the object—then that patient will fall into a state of melancholic depression.
>
> (Abraham, 1924, p. 439)

From structural and genetic points of view, as will be shown in the case material, the threatened loss of the loved object is something that ultimately has to be traced back to these patients' damaged primary relationships, basically in an experience of an impaired rhythm of presence and absence of the object, as well as in the specific quality of the presence that makes reverie highly problematic. However, the threatened loss also has an unavoidable, minute by minute translation in the unfolding of the analytic process. The patient has to suffer the end of each session, the interval between sessions, and the evidence of not being able to control the analyst and take possession of the analyst's life. This is common to all patients, but for the obsessionals it is particularly hard. Fantasies about the absent analyst are forcefully suppressed, and pretended indifference to separations is the strongest shield they use to protect themselves. But it is especially the analyst's unpredictability and liveliness of thinking that shows as nothing else does that the object is not under their control, that it does not belong to them. Obsessionals fiercely oppose surprise, change, freedom of thought, variations, asymmetry, dialectics, and all possible manifestations of otherness that could imply a sense of respect and recognition of the other's dignity and independence. The other has to be dominated, cruelly condemned to rigid symmetry and immobility, as well as turned into being affectively indifferent, and emotionally expelled. The impact on the rhythm of speech, on the countertransference, and on the genesis and quality of psychoanalytic interpretation will be described in the case material.

To go back to the issue of the supposed primacy of sadism, a notion that is common to Freud and Abraham and is grounded in the theory of libido, it is far from my purposes to exhume any sort of Controversial Discussions upon this problem, let alone on the death instinct, or follow the letter of Freud's statement on hate being a precursor to love and all the Kleinian speculations on primary envy and its derivatives.

However, among Jung's legacies which I consider as an indispensable part of my internal equipment, I must underline that the *shadow*, a concept that implies different levels and structures of the individual's mind, has a component that Jung considers *ontological*. Jung never put at the centre of human nature any sense of particular goodness, nor did he do the opposite by posing evil at the centre. When considering the shadow as being substantially equivalent to the personal repressed psychic elements, things look relatively easy. Jung says:

> Unfortunately there can be no doubt that man is, on the whole, less good than he imagines himself or wants to be. Everyone carries a shadow, and the less it is embodied in the individual's conscious life, the blacker and denser it is. If inferiority is conscious, one always has a chance to correct it. Furthermore, it is constantly in contact with other interests, so that it is continually subjected to modifications. But if it is repressed and isolated from consciousness, it never gets corrected, and is liable to burst forth suddenly in a moment of unawareness. At all events, it forms an unconscious snag, thwarting our most well-meant intentions.
>
> We carry our past with us, to wit, the primitive and inferior man with his desires and emotions, and it is only with an enormous effort that we can detach ourselves from this burden.
>
> (Jung, 1938, p. 76)

Much more challenging are these words:

> The Christian answer is that evil is a *privatio boni*. This classic formula robs evil of absolute existence and makes it a shadow that has only a relative existence depending on light. Good, on the other

hand, is credited with a positive substantiality. But, as psychological experience shows, "good" and "evil" are opposite poles of a moral judgement which, as such, originates in man. [...] How can one speak of "good" at all if there is no "evil"? Or of "light" if there is no "darkness", or of "above" if there is no "below"? There is no getting around the fact that if you allow substantiality to good, you must also allow it to evil. If evil has no substance, good must remain shadowy, for there is no substantial opponent for it to defend itself against, but only a shadow, a mere privation of good. Such a view can hardly be squared with observed reality. It is difficult to avoid the impression that apotropaic tendencies have had a hand in creating this notion, with the understandable intention of settling the painful problem of evil as optimistically as possible. Often it is just as well that we do not know the danger we escape when we rush in where angels fear to tread.

(Jung, 1938, p. 168)

Jung's words leave no uncertainty. The point is not of assuming the centrality or primacy of good or evil, nor to suppose that one comes first and the other follows. Whatever name we give to evil, it is *natural*, it is *substantial*, just as good is. Being Jungian, I cannot but assume, together with an innate disposition of the self coming to be—that is, an agency that develops towards subjectification—as well as with a constitutional endowment of unsaturated archetypes—that is, an ability to represent the unknown—an equally innate disposition to evil. Moreover, if we see the term "apotropaic", used by Jung in his statement, as equivalent to a reaction formation, which is well part of the obsessional equipment, we are confronted all the more with the pervasiveness of the mechanisms we are attempting to describe.

By no means does this view imply that the accidental plays no role. The actual interaction of subjects and the impact of life events do affect prevalences and dispositions; they can twist archetypes and dissolve selves, and leave the field open to destructiveness. Jung's view poses the equivalent naturalness of good and evil, constructiveness and destructiveness, subjectification and dispersion. Both are at play, in an uncertain game that involves us as psychoanalysts with all our being: *Ars requirit totum hominem.*

The structure and style of the book

Following what has been outlined in the present chapter, the book has been divided into three sections, each exploring specific issues. The first section considers obsessive–compulsive disorder in its inter-relatedness with thinking disorders, and investigates from a dynamic perspective the variability of insight and ego-dystonia. With regard to the combined psychoanalytic and pharmacological treatment, different situations are presented and discussed, including those in which, for a number of reasons, I had to play both psychoanalytic and prescribing roles with some patients. These are certainly to be considered as exceptions in the consolidated practice of having two cooperating therapeutic figures. However, exceptions interrogate and challenge our theoretical convictions and our technical instruments and may become experiences from which to learn.

The second section of the book deepens the issue of anal sadism through the use of case material, as well as Pasolini's film *Salò, or The 120 Days of Sodom* (1975). And finally, the third section deals with the connection between obsession and depression.

Having outlined in this first part my main theoretical frames of reference, while presenting the clinical material I have intentionally reduced quotations to the minimum, in order to make the case material as lively and vivid as possible. Theory remains in case descriptions as a present but silent companion, whose influence can be glimpsed discreetly between the lines. Some cases are presented in a more traditional form, by reporting detailed material taken from sessions, while some others are in the shape of a narrative, to pay tribute to my conviction that as psychoanalysts we are at the same time scientists and story-tellers.

PART II

THE PSYCHOTIC THRESHOLD:
OCD AND THINKING DISORDER

CHAPTER THREE

Intersections

Since I was a child,
I have never found it difficult
to hear smells, or taste colours,
to see sounds or touch my bluest moods.

(Anonymous poet, 2006)

Introduction

The aim of this chapter is to highlight the obsessional features observed in an autistic child whom I treated analytically with four-times-weekly sessions for eighteen years (from four to twenty-two years of age), to relate them to the obsessional functioning in the family, particularly that of the mother, and to discuss the severe obsessive–compulsive disorder in my patient's younger brother, which became apparent in the latter's late adolescence. This boy is currently being treated analytically by a colleague whom I regularly see in supervision.

I will mainly focus on the obsessional features in connection with language, without giving an account of other innumerable aspects of my patient's mind as they unfolded over almost two decades of analytic treatment, and will consider the family and the brother as part of what I saw as a reticulum of modes of functioning that all the group members shared.

Giulio and his autism

Giulio developed autism at the age of two, although even in his first year, as emerged from his parents' account, there were occasional signs of avoiding eye contact and a tendency to retreat and need repeated stimulation before being engaged in meaningful relational contact. The symptoms of autism erupted at the time of his brother's birth. Because of the mother's mental condition at that time, combined with other bereavements in the family, the family environment was dominated by powerful death fantasies, which probably contributed to making anxieties unbearable and, given an obvious constitutional predisposition, dramatically triggered the autistic symptoms.

Before the onset of his illness, the patient had developed a relatively age-appropriate but very limited language, being able to name his mother, father, and a few objects, as well as some expressions for feelings of displeasure. When he began psychoanalytic treatment at the age of four, he could only utter mono- or bi-syllabic words that indicated his mother and father but little else, speaking much less and more poorly than he did before his breakdown at the age of two. He completely avoided eye contact, had no sphincter control, and showed stereotypical behaviour and repetitive sounds; he was very glued to his parents, slept between them every night, and regularly burst into floods of tears when faced with the slightest frustration. He displayed no sense of symbolic play, he often handled solid objects without making any distinction between them, and engaged in rubbing activity with soft surfaces or with water.

When he came to me at the age of four, he had just ended a psycho-motor therapy begun one year earlier. No specific interventions in the area of verbal communication were implemented in the following years, partly to avoid colluding with the mother's interventionist and over-technical attitude, but mainly to prevent the risk of increasing the patient's strong tendency to echolalia and non-symbolic verbalisa-tion. Instead, emphasis was placed on encouraging the development of the parents' capacity for emotional empathy in assigning mean-ing to their child's experience and in helping him as much as possi-ble to develop symbolically appropriate elements of communication.

The guiding principle was that he should learn fewer but real words as much as possible.

For the whole period of nursery and primary school (until the age of twelve), the task of stimulating the child's relational life was excellently pursued by teachers and non-specialist volunteers, under my supervision. No specific interventions were needed for any particular behavioural problems, Giulio having always been experienced by people as sweet and lovable. Instead, light anti-psychotic medication became necessary after puberty when the patient developed transitory hallucinatory phenomena.

Over the years, his teachers were able to prompt him, in a sensitive way, to improve relationships, preventing him from resorting to stereotypical repetitions and helping him to gradually adjust to frustrating experiences. This was a child with the potential to develop, who managed to finish third form at the age of fifteen, after which he was placed in a private facility to follow a programme of rehabilitation and development of his residual capacities.

Substantially, in the course of the first five or six years of work, on the basis of four-times-weekly sessions, the patient—in spite of the obvious discontinuity and the fragmentary quality of his achievements—reached some capacity for communicative language, began to use objects in a more three-dimensional way (often in terms of symbolic equation rather than as actual symbols), improved his capacity for relational contact, and began to use the pronoun "I" and to depict himself as a whole figure. He gained control of his sphincters and became generally more aware of space dimensions (internal–external) and of time (before–after), and displayed greater modulation in his responses to the rhythm of presence and absence of the object when compared to the fixed quality of his earlier reactions of falling apart when frustrated.

Giulio as a fantasised giant

Mother: ... because, you know ... he is so powerful ... when he cries endlessly, we don't really know how to deal with him ... and if we touch him or try to comfort him, he reacts vigorously and becomes rigid ... there is nothing we can do ...

The father seemed to be absent-minded while the mother was speaking, having an incongruous smile, and looking around in the room. The fact that I look alternately at him and the mother while she is speaking does not involve him. He seems not to be listening. He seems not to be present. So I ask him directly what he thinks, and if he also thinks that Giulio is so powerful.

Father: [keeping the same smile on his face, which I find slightly irritating] Well, yes ... he always manages to do what he likes ... it seems that there is nothing we can do ... we cannot stand his crying ... so we do everything to avoid his crying ...

Mother: [laughing] And he is so incredibly strong ... he is like a giant ... I really cannot manage him physically.

I say I hardly understand what there can be to laugh about. [The mother immediately stops laughing, while the father continues to have his vague smile.]

Me: I would take very seriously the fact that you experience your child, who is just four years old, as if he were a giant, someone so overwhelmingly powerful.

I ask them how tall Giulio is, and what his weight is. Quite surprised, as if momentarily pulled back to reality, they answer my question. I comment that, given that they are not physically disabled, I hardly believe that such a tiny child can have such powerful control over them.

I ask about his sleep. They say he sleeps very peacefully every night, provided that he lies askew in their bed in between them. I ask if this is also something they think there is nothing they can do about. They reply in unison: Nothing!

Well—I say—let us see if we can manage to make him sleep in his own bed, just as ordinary people do, and possibly before the age of serving in the Army ...

They are astonished. They look at me as if they had just seen a Martian.

This is an excerpt from one of the preliminary sessions I had with the parents before taking the child into my charge. Two elements are relevant, among many possible others. First of all, the father's absent-mindedness. He looked as if he lived in a totally alien dimension, completely detached from what we were saying, although seemingly listening. His dreamy expression, his gaze lost in the mist, his odd smile, were all meaningful elements. Apart from my suspicion that he could have been even more autistic than his child, I came to know that he was at least able to wake up every morning and go to work. I most of all asked myself what kind of father he could be, how he could possibly represent an oedipal antagonist, how he could support my efforts, and how I could have him as an ally.

The mother was extremely rigid. I took note of one fact, while listening to her: what was supposed to be a declaration of helplessness and weakness actually conveyed to me a sense of immobility and power, and of omnipotent control. Giulio must have been quite controlling—I thought—but this mother was second to none in this respect. Every minimal change in her position was extremely slow and hard to achieve.

As an example of this, reaching the goal of making Giulio sleep in his own bed took months of effort and determination on my part, the mother being able to tolerate it only via strict obsessional control and by imposing her timing and pace. She decided that she would first let Giulio sleep on one side of the bed and not in between her and her husband, her side of the bed of course; and she provided a small cot that she kept attached to the main bed. Then she calculated that she would detach the cot five centimetres per week, and in a specific notebook she recorded days, times, and supposed reactions, including how Giulio slept, if he had dreams (by detecting the rapid eye movements), or if he was in a good or bad mood in the morning. As far as I could observe, Giulio did not show any particular reaction to these changes, possibly because he had the most skilled ability to quickly turn any variation into something predictable and immobile, and he learned to sleep in his bed without any theatrics.

I would like to mention that such an attitude of taking notes of every possible detail was usual for this mother, who had recorded all Giulio's episodes regarding health issues as well as developmental or behavioural elements she considered relevant. And apparently she considered almost everything as being relevant, without distinction. Several years later, when we were discussing an episode that had taken place some years before that Giulio was apparently able to remember and precisely locate in terms of date, month, year, and day of the week, to which I had incautiously expressed my doubts regarding the possibility that he truly remembered the timing of a past event so precisely, his mother proudly and unquestionably told me that Giulio was perfectly right, as she had stored that episode in her records, and had checked what Giulio clearly remembered, which was totally correct. I have to confess that around the fifteenth year of analysis, when I felt less strangled by the chains of orthodoxy, facing once again the determination Giulio showed in assuming to precisely remember the day, month, and year of any event, I opened the electronic calendar on my smartphone and started to test him. For instance, the question was: "Giulio, tell me, what day of the week May 5th, 1999 was?" or, more acrobatically: "what day of the week will June 14th, 2019 be?". I asked these questions about thirty times in a row, enquiring about different dates in the past as well as in the future. Giulio replied to each question within two seconds, with no apparent effort or sign of anxiety, perhaps just a little surprised by such a new and unexpected Francesco that he was seeing that day, and he did not make a single mistake. That was a major difference between him and his mother. She needed devices to control time, which was humanly confined to the past, needless to say. Instead, he could have the same kind of control without using any external device, just some mysterious circuit in his brain, and he was also able to expand this capacity to the future. I am not interested in investigating how this was possible, but merely wish to underline the similarities in his and his mother's attitude with regard to storing and classifying events. As far as I could understand, most of the events that his mother recorded were devoid of any real importance or meaning; they were seemingly just bare events and not experiences, and were collected with the purpose of preventing the mind from suffering loss and oblivion. Giulio's memories somewhat rarely would carry slight traces of emotions, usually regarding his father or both parents being angry and fighting with each other or scolding him. His capacity to further work through these memories was generally very poor; facts were recorded and replayed mechanically, with no apparent subjective change between before and after recalling and telling them.

His mother surely took note of Giulio's reactions after every session, and when he started to speak, she asked him to precisely report what he had said and done, and what I had said and done. Every time I met the parents, she started the meeting by recalling the day we had met the previous time, and what I had said on that occasion, which I regularly did not remember.

When I happened to suggest that they could be seen by a colleague to support their hard job as parents of such a difficult child, they invariably laughed as if I were a joker telling a funny story. "Ahahah ... yes yes yes!!! ... we too might have some problems .... Ahahahah ...", and that was it. This was something I did not manage to change over the years. Consequently, all the possible work of containment and elaboration remained under my responsibility, with all the unavoidable limits of an insufficient setting. It would have possibly been more helpful if they had been seen in individual psychotherapy, or at least specifically and frequently as a parental couple, by a colleague. But this was the limitation of the situation, and I could not do more.

One more example of the mother's immobility regarded toilet training and cleaning issues in general. At the age of four, when I started to see Giulio, he still wore a nappy, and toilet training was seen by the parents as an impossible goal to achieve. During the sessions, he frequently defaecated, which occurred with some sort of awareness; I mean that, as far as I understood, defaecating was not a totally automatic activity. I noticed that faeces did not simply pour out unconnected to what was occurring at that particular moment in the session, and I observed that Giulio was somehow aware he was pooing. Over time, I noticed he also tended to hide in or retreat to a certain corner of the room when he felt the stimulus to defaecate. This made me think he had some rudimentary concept of his insides being different from the outside, and that he was partly able to realise that something was *coming out of himself*. This was hypothetically linked to a reaction to what I said and did in the session (and consequently was a sign of a momentary break in the autistic isolation), which in turn activated an attempt at recreating the non-separating sensuousness of contact between faeces and skin (and in so doing, he built up his autistic functioning once again). I took these details as being very important, not only in terms of his rudimentary awareness of space but also in terms of the presence of sadism, in what I perceived as an active response to my interventions. The fact that, as I saw it, Giulio did not just innocently and passively dismantle (Meltzer et al., 1975) his self but actively attacked the object was an extremely encouraging element, from which I derived my decision to work with the parents in terms of promoting toilet training. This required time and great effort, of course, considering the starting point, as I shall now describe.

When his mother came to fetch Giulio at the end of the sessions (I had vigorously encouraged her not to stay in the waiting room, but to go out of my office and come back precisely at the end of the session), and realised he had pooed, she was perfectly organised to wash him in the bathroom and change his nappy, which took her exactly and invariably five minutes, never a second more, never a second less. When she ably concluded the operation, she went away with Giulio and left the dirty nappy on the floor in the waiting room, always folded in exactly the same way and placed in the same precise position. As she was not allowed to stay in the waiting room, she let Giulio's excrements—standing for hers—occupy my space.

The smell of Giulio's faeces surely had some variations, likely depending on his dietary regime, but my obsessiveness did not get to the point of classifying smells in connection to the different days of the week and seeing if there was some statistical significance. So, I cannot say more about this detail.

I allowed myself a few months without intervening, in order to better understand the issue of when and how Giulio defaecated in the sessions, as well as how the issue of toilet training and cleaning was apprehended in the mother's mind, and to precisely detect the countertransference in response to all these details. After pulling these factors together and understanding the issue of time and space, as well as the elements of sadism, immobility, and control (which were evident in the ritualised dropping of the dirty nappy on the floor in the waiting room), I first of all suggested that she might dispose of the nappy in the dustbin. "There are appropriate places for rubbish", I said, "… and for things we want to get rid of …". I then said to the parents that, considering Giulio was not neurologically damaged and was five years old, with sufficient awareness of his pooing and his own wish to hide in a sort of private space, I thought toilet training needed to begin with no further delay.

The process took a long time, with much resistance on the part of the mother, accompanied as always by the father's fatuous smile. Similarly to what had happened for the bed, this goal could be achieved via the mother's obsessional modality. She scheduled and recorded times and modes, organising days and hours of "no-nappy moments" and, given that I was inflexible with regard to her objections, the result could eventually, although exhaustingly, be obtained: Giulio, by the age of six, slept in his room, and asked to be taken to the toilet when he needed to relieve himself. A glimpse of normality.

These important achievements did not change the overall controlling attitude of the mother, which of course found millions of other fields to be cultivated over the years, but they were nevertheless appreciated by the parents and reinforced their trust in my work. The parents also appreciated the evidence that Giulio was not a powerful, unmodifiable, and tyrannical giant, and most of all, their belief that they could play a relevant role in promoting his development was reinforced.

It is quite remarkable that Giulio, around the same age and along with the developments in bed and toilet issues, began to pronounce his first words. A better distinction between internal and external space, between self and object, above and below, left and right, which was the constant focus of my interpretative work with him, led to his achieving a capacity for *letting something intentionally and meaningfully go out*. Faeces and urine could be let go off, and got rid off, and words could be released in order to communicate. The orifices were better distinguished from one other, they could be opened and closed with tolerable anxiety, and did not simply leak. Giulio became able to separate himself from his excrements and from his words, with the awareness that they were not always one and the same.

Words

Indeed, the appearance of the first real word, "water", occurred in a moment when a preconception met a realisation and meaningfully regarded an absent object. Separateness, space, distance, and loss are obviously implied in the formation of language, as language is a means to reach someone or something that is, as a prerequisite, a *non-me* at an adequate distance. Not too close, not too far.

This is an excerpt of the session when this occurred, and where the transformations in oral investments are evident:

> Giulio, who has happily come into the room, progressively becomes angry, grinds his teeth and makes aggressive sounds: I comment on this as wanting to make me see that he feels something in his mouth, something like anger in his mouth ...

> He takes, after having searched for a while through the toys, two dinosaurs, makes various roaring sounds, turns to me showing me one of the

dinosaurs, and roaring (looks at me), then after a while he starts a fight between the two dinosaurs, with various bites, always accompanied by gestures with roars ...

He continues in this way for a while, until he finds a string, he puts it in his mouth and pulls it with both hands and grinds his teeth. Then he takes a cow and makes gentle sounds, he shows me the cow and then wraps the string around it. I tell him that "the cow is like mum, mum tied to your mouth, so you feel no more anger now".

He moves towards the sink where he makes unsuccessful attempts at turning on the tap, at times he comes to me for help, he moves as if he wants to take my hand and says, once, "a-t ... wa-t ... wa-ter".

I say that he wants me to give him water, that he was able to name it, and that now that he has got some, he feels like a happy baby that has mummy's milk. [When I turn the tap, he immediately welcomes the water, making a pleased ecstatic sound.]

The achievement of Giulio's capacity to name an absent object, and therefore to use proper language, was of course momentary and discontinuous, but it nevertheless marked a divide. From that point on, I myself could first of all remember his capacity and then remind him of it, therefore pulling him vigorously back to meaningful language every time he withdrew to echolalia and stereotyped phrasing, which continued to occur until the end of our eighteen years together.

The issue of language was of course a major concern for the parents. For years, they had been deprived of meaningful contact with him, as he had not shown *interest* in them but only a tyrannical use of their bodies and functions. Consequently, language was a considerable worry for these parents in what I perceived as their true desire to be in a live relational exchange with him. They fully appreciated the fact that, starting from the first word, Giulio slowly learned other words that sounded meaningful to them, and their efforts to interpret him and detect some meaning in his at times bizarre speech was remarkable.

Nothing was easy, though. The mother secretly engaged Giulio in all sorts of methods aimed at improving his language. I say secretly, because I had recommended not to overstimulate Giulio with those kinds of procedures, underlining the risk that he could mechanically learn millions of words, even the entire *Divine Comedy*, without understanding the slightest meaning of what he was saying. I knew I was quite unpopular in my position, but I tried to explain to the parents that our goal was to first consolidate his capacity for symbolic language by using only a few words. We would have time afterwards to deal with the quantity of words he could learn.

This was a principle the mother accepted with great difficulty, given that she was of course very well aware of all the latest techniques for the treatment of autistic children. As she confessed a few years later, she applied these methods with Giulio after school, as if she were a teacher (notwithstanding my continuously underlining that she was a parent, and her job was to empathetically understand and not teach), with all her obsessional preciseness and constancy.

In one way or another, Giulio learned to speak. My effort was constantly in the direction of making words meaningful: and to dribble, as if I were a skilled footballer, all the tricky traps of his stereotypical and pseudo-adequate language.

An intermediate passage: from echolalia to verbal fragmentation

Around the seventh year of analysis, when the patient was eleven years old, a very manifest phenomenon of formal thought fragmentation began to develop, so that the patient's speech took the form of a "word salad", even though it was not associated with states of hyper-excitement. The sentences he uttered looked different not only from the apparently meaningful words or phrase-words he had produced on previous occasions, but also from simple echolalia and stereotypical repetitions which might echo sentences spoken by adults or words from films or cartoons. I could envisage in this manner of speech a kind of fluid state that might allow meaningful elements to solidify, in a sort of foreshadowing of a more complete language and a new organisation of thinking.

From a session in that period:

Giulio looks at me and starts saying a succession of words like "the cheese tiger lives Paloo they are all participation the brontosaurus grr..grr..ahhh sea the coffee-pot of the day with string we made ten the crow moves concentrating lion ahhh ahhh they are all dead turn it off spaghetti with sauce little green monster ...", and so on for about twenty minutes. I feel he is somehow in contact with me, more than he was when uttering ste-reotypical phrases at the beginning of the session. I am of the idea that he is trying to tell me something, and as I make a comment on all these words which are mixed up together, I find myself making the effort to bring together some meaning. I put together the names of some fierce animals with some expressions of anxiety which appear here and there and then I name these fierce beasts and the fear they might cause him. Knowing that Paloo was his grandparents' dog, who died not long beforehand and to whom the patient was very attached, I try to say something about this death and how the fact that Paloo has disappeared perhaps frightens him, as does the idea that, like Paloo, I could disappear as well ...

I mainly understood the stereotypical utterances and the echolalia produced in the first unquoted part of this session, and in many others, as a means to control and nullify possible contact with me as a meaningful object (this is a sort of obsessional operation carried to the extreme, although not as extreme as the violent pulverisation of the object and the creation of mental urine would be) and retreat into the bi-dimensional realm of autistic objects and shapes. I always took such an operation as driven by a form of primitive sadistic anti-vital functioning, which was most likely rooted, however, in constitutional/biological factors. Beyond all possible environmental causes, either pre-natal or post-natal, this is a sort of *objective* sadism, where even biological factors are *naturally* oriented against the biological naturalness of making bonds. This is not so different conceptually from what occurs in the most severe states of catatonia that we happened to observe in adult patients in the pre-pharmacological era. By no means could I consider such an operation as the result of a passive—and somehow innocent—process of dismantling. There can be no innocence in making bonds impossible, even if nobody can be subjectively held responsible. Contrary to that, the part of the session quoted above, when the verbal fragmentation appeared, evoked a desire to make sense of the experience, activating my effort to tune into a possible O in the patient, at the very moment when O was attempting—through scattered bits of words and splintered emotional states—to change into K. The fragmentation of the verbal connections was not perceived in the countertransference as a sign of destructiveness but conveyed two main elements that were intertwined: first, the evidence that the mind is able to make an effort to create meaning and order, starting from a state of disorganisation and chaos; second, the fact that every link evokes the risk of loss. I think it is also remarkable that the effort to coagulate meaning via projective identification includes Paloo as a lost object. This is, strictly speaking, a totally anti-obsessional operation.

If the Paloo-analyst figure is loved as a live object and not turned into a lifeless, stereotyped object if and when he is not brought under sadistic control, then he might die and be lost. Here, one might envisage the dawn of the work of mourning, where the missing object is no longer completely fragmented and evacuated like mental urine in order to be emotionally and perceptually neutralised, or omnipotently controlled via obsessional operations.

Dribbling repetitiveness

Both Giulio and his mother were extremely skilled in turning variations into the most boring and dull repetitive acts. It took them just hours, if not minutes, to turn any surprise into a lifeless wreck and make it look as if it had always been that way.

The constancy of the analytic setting was itself turned into a high-security prison, all the gestures related to saying hello or goodbye, the way the door bell was rung, the mode of taking off one's coat, or of walking into the room, my voice and gestures, my words and my mimicry, all had the same destiny.

There was a way to respond to this state of affairs, which implied a careful monitoring of the countertransference. As a clearer example of this, I shall quote a common situation that would occur when Giulio was already well into adolescence, and his language was more complex and better articulated.

Here is the beginning of a session when Giulio is eighteen years old:

Giulio rings the doorbell perfectly on time. I realise that I walk along the corridor to open the door as if I were perfectly synchronised with him—a sort of automatic conforming to an unofficial schedule. This makes me feel slightly irritated and quite claustrophobic. I open the door and he comes in, waving his right hand and saying Hello Francesco in a way that is perfectly identical to what I have seen and heard for who knows how long, to which I tend to automatically reply Hello Giulio in the same flat and dull way. As usual he would tend to pour into the corridor, and quickly walk into—or leak-drip into—the consulting room. I remember that several years before, his way of coming in reminded me of the cork of a bottle of sparkling wine when you open it. After interpreting that manner innumerable times,

I imposed a different pace. But Giulio still entered the main door in the same cap-of-a-bottle way, learning, however, to slow down after a few steps, and slightly turning his head towards me to wait for a wave of my hand to go into the consulting room. But all this highly important succession of gestures and rhythms soon became repetitive and lifeless. So today I decided to make a change. First, I did not say Hello Giulio, but Ah! Here you are! and I noticed he slightly shivered. He was surprised: he was no longer able to make me non-existent as he had skilfully done in the past. So what I do and say did matter to him now. Second, when he stopped to wait for my wave and proceed, I did something different. I stopped. I took a few seconds more. I said Wait a minute! And then I moved a few steps towards him. I then said Hey, Look at me! He turns his face and looks at me. As soon as I realised he was a little embarrassed, I was satisfied. Ok, now you can go in!

This is a very simple example of how important the work on the subtle seduction of repetitiveness is, beyond the mere and yet essential interpretative activity in the transference. The way the patient controls his anxiety, or any other emotional state connected with re-encountering me, involves a number of mental operations that determine the exasperation of the natural tendency to make things recognisable and usual, to the extent of nullifying every potential element of surprise and variation. The psychic work here is to make the invariant absolute, and to block transformations. If we imagine the interplay between invariant and transformation as a balanced dialogue between the tendency towards stability and order, on the one hand, and the chaotic and unpredictable autonomy of a non-me object, on the other, the latter is virtually deleted in favour of an absolute state of immobility. This violent and subtle project is precisely what makes me feel uncomfortable and claustrophobic at the beginning of the session. Autistic children are second to none in challenging their analysts on this battlefield, and I have learned from them to respond to the same poisonous strategy when performed by other categories of patients.

Without proper interpretative work in the transference, nothing changes in this respect, but actions—unlike enactments—are also required on the part of the analyst to continuously and patently affirm that we are not open to being easily killed. As the quoted vignette shows, it is not necessary to do anything special. Listening to the countertransference is of course a prerequisite. Then it is just a case of dribbling the ball, like a good footballer, against your opponent whose game is so predictable.

I perfectly knew that if I played in the same way, and used the same words and gestures for a couple more times in the following days, Giulio would have quickly learned my behaviour and would have adapted to it without any difficulty, killing all its potential to create surprise. I did not assume I could be creative every day, knowing that my capacity to be inventive was limited. Playing this way every now and then was enough, I thought, and considering that Giulio presumed he had a perfectly functioning memory, I trusted his capacity to remember that Francesco was not always predictable, and most of all that he was still alive.

Even more tricky was the work with words. By the age of eighteen, Giulio was fairly well able to express himself appropriately. His mimicry and body posture were still quite rigid, he tended to keep the same position on his chair in front of me, trying to restrain some automatic movements and slight trembling, which I had commented upon several times. As he supposed I did not like his movements, he tried to block them, despite my comments on this fantasy. At that stage of his analysis, after taking a seat in his usual manner, slightly in the guise of a leaning tower, he invariably said "Alright …", and then started to tell me about what he had done at school, which was often about some fights with other schoolmates, or he talked about some difficulties at home with his parents. Incidentally, I came to know that the fatuous smile of the father was only one side of the coin. This man was apparently quite aggressive, often verbally and at times also physically violent with the two children. He easily lost his temper.

In any event, Giulio's speech sounded coherent and at times interesting, and he seemed to be willing to tell Francesco—whom he certainly considered part of his consolidated habits—about his everyday life. However, beyond my comments every now and then, and beyond the specific content of what he said, I always felt as if the act of telling was itself a habit, something that had become a consolidated ritual, like brushing your teeth in the morning or going to the toilet before going to bed. Again, my discomfort helped me to intervene with a crucial question, after patiently listening to his account: *Giulio, why are you telling me this story?* The answer was not the most encouraging one I would have liked to hear: *Mum told me to.*

The mother's planning and strategies had not yet ended. Obviously, this was not episodic. As usual, I took my time to verify this issue and to understand that the collusion between the two was still very strong. Despite dozens of comments to the parents, the ritual still ran as follows: mother asked Giulio to tell her what we had said in the session, Giulio told her everything, then, before the following session she suggested what to tell me, which he did, and after the session she checked if he had told me what she had suggested, and what my comments had been.

My intervention with Giulio was similar to what I did when he used words that he simply repeated without knowing the meaning, which I had interpreted in terms of adhesive identification and openly contrasted by saying that words must mean something, *they are not simple sounds*. Now, my intervention was apparently very simple: I said that, although he might think he was the same as Mum, I thought they were different people. Mum is mum and Giulio is Giulio. And then I asked: "Who is in front of me now? Mum or you?" Giulio, quite astonished, with a firm voice and raising his hand: "Me!" To which I added: "Perfect, Giulio. So I want to listen to what you have to say, your thoughts. When I want to listen to Mum's and Dad's thoughts, I meet them. Simple, isn't it?" "Simple!", he replied, with no hesitation.

For a long time, I continued my dribbling work with Giulio, trying to patiently and tirelessly redefine the contours of his mind, having to face a complexity—now that he was grown up—that was surely not present when he was more deeply in an autistic state. At this point, the issue at stake was not only that of adhesive identification and bi-dimensional adjustment to the surface of objects or to their texture or to the sensuousness of lights and sounds. Now projective identification was fully operating, in a totally tri-dimensional world full of all sorts of complexities. Complexities that included, last but not least, the intrusive projections operated by the family, by the hidden and unpredictable aggressiveness of a smiling father, and by the mercilessly intrusive and controlling obsessiveness of a mother.

On my subsequent meeting with the parents, in my umpteenth attempt to create some sense of separateness and respect, I confronted them once again. Not a smile, not a sign of friendliness. Unfortunately, my occasional unfriendliness had become a consolidated habit for them. It was no scandal.

Antonio

One year after having terminated my work with Giulio, I received an unexpected message from the mother, who asked me to see Antonio,

Giulio's younger brother, eighteen years old at that time. I first saw the parents, who told me that Antonio was getting worse and worse. Antonio was apparently blocked in a series of ruminations that regarded almost every aspect of his life, but particularly when he had aggressive thoughts about the people he met, including friends or girls, which he couldn't get rid of. He presented a number of rituals, and the quality of his life had dramatically worsened over the previous months. He was attending his last year of secondary school, and he risked failing his final exams. According to the parents, he had always been brilliant at school and at sport, and they presented his situation as something that had occurred all of a sudden. They said he had never had difficulties or problems. They had no apparent memory of the fact that, many years before, when I was treating Giulio and Antonio was five years old, they had already asked me to see him. At that time, I had not seen Antonio personally but immediately referred him to a child psychotherapist who had suggested starting some work with him, which the family did not take up for economic reasons.

This time, I agreed to see Antonio for a consultation, to assess his state and see if he needed some medication. On principle, the parents were not against the possibility of his needing medication. This was a relevant factor, considering that the family had to be supportive in every respect. I said that I would refer him for psychotherapy to a colleague. They looked quite disappointed, because they had expected me to take him personally into therapy, considering that I had finished my work with Giulio more than one year beforehand. They said they trusted me a great deal, with regard to how much I had helped Giulio, and they wanted the same kind of help for Antonio. The father said: "We did and are still doing everything we can for Giulio. We want to do the same for Antonio, and you know us like nobody else does." When I met them again after three consultation sessions with Antonio, I confirmed the diagnosis and referred him to a skilled colleague who is one of my supervisees. In addition, I planned to implement some pharmacological support, and consequently we agreed that I would meet Antonio occasionally to check the therapy; I would also see them periodically to see how things were developing from their point of view. Having understood that I would be supervising and taking care of the whole situation, they accepted the deal. Of course, I could have washed my hands of the entire issue and simply said I had no space for them. But I think that the treatment of an autistic child implies taking care of the whole family group and dealing with the migration of symptoms and pain within the group. Giulio was doing well; he had developed to the maximum of his capacities, or rather, he had reached the most that could be achieved in our work together. So I had decided to terminate our work one year before the parents raised treatment for Antonio, and to allow Giulio some freedom to find other opportunities for further growth. This did not mean that I stopped taking care of him and his context, directly or indirectly. Now it was Antonio's turn, and I had no doubt that I had to respond in some way; *they* were my patients.

My initial encounters with Antonio were undoubtedly full of interesting features. I was struck by the rigidity of his posture, as well as his mimicry. His face in particular seemed to be made of plaster, his smile fixed and inexpressive, the movements of his neck mechanical and jerky. The tone of his voice remained unmodulated and flat while he was describing his symptoms, with a certain degree of accuracy, even when he talked about his exams, which seemed to worry him the most. He immediately stated that it was his parents' suggestion that he should start a therapy, even though he realised himself that he was blocked and unable to change the situation with his own resources.

The main element I noticed during the three assessment sessions was his tendency to create misunderstandings and to assume that he had not grasped the meaning of what I said. My impression was that most of the time he was just pretending not to understand me, and was playing in the guise of a gambler in order to force me to repeat what I had said.

He talks for some minutes about his difficulties at school and about the fact that he is no longer able to learn.

I try to explore what goes on in his mind in the precise moment he feels he cannot learn, and to understand if there are disturbing thoughts of whatever nature.

He says he has thoughts he cannot stop or restrain, regarding a Chinese girl he likes and the fact that at the same time he prefers Japanese music and culture. This is an unsolvable conflict for him, that is, thinking that appreciating Japanese culture may be a true and concrete offence against his Chinese friend, who may reject him forever because of this. He asks me if, in my opinion, he has to give up his interests in Japanese culture. I immediately feel the huge pressure to respond in terms of yes or no. I comment that he is talking about what he perceives to be an unsolvable conflict, and I understand how difficult it is for him to keep two elements that he thinks do not fit each other, but when he tries to get rid of one of the two elements, he cannot make up his mind and becomes stuck.

He asks, "Can you say it again?" [with a subtle mocking smile]

"Should I?" I say, and add, "Are you sure you did not understand what I said?"

Blushing, evidently embarrassed, "Actually I did," and he repeats what I said.

"The problem is that I am not here to tell you what is right and what is wrong, or what you should or should not do, even though this is what you may expect me to do." He looks at me as if I were an alien.

I soon realised that the aim of such manoeuvres was to turn my comments into an endless succession of pedagogical prescriptions under the dominance of a primitive superego. Things always had to be good or bad, allowed or prohibited, appropriate or inadequate, clean or dirty, morally acceptable or condemnable. Quite clearly, this was the main pattern of his interaction with the parents, particularly the mother. There was a marked collusion and mutual stimulation in continuously asking for reassurance and advice, or in providing judgements and advice even when not explicitly requested.

The parents told me he obsessively asked them how to behave, and they declared they did not want to play that role. What came out in the course of the therapy with my supervisee was quite a different truth.

The hidden destiny: the intended caregiver of the handicapped brother

Within the family, there was a pretended expectation of freedom and separation with regard to Antonio, who was considered the one who had the chance to live an independent life, unlike Giulio. The parents were now in their fifties and were well aware that their ability to take care of Giulio would not be eternal. The issue of how and where Giulio could live some day after their death became more and more difficult to deal with and induced a sense of uncertainty and pain that no obsessional control could diminish.

The official version of the family myth proclaimed that Antonio was not implicated in this issue. He was the healthy and intelligent one, the one who, once the accident of his obsessive–compulsive disorder had been overcome, would go and live freely. But there was a "but".

The choice of a neurosis is never accidental, and it surely cannot be considered accidental that Antonio chose a mental disorder that, among its peculiar traits, has the heavy impairment of the capacity for making a final choice and neatly separating from what one has not chosen, in so doing risking failure. It was not accidental that Antonio introduced himself to me by talking about his inability to choose between his Chinese friend and Japanese music, let alone being able to make the two elements democratically coexist. Democracy implies the capacity to choose and take a position, to say yes to something and no to something else, *before* being able to allow the opposites to interact and coexist.

The façade of considering Antonio as a grown-up led the parents to involve him in the commitment of accompanying Giulio to some of his everyday engagements. Giulio could not use public transportation on his own to move around the city, or at least this was what was thought. So the parents, the mother especially, were continuously involved in taking him here and there. On principle, the idea of involving Antonio in this activity was totally reasonable, but it implicitly corresponded to a strong centripetal force that wanted Antonio to be the successor of the parents in the duty of taking perpetual care of Giulio. This element required cogent work in the individual psychotherapy, in terms of working through persecutory fantasies and guilt in relation to the sense of having the right to live and be healthy.

The family was once again confronted with a powerful entropic force that occluded the whole group in an apparently unsolvable state of immobility. They in fact considered themselves as a handicapped group, as if Giulio's disability had become the unwritten law of the family. Multiple interactions and contaminations between different levels of psychopathology were subtly pervasive and constituted the reticulum of their shared psyche. I will now describe some expressions of the reticulum.

Reticulum: autistic contaminations, obsessive intersections

The occurrence of autistic-like modes in Antonio is evident in a session close to a long holiday break. Such modes regard the sensuousness of rubbing and creating a soothing contact as a defence against separation, and a sort of trans-modal response, similar to what I had observed in my patient Giulio years before, when he was more or less five years old.

In the first part of the session, Antonio talks about his old grandfather, and tells of his fantasies that he may die soon, which he would consider a relief. The sooner he would grieve his death the better. Then he talks of the rhythm of a song that he has in mind and which he had previously tried to memorise, and that now he tries to forget, the song being connected to a girl he likes and who rejects him as a boyfriend. The level of the communication is appropriately dealt with by the therapist in relation to the transference and linked to the forthcoming separation, and includes the feeling of ambivalence as well as rejection. After this interaction, the register changes, as follows:

... Antonio says that his parents say he is indolent ... He actually feels indolent ... Today he used the duster to clean his room, but he was lazy ... as if he had no purpose ... [a few moments of silence] ... He starts rubbing the wall with his fingers, with a dangling movement ...

The analyst comments that he seems to be using the duster here, on the wall.

Antonio smiles, and says no ... then adds he likes touching walls ... to see if they are rough or smooth.

The analyst connects this to the previous issue of remembering and forgetting the song and comments on his trying to keep the memory of some sensations regarding herself in the transference, in preparation of their separation.

The sensuousness of Antonio's moving his fingers back and forth on the wall could be interpreted at different possible levels of his mental functioning. One could be related to the dimension of anal masturbation, which would imply a full tri-dimensional operation based on projective identification, whose contents—if connected to the first part of the session—could be referred to the narcissistic level of the uncertainty regarding *being valuable for the object*, and to the oedipal dimension of exclusion. Anal masturbation, in this respect, could be explored in terms of aggressively penetrating and possessing the abandoning wall-analyst, as well as in terms of multiple identification of self and analyst as faecal objects. This vertex is plausible, and it may have been coherently accompanied by some degree of triumph and excitement, which many times has been palpable in the sessions, but this is not very evident this time. Here, Antonio is in a sort of foggy laziness; he is floppy and indolent.

The second way of reading the material would consider the centrality of adhesiveness as a main functioning mode at this particular moment. Bi-dimensionality in this light would be prevalent, and the mechanism of adhesive identification as a means to possess the object through perceiving its surface qualities would be reminiscent of primitive dimensions of the encounter with the object. Rough or smooth, with no further complexities, virtually with no fantasies; just a *state*.

This is a relatively simple hypothesis, which would not surprise us considering how frequently we observe this kind of autistic-like functioning in patients with prevalently more evolved psychopathologies, unless we consider that Antonio has an autistic brother, two years older than him. Since his birth, Antonio has seen, perceived, smelled, heard, and interacted with a person who was totally different from anybody else he had ever met in the world. Millions of times, Antonio has seen his brother rubbing his fingers, his head, his genitals, his skin against soft or hard surfaces, or becoming ecstatic when his face was beaded with water drops, or bubbling with his saliva, or indolently dangling for hours, lost who knows (no)where. What kind of subtle identification must have taken place? What hidden language unconsciously shared? What sort of shared nothingness or nowhere-ness must have been secretly created between the two? As always occurs with the autistic dimensions, questions may be evocative but answers are more than uncertain, and for each answer one tentatively hypothesises, dozens of further and inextricable questions come to the fore. Nothing challenges the scientific position of the observer more than autistic states.

In any case, I agreed with my supervisee's comment regarding the value she gave to her countertransference, having picked up on the patient's idleness and sensuousness of his rubbing against the wall. She then appropriately, although rather scholastically, connected this element to separation and to the issue of remembering and forgetting. The territory of narcissism and the oedipal paradigm are always safe as they are well tried and tested—every analyst's consolidated resource. Enough has been said to the patient in order to make him feel at least *somehow reached* in his dimension of sensuousness and adhesiveness.

However, a prompter interpretation at that level and a more incisive investigation—in order to make the patient realise that the analyst is truly interested in that psychic dimension—would have been advisable.

Let us proceed now to analyse how the session develops:

> After some silence, the patient says that for a few days, if he cannot brush his teeth straight after eating, he feels the dirt in the lower incisors and gnashes his teeth. [He does that repeatedly now in the session, which causes a certain degree of discomfort in the analyst.]
>
> The analyst underlines, with an interrogative tone, that he feels dirty when he eats. Antonio replies he does not know why. The analyst makes some comments regarding the fact that when he has to satisfy his basic needs, he feels dirty. Again, Antonio says he does not know why, but when he eats or drinks something he feels dirty, and has the impulse to scratch his skin. The analyst is quite surprised and a little confused at this point and asks the patient if gnashing and scratching are the same. Antonio asks her if she can repeat what she has said.
>
> The analyst tries to understand why he has not understood. Antonio says he thinks the analyst eats her own words "… well no … it is not you who eats your words, it's me who picks up only on some."

Similarly to my comments regarding the previous part of the session, the material can be interpreted in different ways and at different levels.

There is a more sophisticated way to consider the issue of feeling dirty, which may regard oral and anal aggression in connection with the analytic food that is about to be taken away for the summer break. But there is another vertex, which takes the trans-modal communication into account, together with the evidence that the analyst in this precise moment becomes confused and seems to fumble.

Although the level of verbal communication is present, Antonio seems to be captured in a twisted and incoherent verbalisation where two levels of sensory and motor response are intertwined: the gnashing, linked to some discomfort perceived in the lower incisors, and the scratching, supposedly linked to the expansion of discomfort to the surface of the skin. Here, dirt is similar to the general sense of discomfort that a small baby may experience in terms of mouth/skin/hunger/bad sensation. In a trans-modal involvement of different sensory-motor levels, which affects the analyst similarly to how a neonate affects the mother's sensory-motor systems, a series of reactions become apparent in the session. Discomfort is the first reaction to gnashing, together with a subtle sense of rejection: the analyst in the countertransference thinks the patient is greedy, but she is not truly empathetic with the supposed greed; rather, she is subtly irritated. Second, the analyst is somehow in contact with the idea that the patient feels dirty when he wants to satisfy his basic needs, but is confused when faced with the sensorial mixing up of gnashing and scratching. She defensively tries to be logical and asks the patient if gnashing and scratching are the same, to which the patient cannot but say he does not know. If a two-week-old baby could speak, he would also respond "I do not know" if the mother asked him something like: "Do you think that the burning sensation of your icy pee on your genitals is the same as the devouring monster that you feel in your belly because I keep you waiting too much to give you the breast?"

The fumbling at this point becomes paramount. Mother and baby do not meet. Interestingly, the patient says the analyst eats her words and then defensively says that he drops some of the analyst's words. We see a fumbling mother trying to obsessively rationalise the baby's needs and trans-modal messages, without being able to apprehend them and respond with the complexity of her own embodied mind.

By the end of the session, however, the analyst is able to say something about the relevance of the appearance of two issues of "eating words" and "feeling dirty when he eats", and empathetically says they would have the opportunity to understand better in the future. In other words, the analyst is able to say that the fracture in their communication is not irremediable and absolute, but that they can learn something from it. Placing the idea of the future and of learning from experience, the analyst implements a truly anti-obsessional position.

Conclusion: hearing sights, seeing voices

After the supervisory hour with my young colleague, I had an unforeseen and sudden memory of a session with Giulio that occurred some fifteen years before when my patient was more or less five years old. I quote only a short vignette taken from that session.

I speak to Giulio, who is silently watching me, and I say something about some hard toys (two dinosaurs) that he has been holding tightly in his hands. Although I pay great attention to my tone of voice, I realise that at some point my voice becomes a little too sharp. I realise I am tired, and likely a little oppressed by the harshness of the work with this patient. So my voice is a little too high and sharp, and probably conveys my fatigue. Giulio, who had been quiet up to that point, suddenly gets a bit agitated, and brings his hands up to shut his eyes. I immediately have the impression that my voice, my sounds, have penetrated his eyes rather than his ears, as it were. I interpret that "Francesco has made an ugly sharpened sound. Ugly sound has got into Giulio's eyes. And it hurts. So Giulio shuts his eyes and bad sound stays out." He seems to relax.

A few minutes later, I feel pins and needles in my leg. I realise I had stayed contracted and still for an undetectable length of time. So I slightly move, in an attempt to feel more comfortable. It is a moment of silence between the two of us, so my movement takes a couple of seconds and is carried out in an absolute absence of sounds. I just realise that my mimicry expresses the pain in my leg and my discomfort, including a sudden and subtle sense of protest because the patient has succeeded in making me immobile and as hard as stone. My movement, I notice, is in the direction of Giulio, who is sitting on the floor in front of me and seems to be looking askance, at a distance of one and a half metres away from me. But everything is absolutely soundless. And takes no longer than three seconds. In response to my movement, Giulio becomes anxious, he watches me for a second and puts his hands on his ears. My movement, I think, apparently has silently entered his ears. And I tell him so, with the calmest possible voice. Again, he seems to relax.

At innumerable as well as obvious levels, there is little to compare between a five-year-old deeply autistic child, still unable to speak at that age, and an obsessional teenager who, despite his illness, had been able to develop a lot of skills throughout his life, certainly much more so than his brother would ever be able to achieve. However, a kind of never-abandoned habit in, so to speak, hearing movements, seeing sounds, smelling colours, perceiving the physical shape of emotions must have survived in both these children, as if a part of their brains continued to work in the same way as we all do at the beginning of our lives.

Control, by contrast, looks rather trivial, and in so far as it works in favour of the avoidance of the painful experience of loss, it operates in the service of psychic death and immobility. Through the power of contagion, Giulio is able to block me and turn me into stone for a lapse of undefinable time. Antonio is able to force his analyst to defensively work as an obsessional mother attempting to bridle his irreducible chaos.

The reticulum of obsessional and autistic patterns in the family is the representation of intended absolute invariance that threatens to leave no space for transformations. The potential provided by the psychoanalytic trans-modal response, its indomitable determination to create movement in the invariant, and to give meaning to meaninglessness, constitute a tentative vital response on the complex pathways to mourning.

CHAPTER FOUR

The case of Marcelino: early adoption and ongoing intrusion

Introduction

I was alone on a boat without oars, at night, on a lake. The boat was moving, pushed by the current. I saw a pier approaching. On the pier there were two people. At one point, behind me on the boat, my adoptive parents appeared, and told me that the two people on the dock were my natural mother and father. My mother was dirty and ragged, she looked at me with contempt and turned her head away. My father was drunk, belching and laughing. I felt very anxious. I beg my adoptive parents to take me away from there. Immediately.

This is the dream of a seventeen-year-old adopted boy, at a well-developed stage of his three-times-a-week psychoanalysis. The dream tells of his encountering his original wound, with the representation of an experiential hole made up of neglect and contempt, similarly to what we observe in all adopted children, which is the internal scar that subtly supports a sense of perpetual anguish.

The dream depicts a sort of Dantesque atmosphere, like a journey to the underworld of the mind. Adoptive parents are as Virgil is to Dante and—in the transference—stand for the analyst, in a journey that can only be temporary, just enough to see and acknowledge the horror and then return to daylight and to the familiar and known objects of everyday life.

However, things were not that simple for this young patient. The dirty and ragged mother, and the drunk father represent subtler elements that needed to be worked through during the analytic work, which I will consider further on when describing the adoptive family and its dynamics.

I choose to name this patient Marcelino, following my memory of the famous Spanish film *Marcelino, pan y vino* (Vajda, 1954), the story of a baby abandoned on the steps of a monastery and raised by the monks. In the film, Marcelino endlessly searches for his mother, and eventually the statue of Christ, to whom Marcelino secretly donated bread and wine, thinking he was starving, comes to life because of this gesture and makes Marcelino peacefully die so that he can meet his mother in heaven.

Our Marcelino, my patient, found an undoubtedly preferable solution to his internal starvation and is happily alive, thanks to our all-human capacity to write a better plot over eleven years of our work together. The interminable question about his origin, however, is the same as in the film.

Marcelino

The patient was referred to me at the age of fourteen by a colleague who had seen him in psychotherapy since he was six years old. The colleague had considered that, given the pubertal phase and some difficulties in dealing with severe symptoms and behaviour, Marcelino would require further analytic work with a male analyst who, being also a psychiatrist, could somehow deal with the issue of medication. Unlike other cases described in this book, adequate prescriptions had already been suggested by the general practitioner, and consequently I did not need to intervene directly but could limit myself to coordinating my observations with my colleague, who easily adjusted his prescriptions accordingly. Before being seen in the previous analytically oriented psychotherapy, Marcelino had been in a sort of psychomotor supportive treatment since he was three years old.

He was just one week old when he was adopted. Notwithstanding this seemingly favourable condition, with the early stabilisation of the parental figures, he had always been a difficult child. As a baby, and in the absence of any physical pathology or distress, he would frequently cry and the parents always found it very hard to comfort him. In his adoptive parents' words, he was never relaxed and he continuously looked unhappy and seemingly unable to experience joy and satisfaction. Since his early childhood, he showed extreme difficulty relating to adults other than his parents, even those belonging to the wider family, and in particular he had great problems with his peers, with whom he seemed to experience a continuous sense of threat and hostility. As well as nursery school, he had great difficulty adapting to primary school. He showed a poor capacity to adequately relate to teachers, essentially trying to establish exclusive and involving contact with a limited number of female teachers, while experiencing all the others, both male and female, as hostile. He basically remained isolated at school, imprisoned in his thoughts with no meaningful contact with the context.

Marcelino's difficulties increased progressively over the years, and through various tests he was diagnosed as suffering from moderate cognitive impairments, especially in the logical-mathematical areas, in his capacity for abstract thinking, and in appropriately providing mental representations for emotions and internal stimuli. Contrary to this, his verbal language seemed appropriate, even sophisticated at times. However, my understanding of his way of speaking was that he had learned to imitatively use appropriate and seemingly refined language in his cultured family, but he did not always fully understand what he was saying, nor fully comprehend the complexities of what he was told. He clearly missed the nuances of language, especially when it was potentially descriptive of subtle emotions and feelings, or when he should have been more truly logical. His pseudo-sophisticated language was an aspect of his obsessive adaptation and the result of an imitative incorporation of the family styles, at the service of his extreme anxiety about being accepted and welcome.

His intellectual disability, although disharmonious, was overall classified as mild to moderate, and—especially due to his behavioural problems at school—he was provided with a special needs teacher for many years. The issue of shame, which was so relevant for this patient, was certainly intertwined with his being certified as "different" from his peers. The obvious advantages of being assessed as mentally retarded or psychologically suffering, such as having a specific curriculum at school and designated teachers, enhances, as a counterpart, the feeling of shame and exclusion. This is especially so for those children who are mildly handicapped, as in Marcelino's case, since they are totally aware of the differences between themselves and their peers.

Since the age of five, Marcelino had developed frank obsessive traits that progressively impinged upon his development: intrusive thoughts of being dirty and smelly, of being punished by the adoptive mother, the fear that the adoptive father could die abruptly, and the fear that his siblings—the younger biological children of his adoptive parents—could harm him in some way. When I met him, he was fully pubertal, his ideation was centred on the fantasy that his mobile phone had damaged his testicles, thus making him sterile forever. I will present some specific material on this meaningful element in the following pages, after providing some more general details.

The second prevalent idea in the first stages of his analytic work with me was his concern about being smelly, which activated compulsive rituals of continuously washing and double-checking through tics and bizarre manoeuvres that he was not giving off a bad smell. Among the various contents of his ideation, the damage to his testicles and the fear of being smelly were the only elements that at times took the shape of quasi-delusional or hallucinatory phenomena. His insight on certain occasions seemed to decrease, and the level of persecution became dramatically pervasive. However, a truly delusional or hallucinatory quality to his ideation was never easy to detect; his cognitive development and his low capacity for symbolisation processes and abstract thinking gave me the typical impression of poverty of expression and concreteness that we commonly see in young patients with mild deficits and which is hard to clearly define as psychotic. He was certainly on the edge of concreteness and magic thinking, the level of anxiety varying according to the circumstances. Contrary to what one would expect in frankly psychotic conditions, it is undoubtedly meaningful, in terms of a retrospective diagnosis, that he was able to dramatically decrease his medication as early as the first year of the analysis, and stop completely after three years, with the only exception of four months of neuroleptic medication at low doses in the sixth year, due to the impact of very difficult external events. In general, as I shall show, the evolution of the case was favourable, thus depicting a clinical condition quite different from some typical chronic psychotic developments that are observable in certain intellectually disabled patients.

The adoptive mother

Two unmourned events were present in the adoptive mother's emotional biography that appeared to have a deep impact on my patient.

When this woman was twenty, her beloved and idealised brother, who had been two years her elder, tragically died in a car accident. When describing this event in front of me, despite it having occurred approximately twenty-five years beforehand, she burst out crying as if time had not passed, giving me the clear impression that the loss of her brother was still a living torment in her mind. That was confirmed by the husband, who affirmed that "without a doubt" she was suffering as if her beloved brother had died the day before. With no apparent insight or questioning, they both decided to give Marcelino the same name as the dead uncle. This choice looked obvious to them.

The second relevant issue is that one year before Marcelino's arrival, the adoptive mother became pregnant. The pregnancy was dramatically interrupted in the eighth month, due to the sudden and unforeseen intrauterine death of the foetus. The delivery was induced pharmacologically, so this mother had the experience of giving birth to a dead baby. Again, she cried when recalling this event in front of me, particularly when she remembered the burden of the heavy silence in the delivery room. No cry of the baby, no words from the nurses or the obstetricians. "I never experienced such a painful silence before or after that day, the horrific sense of being dead myself", she said.

As frequently occurs after a stillbirth, the mother herself and all the family group, as well as friends and neighbours, were there advising her to try to become pregnant again as soon as possible, because by their definition a foetus does not deserve any grieving; a stillbirth is just considered a mistake of Mother Nature that does not require any further waste of time. The simple idea that this loss could and should have been taken care of was miles away from this family's mentality. The couple tried for some months to conceive another baby, with no success. Thinking they had some physical impediment, they resolved to adopt a baby. So Marcelino arrived, at one week of age, exactly one year after his nameless brother's death, with the heavy burden of two unmourned losses in the adoptive mother's mind.

One more meaningful element is worth considering with regard to this mother's character and her general attitude towards life and relations. She was professionally involved with genetics and had a scientific mentality, as she would define it. To her, facts were facts, and especially, anything problematic in people was viewed as the outcome of some biological factor, even a genetic mutation. The difficulties Marcelino had shown since his birth were therefore firmly regarded as connected to some genetically hardwired and inherited factor, the biological parents supposedly being mentally disturbed or addicts or criminals. Psychological factors were generically considered as "the influence of environment", provided that, within the concept of environment, her role was not included. She was quite critical towards her husband having been in analysis for about ten years, something she considered a total waste of time and money, and she decided to trust me purely because I was a psychiatrist, and consequently must—in her words—have had some sense of reality; my being a psychoanalyst was therefore considered as tolerable.

She acknowledged that Marcelino had a more significant bond with his adoptive father than with herself. Again, this was considered as a sort of innate characteristic of the child, she herself having no influence whatsoever on this, and there being no particular meaning to explore. The fact that she had given birth to two children after the arrival of Marcelino, thus disproving the supposed biological impairment to conception after the stillbirth, was not considered a possible source of fantasies or difficulties: "We certainly love Marcelino in exactly the same way we love our other two children, there is no difference for us." And that was it.

The genetic element played a relevant role in Marcelino's fantasies throughout the years of his analysis. He was very curious regarding what his adoptive mother had to say about genetic transmission, and took her explanations as being something magical and mysteriously powerful. This included the fantasies regarding his origin, potentiating in particular the idea that his real mother must have been a prostitute and his real father an alcoholic. On the other hand, the genetic issue was part of a complex system of partial denial of the reality of adoption, with the fantasy, shared by the entire family, that Marcelino and his adoptive father looked physically alike.

The adoptive father

The adoptive father had an extremely controlling personality. He tenaciously assumed I had to inform him about everything Marcelino did in the sessions, and he could not refrain from investigating with him every possible detail after each session. Marcelino took years to learn not to comply and collude with the adoptive father's demands, and I took years trying to make the adoptive father understand that Marcelino was not his exclusive property and that there is a substantial difference between keeping poisonous secrets and claiming a legitimate sense of privacy. Although I used to see both adoptive parents regularly, and this man was apparently in his own analysis, he seemed incapable of respecting the boundaries and continuously invaded me with messages and emails in which he asked me how to manage one behaviour or another that he observed in Marcelino. During our meetings, he seemed quite arrogant and continuously tried to put his wife down and take the stage with me in a sort of continuous phallic challenge that sounded slightly erotised to my ears. The work of overcoming his idealised fantasies of Marcelino took him a very long time, but he eventually realised his child had all the difficulties and limits he had desperately tried to deny.

Parallel to what his wife said, he proclaimed Marcelino had always had a special bond with him, which he said was totally reciprocal. In saying so, he seemed not to limit himself to a simple declaration of a special love: instead, he became triumphant, as if describing something that belonged to the two of them in an exclusive and magical way, something that excluded the rest of the world, and that sounded heavily erotised. When he recounted their wrestling or other physical games they had always shared, I noticed his complacency. Along with it, he had always been physically intrusive with Marcelino, "taking care of" and "exploring and checking" his body parts, including his genitals and his bottom, with the excuse of health issues. When Marcelino developed his obsessive fantasy of having his genitals damaged by the phone, the adoptive father did not hesitate to directly check his genitals and, in order to reassure Marcelino, to suggest a lab test on his sperm. As far as I understood, he did not concretely "help" take the sample, but his intervention was nevertheless quite explicit.

Marcelino certainly colluded, however, by insistently asking for continuous reassurance and demanding physical contact with his adoptive father, and the sensuousness he shared with him was somehow replicated in some of his gestures and tics, in the movements of his hands, or his dangling and slightly rubbing which I observed in the sessions. However, it also became progressively clear that part of Marcelino's compliance to the adoptive father was motivated by the anxiety of losing what was felt as an exclusive object, and reinforced by the fact that this man had suffered from cancer when Marcelino was five years old. He remembered the adoptive father having become extremely thin and losing his hair because of chemotherapy, and distinctly the terror that he would die. The terror of his possible death had remained as an obsessional thought throughout many years of the analysis. So, I understood Marcelino's sensuousness as partly supported by this anxiety, which explained the obsessional quality and repetitiveness of the fantasy, beyond his acting concordantly to the adoptive father's incestuous attitude. In parallel, the occasional appearance of a glimpse of homosexual fantasy caused Marcelino the greatest anxiety, also in relation to the fact that the adoptive father was defensively extremely homophobic. No average ambivalence was possible for the patient, and the slightest awareness of aggressive fantasy was immediately inserted into the circle of magical thinking and had to be strenuously defended against through mechanisms of isolation and ritualised pseudo-reparative manoeuvres. The sense of being imprisoned in the adoptive father's fantasies and actions was very strong for Marcelino, and required, together with obsessional mechanisms of control—which, however, were themselves imprisoning—further massive splits and projections. The unknown biological father had to be fantasised as the drunk, the addict, the criminal, the receptacle of evil. The analyst had to be conceived as the one who wanted to kidnap poor Marcelino, and bind him perversely for his subtle purposes of making money and exerting power.

One more significant element regarding this man was that his own father, quite a powerful and well-known person in town, had been extremely tyrannical and had always humiliated him and treated him as being stupid, while idealising the elder brother. His fragility and sense of devaluation came to the fore over the years, which was progressively of great help to Marcelino with regard to accepting himself and feeling accepted in his own nature.

Session on damage to the testicles (sixteen years old, two years into treatment)

He walks into the consulting room with his usual pace, moving rigidly and keeping his hands tightly together. He seems to keep his fingers contracted, as if he wanted to couple and tighten the small and ring fingers, to leave a V-shaped space and then tighten the index and middle fingers to each other in the same way. He does this with both hands. He takes off his coat with slow, mechanical movements, folds his coat and puts it very carefully on the couch. He finally sits in front of me. He gazes at me for a few seconds while remaining quiet. He keeps his legs wide open in front of me, showing a prominent bulge. [I remember he had told me several times he frequently wears a jockstrap, as suggested by his father, which he had connected to his fear that his genitals might get accidentally damaged.]

He starts talking in a tortuous way about a place he had gone to the previous day with his father and brother to do some shopping. He spends minutes complaining about how crowded and noisy that place was, and repeatedly says he was afraid of touching people and objects but also of being touched and hurt accidentally. He mixes up the account of the shopping mall with apparently incoherent statements regarding the fact that when he takes the underground he never touches doors or metallic supports with his hands. While he talks, I notice he is quite anxious, and gesticulates in a bizarre way, keeping both hands in this V shape. Although he gesticulates and moves his forearms and wrists with wide but snapping gestures, it seems that he keeps his fingers rigidly firm in the V position.

I interrupt his potentially endless speech and say that it seems he is very scared that his body may be damaged. "Are hands doing something bad?" I ask. [I intentionally avoid saying "your hands", but say "hands" in general.] I then say that, "fingers seem to be coupled, like two people touching each other."

He immediately says he has had his thoughts about the mobile phone he used to keep in his pocket, and the doubt that this might have caused some damage to his testicles, making him impotent and sterile forever. He admits he has bombarded his father with questions in order to be reassured, which he was, his father reminding him of the sperm test and of how his pubic hairs are very thick, as well as the fact that he has erections and that his sperm is normal. When saying this, I notice his gesticulation becomes less evident, and he relaxes his fingers slightly.

I comment that I know about these thoughts, and that he must surely be upset by my not reassuring him in the same way his father does, and by not asking him to take off his pants to check his genitals. I say that I am sure he expects me not to be harmful and that it might be important to understand why he is so scared of not being able to give birth to children. "There is something here about giving birth, isn't there?" I say.

He immediately says, with a tone of contempt, that he would never adopt a child, never in his life! He wants to make children with his sperm and transmit his genes to his children!

"So there is something you dislike about being adopted," I say. "It seems that you think being adopted implies a sense of shame. That is why testicles are so important to you; if they work, you and your future children will never feel ashamed."

When I announce the session ends, he gets anxious as usual and hurries to put on his coat and go. He says his usual "Buonasera Dottore," [Goodbye Doctor] with his pseudo-adult affectation and leaves the office.

Session ends.

One relevant element of the countertransference I have taken note of in this session, as well as in many others, is when Marcelino sits in front of me with his legs wide open and shows me his bulge. I obviously consider, in general terms, that there is something sexual in this position. The sense conveyed, however, is not precisely seductive in an explicitly erotic sense; rather, it feels like being in front of a miserable body exposed to the indecent sight of a voyeur, like the nudity of a beggar, or of a victim of torture. In other words, the subtle element of contempt, violence, belittlement, reification, and nullification of the person's identity is made clear by the nuances of the countertransference. The issue of "exposure" is also relevant, in terms of an incommensurable experience of non-protection, abandonment, and nudity. It is the nudity of the soul, the misery of desperate humanity.

We are still in the initial stage of the treatment here, and I do not think I can directly address at this point the issue of the likely incestuous relationship between Marcelino and his adoptive father. This is enough for the time being of addressing couplings, hands, harm, and shame, and the expectation in the transference that I could be a respectful interlocutor.

The issue of humiliation, which crosses the patient's communications and the countertransference, seems to be related—as I came to understand over time—to a specific problem in the adoptive father, in connection with his own father. Marcelino's adoptive father seemed to have responded internally to his paternal problem by developing a strong controlling attitude, and the position of relating to people by exerting dictatorial power. Exchange was not truly possible with this man, the paradigm always being dominated or dominating, imprisoning or expelling. This attitude is specifically obsessional, in the sense of anal control, where the other—or dangerously the self—is substantially equated to the faeces. Sensuousness and subtly incestuous behaviours are part of the mechanism. More specifically, it would be simplistic and generic to say that the adoptive father was a repressed homosexual, especially because the term "homosexual"—used in this context—would resemble an outdated view that equated homosexuality with perversion. This man was, more specifically, a voyeur, in the double sense of secretly watching the primal scene and spying on the anal activities.

Session on being smelly (sixteen years old: two and a half years into treatment)

He is recalling when he was a child, and used to spend hours sniffing his hands. I comment that he seems to have enjoyed that smell and he confirms that he did enjoy his smell, finding it inebriant. When I say that smells seem to be important to him, he gets progressively anxious and says he takes a shower twice a day and always washes his hair and his pubic hairs with precision and consolidated gestures. The same applies to when he dries his hair and hairs; so I understand there are complex rituals. He says that when he goes to the toilet, he cannot sit on the WC and the process of cleaning his penis and anus is always very complicated.

"What you are scared of?" I ask.

He says he is scared of being smelly. He tries continuously to test if he gives off bad smells, but he knows that one cannot detect one's owns smells precisely, so again he engages his adoptive father to check many times a day. He says he is afraid of smelling bad especially here with me, and he always washes himself carefully before coming to the session. He gesticulates while saying this, and he accidentally bumps into a lampshade close to his chair. He gets very anxious, and repeatedly says he is sorry. I comment he seems to be afraid of me finding him disgusting and smelly, and that I may feel contaminated by him.

It takes minutes to calm him down, I have to repeat many times that he suspects that I find him disgusting and wants to make sure I do not expel him as one would do with one's faeces. I also comment that the fact that he has accidentally touched the lamp makes him feel dangerous, as if he had really wounded and hurt me. He eventually calms down.

The quality of Marcelino's thoughts in this session is certainly on the edge of being clearly psychotic. He is somehow able to acknowledge that he does not *actually* stink, he does not make me suspect that he concretely *senses* anomalous smells in a fully hallucinatory way. Even when he recalls how he continuously sniffed his hands in the past, he seems to recognise that there was no alteration to his perception; rather, he masturbatorily *used* his *true* perceptions. So, with regard to the perceptive level, we may reasonably say that Marcelino did not have hallucinations. On a strictly ideation level, although able to be partly critical with regard to the *certainty* of being *smelly*, he was nevertheless extremely anxious, and his thoughts had a massive impact on his general mental state and significantly impinged on his daily activities. The effects of accidentally touching the lampshade show how close to a delusional state he was. In fact, my intervention here does not substantially differ from what I commonly do with delusional or hallucinatory phenomena in the transference, which is to directly interpret persecution. At the same time, it was interpreting persecution, magical thinking, and omnipotence, as well as the reinforcement of the container that technically worked and allowed me to progressively approach more complex issues linked to humiliation and sexuality. In general, I would say that insight became poorer in Marcelino, and was directly proportional to incestuous and erotised situations occurring with the adoptive father. It was the relationship between the two that had a psychotic nature, and when the father learned to withdraw and be less intrusive, Marcelino showed healthier development.

Concluding remarks

The genetically transmitted element—in a strict biological sense—in Marcelino's psychopathology is scientifically unprovable. We do not have any knowledge of the biological parents; we do not know if there were psychiatric conditions or other organic factors in their genealogy to underpin Marcelino's fragility. Nor do we have any information regarding how the biological mother may have carried through her pregnancy, in what environmental and subjective conditions those nine months were spent, or if there was a father, or what kind of father he was. We do not know how conflictual the decision of this mother to abandon her child may have been; we do not know how and when the decision was taken, if she was alone or not, if she was aware or not, if she had any contact with her own pain or not, or what she did with her sense of guilt. We do not know if she saw Marcelino or had any contact with him in the first minutes after his birth, enough time to create a bond that had already been planned to be disrupted. So we do not know whether or how the two actually experienced a bond and a sudden caesura. The extreme fear of abandonment, and the sense of being an excrement in the other's mind, his tenaciously clinging to the object, were so evident in Marcelino as to allow us to hypothesise that *something* between himself and his biological mother must have occurred and left traces. But these are hypotheses that cannot be verified. Certainly, the fantasies regarding the biological family were very powerful in Marcelino and in the entire family group, and this was surely a psychic fact.

What could be observed and verified was the influence of the adoptive parents, of their personalities and their history, on Marcelino's development. If a transgenerational transmission can be hypothesised, it can be seen in the past of the two adoptive parents, beyond any possible biological element. The dream quoted at the beginning of this chapter is more complicated than may be considered at first sight. Who is the ragged and dirty mother? Who is the drunk, insulting, and belching father? Which internal family do those parental images truly belong to?

The adoptive mother was a deeply suffering woman. She recalled her own parents as being extremely rigid and emotionally detached, as if they were always very distant. She said that "it was always like watching them in a photograph, or from the balcony of the building opposite, even if we were in the same room". She remembers the deep bond she developed with her three siblings, but especially with her elder brother, the one who tragically died. Her words made me think of Hansel and Gretel, or of the special bond that children create among themselves in orphanages. For this woman, who defensively grew up as a hyper-rationalistic scientist, reality and emotions could be mastered and controlled, but never transformed. Her interest in genetic determinism and in incurable diseases stood for a sense of immobility and irreparability of her inner world. She gave Marcelino the experience that things cannot really be changed, that there is no hope. Losses are like stones. Pain is incurable. At the same time, she replicated with him, but not with the other two, biological children, the same distance she experienced with her own parents. So for Marcelino, she actually was experienced, and not simply thought of, as an abandoning mother who preferred her other children. Whether or not this replicated the first abandonment suffered by Marcelino is hard to say: thanks to displacement, it surely reinforced the fantasy shared in the family group that the problem lay in the abandonment effected by the biological mother.

The double death, of her brother and the first baby *in utero*, potentiated the subjective experience of irremediable loss. The symbolic relevance of giving Marcelino the same name as the dead uncle, and the timing of his adoption precisely one year after the previous stillbirth, are surely meaningful. That was a kind of stigma: Marcelino stood for the dead, without being able to repair the loss. His name *presented* the past, but the past was imprisoning and unmodifiable.

Marcelino could not but move to the father in search of a living object. He undoubtedly found some *warmth* in the sensuousness of their contact, in the stickiness of endlessly engaging and controlling each other. Marcelino in some way felt *wanted* by the adoptive father's idealising him and his tenacity in pushing him forward and wanting him to be "normal". All this was deeply contaminated by the adoptive father's wounds, by his feeling devalued by his own father, by his voyeurism and pathological possessiveness. But I can reasonably say that the adoptive father, unlike the adoptive mother, was not depressed, and that by the end of the story, he played some sort of positive role in stimulating Marcelino not to give up. Despite his conflictual position towards me, and the hatred he felt when the transference took Marcelino away from him, he was also somehow an ally. I think he realised I was working for Marcelino's growth, even though it was not the growth he had imagined. The deep sense of being an excrement, which had crossed the generations in his family, was hard to clean. The death of his father and a severe car accident, which led to him losing his job, turned this man into a weaker and overtly fragile person who was more willing to let Marcelino be free and choose his own life. Unlike his wife, this man could learn from loss and pain.

Marcelino, over more than a decade, grew more than one would have expected from a so-called "deficit" patient, especially when affected by such an impairing disease. He was on social security and, as a member of a so-called "protected category", he had the opportunity to find a job. Working in a back office was very simple, but thanks to the advantages of obsessional functioning and character, he was very meticulous and carried out his duties with extreme precision. Although he was at times bullied by some colleagues at work, he learned to stand up for himself without feeling too persecuted. He was a sweet guy, that was his gift, and he always managed to stimulate some welcoming attitude in other people. Of course, I cannot say to what extent this capacity was innate, or the trace of some good primary object, or the result of a long analytic experience, or some of all of these. It was in fact a blessing.

As soon as his bizarre behaviour lessened, he could find friends who helped him experience some sort of normal social life. He got his driving licence and learned to drive his own car and explore the world around him. He could only drive automatic cars, saying he could not coordinate his movements to use the mechanical gear. He felt he was not gifted enough to do more than one thing at a time. Paying attention to the traffic and using the gear stick at the same time was too much for him.

What I consider his greatest achievement was that, after finding his job, he went to live by himself. He chose the furniture and colour scheme, and he learned how to do housework and the laundry, which of course he did with the greatest precision. It is worth noting that he managed not to be invaded by his father, who by that time was ill and old, without feeling guilty about choosing his own habits.

He carried on with his life in a simple and precise way. Work, friends, cooking, cleaning, watching films. Nothing special, seen from the outside. Very special, from his point of view.

Sexuality was very hard to cope with. Over the years, he had learned to masturbate without getting lost in confused and aggressive fantasies, and he had slowly learned not to be terrified by women. Initially, he could not bear any eye contact with girls, and the idea of sexual intercourse was full of persecution. I repeatedly worked on that over the years, trying to work through persecution and the most horrific and devouring fantasies linked to the female genitals, as well as to the fantasies of a murderous penis. I have to be honest. I did my job on the sexual fantasies with professional scrupulosity, we may say obsessionally, thinking it could be helpful to evolve some element of persecution in a general sense. But I never thought my work would lead to the development of a true sexual life in Marcelino. I felt that my interpretations somehow worked, but in general Marcelino remained a bizarre, although somewhat lovely, weird guy. So who on earth could feel sexual desire towards him, let alone fall in love with him? Like his adoptive mother, I felt the situation was unchangeable in this respect.

Instead, Marcelino truly surprised me when he announced that he was seeing a girl of his age, he was twenty-five at this point. She was a physically handicapped girl, who was very clever and well educated. I remember I was worried about the possible pathological implications of such a relationship. I decided I would not comment on this and simply wait over the following weeks to see how things developed. Thinking of the way he drives his car, I decided not to make things too complicated for Marcelino, as if my thoughts could disturb him this time. Let me see what *he does on his own*, I said to myself. As a father who does not intervene. As a mother who silently waits.

One surprise after another, Marcelino gave life to immobility and moved the stone. The two fell in love, and made love; he dedicated himself to this girl in an extraordinarily warm way, and learned to stand her temper and his own fear of losing her. We could not ask for more. Retarded, disabled: we define these patients. With these terms in mind, I silently and joyfully laughed during our last session when I said goodbye and wished him good luck. Marcelino, bread and wine, who made the stone alive, and wrote a better plot.

CHAPTER FIVE

Marco and Maria: OCD and developmental breakdown at puberty

Introduction

In the present chapter, I wish to reflect upon the violent onset of obsessional symptoms in the context of a psychic breakdown at puberty. Marco, one of my patients, had developed rigid obsessive personality traits during latency in order to cope with extreme conflicts between his parents, and to comply with the pervasive idealised/incestuous fantasies his mother had of him. The other patient, Maria, had also developed hidden obsessional thinking during latency, characterised by intensely erotised aggressive fantasies. These fantasies were kept secret by the child, and she developed overly rigid latency traits, especially perfectionism, order, and control.

Both situations underwent violent breakdown when these children were twelve years old: at that point, obsessional ideation could no longer be controlled through compulsive rituals; the level of insight dramatically decreased to a quasi-delusional quality, although the psychiatric diagnosis of OCD was still confirmed, ideation having remained substantially ego-dystonic with neither concomitant altered perceptions nor other features typical of schizophrenic conditions. The level of anxiety and, in the case of the boy, of psycho-motor agitation and self-harm behaviour, became rapidly unmanageable, and the children had to be hospitalised in a child psychiatry unit. They were both referred to me after being discharged from hospital. Both were heavily medicated and required continuing maintenance medication for several years.

The two cases are an exception in my practice, in that both children wanted me to deal with medication and strongly refused to see another psychiatrist while I was seeing them in intensive psychoanalytic psychotherapy.

Although the issue of combined psychoanalytic/pharmacological treatment is more widely discussed in Chapter Six, the relevance of medication as a meaningful element of the transference is quite evident in the description of both clinical situations illustrated in this chapter.

As already mentioned in Chapter One, when OCD starts in childhood or adolescence, young people may avoid socialising with peers or become unable to live independently. Being able to go to school and develop cognitive skills, as well as having meaningful contacts with peers, is vital for children and adolescents. Such schooling cannot be considered an option, nor can it be postponed or replaced by something else. Consequently, when a child or an adolescent develops severe symptoms, of whatever nature, that turn out to have a substantial impact upon these vital aspects of their lives, there is an issue of urgency and responsibility that, as psychodynamically oriented clinicians, claims our attention. Psychoanalytic orthodoxy, whatever it may be, or the supposed primacy of technical purity, cannot come first. What comes first is the duty to make life reasonably possible, in the shape children and adolescents strongly require.

Obsessive–compulsive symptoms, unlike general obsessive personality traits, are only slightly influenced by exclusive psychotherapeutic interventions and require medication to be decreased and managed, even in children and adolescents, as the stories that follow clearly illustrate. Symptoms can be weakened sufficiently to make social and emotional life reasonably possible, while being kept strong enough to be investigated analytically. The more traditional way of dealing with a combined therapy—with the psychiatrist and the psychotherapist working in cooperation—presents advantages and disadvantages. Being the only therapist for both analytic and pharmacological treatments, as in the two cases presented in this chapter, also has advantages and disadvantages. It surely requires a degree of flexibility and accurateness in considering a number of factors. The priority, however, belongs to the transference, not to the purity of technicalities.

Medicines are part of the transference, as well as all the factors interacting with one another in the analytic situation. Although the main issue in the two cases presented regards, psychiatrically speaking, thinking disorders and the contiguity of obsessional ideation with delusional formations, we can also see how the presence of tics, skin excoriation, and body dysmorphic phobias in the female patient, and of depressive traits in the male patient, provide us with a clue as to the complexity of so-called comorbid conditions.

Marco: violence and tenderness

Marco is twelve years old when he is hospitalised in a child psychiatry department, following a violent outburst of severe obsessional ideation, centred on the impulse to kill his mother and father. For several months before this acute episode, he had tried to control his obsessions through increasingly paralysing and exhausting rituals and mental ruminations, such as counting books on shelves, placing toys on the floor in a precise order, playing a sort of ritual dance in his room before being able to go out, turning the chair a number of times and placing it in a perfectly precise position before being able to eat, and innumerable lullabies and magical formulas to ensure that he would not kill anyone. These obsessive thoughts and rituals deeply affected his capacity to interact with his peers as well as his performance at school.

However, Marco is a very intelligent boy, with remarkable creative resources. He is very skilled in painting and drawing, especially in the way of a cartoonist or a street artist, but he also loves contemporary design and architecture, with excellent results in these areas at school. Since his early childhood, he has also shown a great passion for music, especially singing.

Representing the breakdown

I have just a few of his drawings (the only ones he wanted me to keep), some dated a few weeks before the breakdown, and others several weeks after the breakdown, when he started to feel better and was already in therapy with me.

His drawings in the weeks before the breakdown looked very meaningful.

In Drawing 1, we can see a number of bizarre puppets, most of which are represented without mouths and with huge empty eyes, drawn in black with no background and no connection to one another, as if floating in an empty space of unrelatedness. Among many possible interpretations, one may speculate whether one of the typical aspects of obsessions, which is inextricably linking thoughts and words together crookedly, may work as a defence against a sense of separateness, felt—as shown in this drawing—as a sense of total fragmentation. Marco described his obsessions, however, as sudden incursions of thoughts that were apparently unrelated to one another or to other more realistic thoughts or activities that he recognised as "coming from somewhere", and the obsessions were felt as totally unwanted and disturbing. In this respect, in psychiatric terms, his insight was quite fair, at least in the weeks before the breakdown and when he was already in therapy with me, during which time he was also under the influence of medication. Instead, during the days of the acute breakdown,

Drawing 1. Bizarre puppets.

the apperception of his obsessional thinking had actually turned to a quasi-delusional quality.

One may also notice here the name LU—or LUMEN, which is his nickname. Interestingly, he seemed to find a sort of self-cohesion, as it were, through the nickname and not his real name. A hypothesis is that the nickname links Marco to his group of schoolmates and peers, which was terribly important to him and was felt as a chance to live a normal life, while his real name was the name of his difficult infancy and childhood.

It is noteworthy that for a limited time before the breakdown, the simple fact of being able to draw these figures on paper (and to defensively use just a black pencil) helped him to contain and somehow provide a representation of his internal world, especially the unspeakable and fragmented series of fantasies, but most of all his fragmented sense of self as unable to speak, which he just barely controlled through his rituals. In some way, bizarre obsessional "connections" (beyond the function of control) could also represent a pathological and almost desperate attempt at "making links" and "giving words" to such a desolated, fragmented, and speechless internal world.

In Drawing 2, the only mouth belongs to the desperate monster created by Dr Frankenstein, a cluster of dead pieces, yet with some possible

Drawing 2. Lu.

thoughts hidden in the skull. Some spray cans stand for a wish to give expression to some sort of internal state, and the black stain may refer to a hidden sense of death and depression. Again, his identity is drawn in fragments. Lu is still there. "*Scansafatiche!*"—loafer—could possibly refer to avoidance, disinvestment, and disavowal, which can stand for the patient's attempt to keep his internal world at a safe distance and somehow under control. However, beyond the meaning of this mental position in the weeks before the breakdown, the same mechanisms would be a consistent part of the mental tools of this patient over the years, with a significant impact on the transference.

Drawing 3 is the last drawing before the breakdown. Bombs are falling "upwards" on a world that is already subverted and bizarre. Faces look blind and the nickname is dispersed in the multiplicity of unconnected selves and objects. Some shapes are sharp and pointed, some others are roundish and soft. Marco always showed me a combination of the two ways of presenting himself, extremely defensive and difficult to reach on many occasions, tender and fragile on others.

Marco brought me these three drawings, which he had made in the weeks before the breakdown, during a session around three months into treatment, as a sign of trust in my capacity to contain, but also as a way to place a sort of in-between object, which kept me at a safe distance, an object he could hide behind but through which he could also tell me about himself at the same time. On one level, he pretended to be unaware of any possible meaning of his drawings and of any connection to his state of mind before the breakdown, and assumed to be simply showing me his technical skills and his interest in street art. In this respect, I showed him true interest in his technical abilities, and felt really curious about the new developments of street art in town, which he showed he was quite in the know about. Adolescents always need—independently of any specific problem in the narcissistic area they might have experienced with their parents—to feel that the analyst is truly interested in their vicissitudes and in their passions. On this specific occasion, I followed Marco in his defensive communication and did not challenge him directly on the grounds of what the representations in the drawings might mean. I showed genuine interest in what he was saying, and in the way he was showing me what he had done, I was *pleased* that he was showing me something so personal and intimate, thus reinforcing his sense of trust. While interacting with his explicit communication, I commented incidentally, as in a sort of

Drawing 3. Bombs falling upwards.

delicate and unapparent soundtrack, something like … "Oh … those figures have no mouth … so they cannot speak, can they?" or "Ah! … the monster of Frankenstein, made up of different assembled pieces … look at him …," and "… uh! What's that black stain?" or "… ah! That's quite scary … isn't it? … being bombed … that's scary! Upside down … that's peculiar!" and the like.

Beyond what I commented in the session a few months after he had drawn these pictures, it is meaningful that the third drawing had been the last of the series, after which his mental state dramatically worsened. Marco then became totally unable to draw, and even to talk, sleep, or eat, and his mind quickly became overwhelmed by terrifying obsessions: after a couple of days, hospitalisation became necessary, with heavy medication and physical restraint. He experienced overwhelming fantasies of killing his mother and father, as well as the people at school, and he felt as if every thought he had could produce actual effects on the people around him, especially his parents. A severe state of psycho-motor agitation became evident at that point, together with self-harm acts, such as violently banging his head against the wall and a couple of attempts to commit suicide through defenestration. When doctors arrived at his home, this boy of twelve required two strong male nurses to restrain him and place him in the ambulance. In the child psychiatry unit, it took three days of heavy medication to sedate him sufficiently. After two weeks, he was eventually discharged from hospital, with a robust prescription of neuroleptics and antidepressants, which worked in terms of decreasing his anxiety and obsessional ideation as well as his psycho-motor agitation. Marco was referred to me for psychotherapeutic treatment, and I saw him three times a week for eight years.

Initial sessions

During our first meetings, although in an evident state of mental suffering and anxiety, and a robust defensive armour, Marco showed me a strong wish to go back to his normal life, especially to school and his friends, which he immediately described as something extremely important to him, like the air he breathes. Medication, in this respect, was something we all considered essential, despite it being experienced by Marco with obvious ambivalence. He showed a remarkable degree of compliance in taking his pills every day, supported by his wish to be good at school and have his close friends with him—which I totally agreed with—and by my openly declaring that my aim was to hopefully help him come off his medication some day. No promises, but I would do my best, I said. And my condition for taking him as a patient was that he should come at least three times a week for psychotherapy. As a matter of fact, his condition was that three times was the maximum, considering school, sports, and other activities, and that I should be the one to deal with his medication. He firmly refused to see another psychiatrist for pharmacological support. Having to choose between defending orthodoxy or losing the patient, I agreed to Marco's conditions, and this was the deal. I appreciated his being so assertive, without denying a subtle sense of harshness and control that I experienced during our negotiation. *One wins and one loses, there is no space for two.* This is a paradigm continuously operating in the background of Marco's mind: and it quite clearly challenged my ability to stay on a subtle edge, without surrendering to *his* condition and without imposing *mine*. Therefore, the simple fact of negotiating and making an agreement at our first meeting was not something to be taken for granted at all.

I must add, I decided to see him in the room I normally use for adults and not in the child room. I wanted to consider him as a grown-up, as it were, being almost sure he would not appreciate being treated as a small child, given toys or plasticine to express himself with. Words would be undoubtedly strenuous, considering that obsessions themselves were "in words". Battles must be fought on the same battlefield, and the enemy always makes the initial choice of weapons.

These are my brief notes of a session just three weeks into treatment, including some meaningful details of the countertransference at that moment:

Marco is on time as usual. He is quiet for a few minutes, I fantasise that his being on time is certainly due to his mother accompanying him to sessions, but I realise I *like* thinking that he himself wishes to have *all* his time with me.

He looks down at the floor, his expression is gloomy. My impression is that he is looking at the figures on my carpet. It is an oriental carpet, with some crooked geometric lines and also flowers and birds. I feel slightly uncomfortable, thinking he might get lost in the twisted lines and shapes of the carpet, they too dangerously resembling his ruminations. Would he get lost in my ruminations? How much time has passed since the beginning of the session?

After an (undetermined) period of time, I say:
"... Well... maybe you expect me to keep you alive, and not let you get lost somewhere..."
He turns his head slightly and watches me for a few seconds. His eyes are full of what I perceive as intense sadness. He moves his body imperceptibly, as if shivering all over. Sleeping babies come to my mind, when mothers

gently touch them, and wake them up. By contrast, I remember the sharp voice and aggressive attitude of his mother and the interminable fights between the parents—also in my presence—and the sense of intrusiveness and violence that I perceived while listening to them.

"There is no rush..." I say to Marco. "... We have time..." And after a pause... "Thoughts are difficult to manage at times, aren't they...?"

He sighs. After a couple of minutes, he starts telling me he has finally returned to school. All his friends have welcomed him, and asked how he was doing... "Everything looks OK... but I'm scared... I suspect they think I'm crazy..." He keeps talking about this issue until the end of the session, his tone of voice is a little flat, and I feel slightly numb while listening to him.

I comment that moments like the ones he is describing are often quite difficult to bear, so one might prefer to switch the light off and simply not think of them. He nods, but he does not look at me when the session ends and we say goodbye.

As a comment to this vignette, I wish to underline some elements in the countertransference. According to my usual viewpoint, there is a particular value—yet not devoid of risk—in the capacity of the patient to be liked, or to evoke some sort of pleasure in the analyst regarding what he or she actually does or is imagined to be doing. Such a capacity is rooted in the preconception of a pleasurable encounter, which in normal conditions is firstly and satisfactorily realised between mother and baby. The preconception of a pleasurable bond, although innate and supposedly genetically hardwired, or archetypal—as we may also say—can undergo massive deterioration, if not total disruption, when life events and actual encounters variably combined with subjective disposition, negatively impinge on the subject. People may become unable to evoke love, hope, and pleasure, and addictively force their interlocutors to see them as evil by killing in the object every glimpse of hope and sense of future development. I do not overlook the possible impact of seductiveness and collusive manoeuvres that may be enacted in *liking* the patient, with the purpose of denying/controlling/splitting anxieties related to aggressive fantasies, but I assume that being liked and loved cannot of course be reduced to mere pathology.

Drawings in the first months of therapy

These are some drawings he made in the first months of our therapeutic relationship. He continued to draw in the following months, and brought his drawings to me in the sessions, but he then wanted to take them back home. I took this as a sign of a slight capacity to keep something inside, as it were, as opposed to a strong tendency to evacuate, which was a sign of a massive identification with both his parents. Therefore, the following are the last drawings he allowed me to keep.

Drawing 4 was the first of this new series, when he resumed drawing after hospitalisation. It is quite similar to the previous one. But blood became visible in red (the marks and spots at the top along with some others being red in the original), with all the possible meanings in terms of *hot* violence and suffering. As I discuss further on, the presence of *heat* was a prognostically favourable sign. In the course of the treatment, Marco always showed some kind of *warm temperatures* in front of me, although at times he would strongly defend against this. As for myself, I always paid attention to keeping *my temperatures* sufficiently warm when relating to him, and to *warming him up* when he tended to become slightly cynical or emotionally detached. I always preferred to see him angry rather than icy.

In this drawing, the black stain is still present, but blood is inevitably alive. When a person bleeds, he is unavoidably in contact with pain. Pain was mainly felt through the countertransference at that time, Marco still being closed up in a strong armour of pretended icy withdrawal. I simply commented in terms of "there's blood here... someone must feel pain", because saying "you are suffering" or "you are bleeding" would obviously have been too much for him, let alone saying something like "you want to hurt and wound me ..." or the like. But when I said "someone must feel pain", he looked at me intensely for a few seconds, as in a moment of unexpected contact. There is a single word in the drawing: "oink", possibly the sound of sea lions (in my fantasy), which I usually perceive as something tender, desperate, and assertive at the same time. These are features that I learned to recognise and understand in Marco over the years.

Drawing 5 marks the presence of "warm pink" (all the details being outlined in pink in the original), a sort of lighter blood, blood kept under control but usually associated with femininity, too, which surprised me a lot, and the remarkable fact that the hand of the puppet is releasing

Drawing 4. Blood and pain.

some objects. For an obsessional person, the experience of being able to release something—and accepting some degree of separation—is surely meaningful. Considering that this occurred in the first months of therapy, I took it as a sign of encouragement and also as a sign of plasticity in his defensive system—which is less commonly observed

Drawing 5. Warm pink.

in obsessional adult patients. It is obviously important to carefully distinguish between releasing and evacuating, or between separating from an object and denying its value by simply getting rid of it. But given the situation of this patient at that particular moment, I took his ability to *let* internal objects *go* and not remain stuck in a sort of imprisoning mental constipation as a good sign.

Drawing 6 (the contents of the bubble being red and the rest of the drawing scattered with small yellow marks) is relevant for two details, the words "fuck" and "help". One may easily imagine how the word

Drawing 6. Fuck or help.

"fuck" is a condensation of sexual fantasies as well as the wish to make his parents and myself fuck off, which was worked through over the years. The word is iconic. It contains the past as well as the present of his difficult relationship with his parents, and a non-secondary part of the transference. Over the years, even the breakdown was interpreted as a desperate attempt to violently—and masochistically—get rid of his mother's idealising him and entrapping him in a deadly bond, which included sleeping in the same bed and keeping him under rigid and ambiguous control.

The word "help" is equally important. As I previously considered, his ability to ask for help, the survival of the preconception of a helping object waiting for the realisation of actual help, was not at all obvious.

Drawing 7 is the picture of an internal state of mess and despair, with the twisted objects invading the mental space. One may notice the two crying figures, the small one threatened by the monster on the left side, and the big one on the right, outside the crooked world. I took the latter as a possible representation of myself in the transference, as the one who "cries in unison" with Marco—a consequence of projective identification—but is nevertheless safe, being *outside* the crooked world where the devouring monster is.

Marco made this drawing a few days after a dream, for which he could not provide verbal association, and so I stimulated him to draw the dream and see what would emerge. The drawing can be considered as a pictorial associative/amplification work in connection to the dream.

Drawing 7. Crying at unison.

The dream was:

There are two monsters, the big one is blocked behind bars, the small one is at large and scares the people around it. The big monster is freed, it kills the small one and starts chasing me. I'm terrified and try to escape, the monster has a red book. There's a revolving door and the monster starts chasing me inside the revolving door. I take the red book from the monster and throw it as far as I can, so the monster runs after the book and I can escape and run up the stairs...

Marco could not provide associations, he was quite blocked and looked at the floor with a gloomy expression on his face. He was seemingly scared that I—as a monster—would entrap him in the spinning movement of my red thoughts. I said: "Thinking is difficult here at times, it may be scary..." and after a pause, "I understand I myself would wish to escape if I were in front of a monster... it is good that in the dream you find the way out and do not remain entrapped, but it is also good that we are both sitting here now in my room, you are not escaping... and neither am I." I was keeping my fingers crossed while saying this, and fortunately we could come to the natural end of the session. The atmosphere remained nevertheless quite heavy, with no words. Around the end, I suggested he might draw the dream, just in case he liked that, but that there was no obligation. He felt relieved, and in the last couple of minutes he started telling me about school.

The following session, he arrived with the drawing. Significantly, he added me as the crying man on the right side—I was not present in the dream in that shape—by replacing the second monster with me-as-a-crying-man, and he also added tears to the small human figure in the centre. Only fear and anxiety were actually present in the dream, but no tears. This is an interesting development of the dream material, also in terms of the issue of psychic pain and depression, which would be extensively present in our work over the years.

The role of medication in the first period of the analytic work

The material regarding the first months of Marco's therapy shows that medication with antidepressants and neuroleptics was implemented in order to decrease the intensity of obsessive–compulsive ideation, especially the circularity of purposeless ruminations, with the aim of allowing him to go back to his everyday life as much as possible: however, doses were set in order to allow ideation to be reasonably florid, in terms of content, and especially to keep emotions as alive as we could. An example of a certain degree of plasticity is shown by Marco's ability to amplify the dream material through his drawing. In general, he could not only critically work through his former ruminations with a good degree of insight, but he also showed me an ability not to remain blocked and to adequately respond—despite being extremely defensive at times—to my comments.

He was perfectly compliant, being able to take care of his twice-a-day medication without being helped or prompted by his mother. Over time, medication became a normal part of the transference interplay, conveying idealised and omnipotent expectations as well as the persecutory fantasy of getting better not because of *our* resources but as a precarious result of biochemistry. This allowed relevant work on narcissism. Interpreting *every* fantasy or thought or complaint regarding the pills as an aspect of the transference reinforced the analytic bond and potentiated the effects of medication itself. Medication had meanings, and Marco was in some way an active interlocutor: this was especially true when— three years into treatment—we decided to gradually decrease the doses and eventually stop altogether. That was the point when Marco realised he had surely been *helped* by his pills, but that *he* himself had done the job with his own resources.

The survival of tenderness

Marco's tenderness and a sort of greed to be reached and understood came up from time to time in the course of the first stages of his therapy, in the shape of a sudden light in his eyes, or an unexpected blushing, or a tear, or a smile. However, he was in general very difficult to reach, which could be referred to his parental identifications as well as to the role of his actual parents on many occasions. His mother adored and idealised him, without properly seeing him as a real and separate person. She even idealised his actual artistic and creative qualities, but always giving Marco a disturbing sense that those qualities did not completely belong to him, as if she was subtly and continuously stealing them. She was very ambivalent towards me, always complaining about me and the therapy (because basically I was not giving her back her beautiful ideal child), and always underlining what was wrong in Marco or poisonously saying that Marco did not completely tell me the truth.

Given the fact that I had to have her as an ally and not as an enemy, I did my best to monitor my countertransference when I periodically met her, or when she called me in a state of anxiety. Her capacity to be provocative and to constantly increase the level of tension and excitement *in the system* was pretty evident in the countertransference, in the same way that it was typically shown in her way of relating to her ex-husband. I had to stop seeing the two parents together, because they kept fighting uncontrollably for the entire session. Significantly, on such occasions, Marco was not only physically absent, but he was also totally expelled from his parents' minds. This was the situation Marco had been exposed to since his infancy: virtually no mind to contain him, and a world full of screams and violent sounds. His attempts at identifying with the mother's idealised child, by becoming submissive and sweet during latency, were not enough to feel wanted and seen as an individual. His creative capacities comforted him, but were somehow *stolen* by the mother's idealisation. His attempts at identifying with his father actually meant being involved in the same fights with his mother, and sleeping in the same bed as her. His mother was emotionally unstable, very controlling and unpredictable in her reactions, easily switching from indulgence to harshness. Similarly to what she had done for years with her ex-husband, she was in general very intrusive and provocative by activating rage and violent emotional reactions in Marco, who often colluded by provoking her to provoke him. At the same time, she was very "practical and concrete", approaching mental suffering as a mere cohort of symptoms to quickly fix. In this respect, I was considered her inadequate servant.

Marco's parents divorced when he was six years old, after years of harsh conflicts, including a few episodes of physical violence perpetrated by his father. After their divorce, they continued to have a conflictual sado-masochistic relationship, Marco's father being economically parasitical towards his ex-wife (in the way addicts usually are). The two were collusively linked in a continuous mutual series of uncontrolled provocations, so, in Marco's experience, they could not but start fighting every time they talked. This was what Marco himself quickly learned to do very well with his mother. His father was an alcoholic, with a delinquent personality, who involved Marco in a sort of subtly sexualised and vulgar alliance, when speaking of sports, cars, or women.

He was unreliable and almost totally unable to show empathy. Many times he did not show up at the appointments he had with Marco, thus continuously frustrating Marco's expectations of meeting a sensitive and affectionate father. As a male model of identification for Marco, he was the prototype of the phallic, erotised, delinquent kind of man.

Marco slept in his mother's bed after his parents' divorce, and beyond idealisation, he was placed by his mother in the same role as the father in terms of continuous provocations and fights. In addition, the mother considered Marco's illness as a biologically inherited disease, the paternal grandfather having being diagnosed as manic-depressive. Over the years, she continuously tried to make me formulate a diagnosis of bipolar disease for Marco, with the purpose of confirming the biological factor, claiming that the paternal family were responsible and totally denying any psychological component, especially one that would imply responsibility on her part. For instance, the fact that she recalled Marco as always crying when he was a baby, and herself as completely overwhelmed and unable to cope with him, was totally meaningless and not considered as somehow linked to Marco's psychological condition. Sleeping in the same bed was regarded as totally normal. She denied being provocative, merely assuming that she was the one who was provoked, and took Marco's reactions to her provocations as evidence of his biologically grounded instability. Over the years, she would interpret every state of excitement or rebellion of her son as a clear sign of his having suddenly and groundlessly switched to mania, or every moment of sadness and withdrawal as depression. I referred her to individual psychotherapy, which she did as a duty for a short period of time with no real insight, and which proved to be quite ineffective. However, she supported Marco's therapy with me for many years. Although in the guise of Penelope's shroud, she allowed me to work with Marco with continuity until the termination of our work.

Such a violent breakdown at puberty could be meaningfully linked to a number of elements. First, the anxiety linked to sexual arousal— potentiated by pubertal growth—because of sharing the same bed with the mother. Second, the failure of latency work, in that normal obsessional control, which requires a certain degree of stability of narcissism and a consequent fluidity of the oedipal situation, could not be established. Third, the intensity of violent fantasies, which could be expressed and kept under control only through massive obsessional formations. Fourth, the sense of imprisonment linked to identifications with *each* of the parents, as well as to the experience of the *parental couple* as a whole: this created a world with no escape routes. Fifth, the increasing sense of imprisonment linked to obsessional symptoms *per se*: when symptoms could no longer serve as protection, there was a summation effect together with the sense of imprisonment Marco experienced with his parents. This caused a mental short-circuit that became totally unmanageable. Sixth, the masochistic response: the experience of being able to escape and move on only through violent self-harming acting out—Marco attempted suicide and banged his head on walls—was dramatic in itself, but progressively became a sort of pattern. Over the years, Marco was constantly on the edge of being heavily self-destructive, and all major changes in his life were announced by some sort of self-harming act.

Regarding the transference, Marco shifted from functioning in identification with his mother, especially when denying feelings and emotions and the meaning of relationships in general, consequently pretending to be "practical and concrete", to subtly functioning in identification with the father by showing a sort of delinquent attitude, which expressed itself in his tendency to "steal and hide" meaningful information and behave as an unreliable smart guy. The combination of the two identifications made my contact with him quite a difficult task for several years. His creative capacities, and his sweet delicacy remain, in many respects, a mystery to me. It seems unlikely that he had developed these qualities via identifications with parental or extra-parental figures. One may hypothesise that they developed as an expression of some innate vital resource that somehow helped him to survive, and for sure helped him to take something good from our eight years together in the analytic room.

During those years, he became in many respects an *average* adolescent, bordering on some delinquent behaviour but always regarding intimate relationships as valuable. Among his symptoms throughout adolescence, I considered as particularly meaningful his compulsive stealing, which caused some issues with the police on a couple of occasions. I interpreted this as an omnipotent, overexcited, and somehow desperate attempt to *steal* good objects he had experienced as unavailable via the normal tools of healthy relationships. This specific symptom, as well as all other delinquent behaviours, were expressed with the quality of *hot* investments; at times brutal excitement, at times with the ingenuous passion of the typical scapegoat. Quite often, such conducts were unconsciously linked to love disillusionments or with what he felt as betrayals. He never developed psychopathic icy delinquent conducts, and when he built up defensive armours of pretended indifference and withdrawal, he was patently relieved when I broke his barriers through interpretations. The best outcome of his therapy was that he did not give up loving people, or at least trying to stimulate affectionate responses, and especially important was his ability to protect himself and not to expiate before allowing himself to proceed. When we considered that these acquisitions were sufficiently solid, we decided to terminate our work.

Maria: what is normal?

I have been seeing Maria for thirteen years, four times a week for the first seven years, then twice a week. Maria was twelve years old when she was hospitalised in a department of child psychiatry. It was a dramatic breakdown with obsessive–compulsive ideation, which followed years of obsessive ruminations that progressively became invasive.

She is overwhelmed by vivid images of her mother naked and tied down to a table, with hooded men that abuse and torture her with their knives. She also obsessively thinks of having sexual intercourse with her mother, or with her father or with them both together and compulsively fantasises that her mother dies. It is enough to think that mum may die for mum to *actually* die. Then the dead mother avenges on her, mostly because when Maria thinks of her mum's death, she happens to laugh. Washing her hands, counting the books on the shelf, ordering the serviettes in the wardrobe, or thinking the dead may be brought back to life just by singing a simple lullaby, is no help at all. The lullaby should be perfect and one always forgets a piece of it. It seems she always makes a mistake in the lullaby. And Maria has to start it all over again. Notwithstanding the intensity of anxiety and the vivid quality of these thoughts (including massive magical thinking), Maria never lost insight, and constantly experienced these thoughts as ego-dystonic.

She also tries to cut her own skin with a razor-blade. But what always comes to her mind is that she is *not* doing that to herself *instead of* doing it to mum. She thinks she is *really* doing it to mum. Maria scratches the scabs from her skin, she gets excited watching blood, and in her thoughts mum always keeps dying.

Mum can never go too far from her—if not physically, at least in her thoughts. And if not by normal means, there is a well-tested repertoire of excitements, provocations, and quarrels that both she and her mum share, and can help the two of them *remember* and *know* that each of them is *here* and is *alive*. Tortured but alive. So torture is a guarantee of existence.

A big penis always reaches Maria's mind. She gets rid of it, and it always comes back. She cannot even name it. Like that word which she cannot even pronounce: *penetration*. Tics are also present, consisting of sudden movements of the mouth and nose, which resemble an expression of disgust and contempt.

When I meet Maria for the first time, she had come out of the hospital just a few days earlier, and feels a little better compared to when she had been admitted, due to heavy medication. Her thoughts are much the same, and arrive in the same way, but are less brutal, with a little less anxiety. And at least at night, Maria is able to fall asleep. She can even tell me that doctors and nurses in the hospital were kind, and that they helped her.

Her main concern now is to be able to go back to school, and not to be called crazy by her classmates. "With all that has happened to me and what I keep having in my mind, how can I study and have relationships that may *look* normal?" She makes me understand that she really wants a normal life, her school and her friends. She lets me know she is capable of gratitude and of accepting a cure. She is clever and intelligent, I understand that she wants to behave as the "grown-up" in front of "the psychologist", as she calls me. She says a couple of very precise and sharp things that make me understand that there is not just deteriorated seductiveness in her. She likes studying. It is her way of protecting and defending herself, but she has an ego-ideal. She is not really *nice*—I cannot ask too much—but she gives me the impression of having her own resources. She helps me to choose to take her as an analysand.

While speaking to me, she rhythmically grips her thighs wrapped in her jeans, compressing her pubis. A slight dangling. She never stops masturbating for a single moment, whatever she is doing or thinking in the meantime. I have a child who is still pre-pubertal in front of me. Maria is heavy, very overweight. Disharmonious, big and bulky like her mother. For that reason, she has been continuously criticised—at least, but likely not *just*, in her fantasy—by her father, which powerfully nourished her body dysmorphic phobias. The menarche will only arrive a year after the beginning of the analysis. So we could have a year of work without the hormones to prematurely make things more complicated than necessary.

For a long time, she was to be very scared. She was often deeply overwhelmed by her thoughts, despite the medication in quite heavy doses. She kept taking her tablets for four years, with remarkable compliance and with just some occasional moments of refusal that had the quality of an imperious and maybe hurried wish for health and normality. It was terribly important that I did not interpret these moments as mere attacks on me, but as a wish to be healthy that I, in the transference, was felt as unable to satisfy omnipotently. She learned to distinguish the valuable wish of gaining her health from the improper, or perhaps premature, means of achieving this. So she kept on taking her medicines as long as was necessary. I will not forget her grateful and joyful smile when eventually she was able to stop. That was the moment when the narcissistic feedback could be intensely reinforced, and the positive transference developed more realistically.

During the first years, she showed many moments of opposition, a subtle way of being seductive, often complaining and moaning with a certain childish voice, which I heard sharper than a blade. Maria had the expectation that adults always and necessarily had to feel captured in a sort of emotional slavery, ready to be manipulated like puppets in her hands. At times, she missed her sessions, often after dramatic phone calls in which I was expected to *do something immediately* in response to her shouts, to her cuttings on the skin, to her threats of suicide.

Obviously, I was expected to magically solve the problems with her mother and father. To her, I was definitively useless, no help at all, and she *of course* was forced to come and see me—essentially, I was the worst human being on earth. These attacks did not simply represent a blind repetition of her primal object relations but evidently asked for new and unforeseen answers. Maria was for sure struck by the simple fact that I did not counter-react to her behaviour, as her mother would usually do, or as she would do towards her mother's behaviour. The relational quality of our encounters sounded very strange to her. Literally *unfamiliar*. I was at times paternally firm and usually assertive. Words are not always knives, or violent penises. I was not really calm, as the tension in the analytic atmosphere was frequently palpable, but as mindful and emotionally stable as I could be. I often responded in a way she did not expect at a certain moment: that is, I was silent and serious when she wanted me to unreflectively and automatically get excited; empathetic when she expected me to be cold and rejecting. I always tried to dribble her expectations. I showed, and at times explicitly said, that her attacks did not make me glad, let alone aroused at all, neither explicitly nor implicitly. Maria knew I had no love in dealing with her—as love is not a necessary ingredient in the analytic position. Rather, I had true dedication and care, even passion. *Joy*, every now and then, which is more essential for an analyst than love is. She knew I saw her willingly. She knew I allowed myself to occasionally and necessarily hate her, as average mothers and fathers commonly do. That was our routine.

It was maybe less simple to find the right way to convey the sense that I let her be free to choose her death, and to make her realise that I would not have done the impossible to prevent her suicide, but only something reasonable. Something humanly and professionally possible. I openly declared that her life did not belong to me, that her life was not a reason for my living, and that her death would not have been a reason for my despair. It was her business, in a certain sense.

Maria's fear of all sexual matters was unquestionably clear. Her attempts to be seductive towards me had the quality of a child's strength when the child assumes that he or she is capable of making illusions real. Mainly the illusion to totally belong to each other. Maria usually wore tight pink shirts and stretchy trousers, glittery shoes, and bows in her hair—in a sort of Japanese cartoon style—like a latency girl. It was impossible not to notice her, considering that we are talking about a one-hundred-and-eighty-pound girl, six feet tall. The whole world had to see her, always, as a mother would be expected to see her baby. As if the world represented an always too ignorant mother, always felt as neglecting and blind, and consequently always needing to be forced to see and possibly understand. Maria was too scared to look feminine, she could just allow herself to look like a freak of nature, seeking compassionate eyes as orphans do.

But in order to better understand Maria's sexual fears, it is necessary to say something more about her parents, Marta and Giuseppe, about their being child-parents and about their mental as well as actual doors.

Marta: a mother with no doors

Marta pants on the telephone when she contacts me to have the first appointment. She is particularly pressing in order to have a meeting with me as soon as possible. If we put ourselves in her shoes, which in some way is our duty, there is nothing wrong or strange about this kind of pressure. It is not an everyday occurrence to have a twelve-year-old daughter hospitalised in a psychiatric department, and to see her after about twenty days walk around with a robust dose of neuroleptics and antidepressants, the kind of medication one surely feels quite scared about. And then there is that well-known expression and tone of voice that only doctors are able to use on certain occasions when they want to be truthful and realistically encouraging: they glance slightly sideways and say that the situation is... "well ... somewhat difficult...". And about the prognosis gravely state... "Madam... for your daughter we need time... a long time...".

"But how long? And if my daughter goes crazy? And if my daughter dies? You know Doctor, my daughter has always been a difficult child. And myself too, after all. And the father... Ah! Forget about the father!... But...Doctor ... The blame! Whose fault is it? I am scared, Doctor ... what if my daughter dies?"

So when Marta calls me, I sense in her anxiety a concern that is in many respects realistic, genuine, and warm, which I notice again from time to time during the meetings that I periodically have with her. I see her deep fear in a typical darkness of her glance, like a shade which certainly goes beyond Maria's problem, and possibly has very much to do with this woman and her entire life: the black glance of a mother, who is the daughter of a mother and a father, who are children of innumerable mothers and fathers from time immemorial. Of whom that blackness is the only living memory that remains.

But, maybe just because of that unredeemed blackness, a kind of childish urgency is intertwined with Marta's preoccupation for Maria. It seems like a kind of urgency with no mediations or ability to wait and think, as if Marta herself were a child inclined to produce automatic acts and induce thoughtless responses. As far as I could get to know this mother during the years of Maria's analysis, Marta did not hesitate to subtly become dishonest and manipulative when she wanted to obtain what she considered to be her absolute and non-delayable needs.

There is an extraordinary physical likeness between Maria, a hypertrophic child, and her mother. But it is not only this likeness that makes me think of two orphan twins: mother and daughter are in fact like two lonely children who get mutually excited through continuous quarrels, triggered like perfectly synchronised time bombs. They are able to masturbatorily stimulate and reposition each other within each other's horizon and fill the void. This is *their* identity, their sense of being one.

Their being in unison seems to be a substitute for feeling at one when necessary, and for being able to separate, when necessary.

Maria's parents had never lived together, and have maintained a very ambiguous relationship since their child's birth, with a lot of fights and at times overt, gluey, sadomasochistic violence. Everyday life was filled with fighting and shouting, threats and acts of revenge. Marta is able to escape if this means her being able to call the other guilty, and she is quick to return if this allows her to provoke a new fight. This way of relating with other people seems to carry no sense of discontinuity, no empty space is allowed, and no separateness either, as if seducing and fighting were a consolidated way of dispersing one's identity into each other's. No mourning is conceivable.

Marta's mother usually goes around half naked in her house in front of her children and grandchildren, including Maria when they lived together, talking about sex and body functions quite explicitly. In this family, a substantial degree of intrusiveness is defensively and ideologically called open-mindedness. Voyeurism and exhibitionism are called intimacy. Closed doors never existed in this house. Neither toilets nor bedrooms are private spaces.

Maria's grandfather, as one may surely expect, is substantially castrated and totally passive within this sort of matriarchal incestuous family group. Marta tells me: "You know… my family is a *real brothel*." She could not be more right.

Within the ongoing *après-coup* in the course of her analysis, at the age of sixteen, Maria recalls a recurring dream she had as a child when she was living at her maternal grandparents' home together with her mother and an uncle.

> At night I hear noises which scare me and I go to ask my grandparents for help. I see them from behind, I call them and they turn towards me. They are zombies. Very scared, I go to my uncle and ask for help. I also see his back and I call him, he turns but he is a zombie, too. I rush and look for my mother, I am too scared to stay alone. Mum is a zombie, too. My mother, my uncle, and my grandparents come close to me and threaten me, I am terrified. I walk back to a window. The dream ends when they are about to assault me.

One of Maria's associations to this dream seems to be especially significant. Is it myself who has remained normal, or are they normal and I am the one who has changed? Who is stranger and unrecognisable? Who is really uncanny?

What Maria says witnesses the summation of a markedly confusional anxiety, related to receiving a threat from an object that is expected to provide protection. This is linked to the experience of being *mirrored* by the *living dead*, with the consequent effects on the normality of the core sense of oneself.

Freud himself showed on a linguistic level how the word *heimlich* (Freud, 1919h) has a dual meaning: familiar-trustful-intimate, on the one hand, and hidden-secret-insidious, on the other. The second meaning makes the word *heimlich* close to its opposite, *unheimlich*. What symbolically connects the two opposite meanings is the infantile element, the fact that what appears unknown and uncanny in the *second instance* is already known in the child's experience. Freud connected the experience of the uncanny to obsession—the case of the Rat Man (1909d), in particular—and especially to magical thinking, where a certain kind of anxiety is raised—among many possible others—out of the uncertainty about the animate or inanimate nature of an object or about its being dead or alive.

To go back to Maria's dream: we can observe that everybody is or looks normal when their back is turned, the position of the one who goes away and possibly disappears. As soon as contact is established, the uncanny comes to the fore. The subsequent allusion to the fantasy of the sexual assault again underlines the subversion of the sense of protective boundaries and elementary ethics, which is the matrix of all possible subsequent ethical confusion.

The shut window of the dream, in a certain sense protects Maria from falling into an empty space, which can be linked to her suicidal fantasies. On the other hand, the shut window dramatically describes the sense of claustrophobic imprisonment in the sexual/violent fantasies that Maria has so intensely suffered since her childhood.

Giuseppe: a father with barred doors

I had been told that the father was more than sceptical of and did not trust those like me, the "headshrinkers". I did not have any doubt about that when I met him for the first time, together with Marta. A man less than forty years old, in his tight tracksuit showing his big muscles, is sitting in front of me. Folded arms, stone face, dark sun-glasses, and few words.

Here, we have another one who needs not to go unnoticed, I think. Another one who is used to impressing the passers-by. And for sure, he looks like a bomb ready to explode.

I make sure that he can quickly and explicitly tell me, which he does without any effort, that he does not trust the psychoanalytic cure, psychiatrists and all the rest. I look at him straight in the eye, trying to get through his dark green lenses, and tell him that I truly thank him for telling me all of that so clearly. This is a great help for me, I say. He is quite surprised, but I notice he appreciates my words. He remains hieratic though. I keep being hot on his heels and say we have to make a deal for Maria, if he trusts me just that little bit, that is. And if not, that it is better to be clear about it right away, in which case they can go elsewhere. I do not want to have my or anybody else's time wasted. Take it or leave it.

He accepts. He likes that we settled it between men. And I like that he likes that. I imagine that something more healthily and paternally sophisticated may slowly grow over time, and things could become less coarse.

It took two years. Two years after this first meeting to have a smile from him. With no green lenses. A smile with a sort of kind delicacy and a bit of trust, even some traces of gratitude—if I am allowed to be optimistic. A smile for sure interspersed with a glimpse of seductiveness that this man surely considers as part of his consolidated and totally automatic mental equipment.

In the meanwhile, I come to know that he lives in a big house together with his elderly adoptive parents, both affected by a neurological disease. They are described as demented and confused, unable to know and recognise people. Incontinent. Such a description makes me immediately suspicious, both regarding the actual severity of their illness and the reason why they are not properly assisted or hospitalised.

Giuseppe keeps them segregated, without any external help, in a condition that is verging on illegality. He feels persecuted by his parents and locks them up. Later in time, I come to know that he occasionally becomes violent towards the father, and that he has always been obsessive, always trying to hide his symptoms, especially his hoarding. He has always refused any kind of treatment whatsoever.

Doors are barred, also to defend himself from the anxiety of becoming exactly like his adoptive parents, beyond any impossible genetic transmission. Sooner or later. Demented. Because fantasies can be more powerful than genes. Being demented and being mindless seem to be intertwined with each other. Giuseppe seems unable to see and think, he can just segregate and lock parts of himself up, including his being able to meet his daughter's wish to have a father. *How can one be a father?*

When Maria goes to her father's house, he locks her up in her room while she studies, with the excuse of protecting her from her molesting grandparents. But he locks her in from the outside, he does not give her the key to lock or unlock the room door. Maria gets scared, she feels imprisoned behind barred doors and masturbates. She has to call daddy on the mobile phone even to be allowed to go to the toilet. These are reported as unchangeable habits. Everybody in the family, including Maria, agrees with no objections.

Giuseppe is used to hiding himself. He cannot find anything really meaningful in the comings and goings of his everyday life. There is nothing he can *really* cope with. He has always been scared but he cannot show it, because this would scare him even more. He has always looked at himself in the mirror, since he was a boy. Now that he is nearly forty and goes to the gym two hours every day five days a week, when he looks into the mirror he still cannot meet himself behind his muscles and his seducer's smile. He is not even able to recognise himself when he looks inside his stretchy clothes, so well designed to show, so well built to hide, his fragile identity. Hidden to himself, hidden to everybody.

Giuseppe did not give his surname to his daughter. The *Nomen Patris* has gone mindless and lost, who knows where. He has not had *time* for this, he justifies. Between a lost name, unfound time, and barred space, how can one become a father? Years later, he would not tolerate Maria's mother emancipating from her financial dependency on him, and started to fantasise that Maria and Marta would spoil his patrimony. Not legally recognising his daughter was not enough at that point, so he actually interrupted every contact with Maria. As expected, he did it in a sadistic and controlling way, by sending text messages in which he promised a future meeting with her that he regularly cancelled. He poisonously kept the hope of having a father alive in his daughter, and continuously frustrated it, sadistically preventing her from mourning him. The bond was cruelly eternal, and cruelly impossible.

I met Giuseppe just a few times, and when he finally decided to break off contact with his daughter, he also refused to see me and never answered any of my messages. The presence of his absence remained for years at the core of the analytic work with Maria, in the shape of the persecutory penis of her dreadful obsessions as well as in the guise of an idealised beloved and longed-for father. He was for Maria the representative of the core obsessional functioning: abandonment/imprisonment was the essential pattern. Cruelty was the affect implied, the main tool for creating suffocating bonds where distance and freedom were unconceivable.

Marta agreed to begin psychotherapeutic work with one of my colleagues, alongside my work with Maria. So, something more about these two parents could be reconstructed through the mother's work in her own therapy. Apparently, the two must have met following roaring erotic passion: Marta, in her search for a *real man*, the one who could free her from her castrated father, but she was not sufficiently free to avoid breathing the same mephitic air and sharing the same promiscuous glance of her mother, and so becoming her double; Giuseppe, in his search for an identity through his muscles and his simulacrum of masculinity, in a desperate attempt to be freed from that threatening and overwhelming dementia.

But how can one become a mother? How can one become a father? And if our daughter is crazy? And if our daughter dies? How can doors be hinged? How can they open and how can they close? How can they separate and how can they connect?

And how can Maria not feel imprisoned in her excited and brutal fantasies? How can she stop getting excited in fantasising to imprison? How can she stop worrying and feeling breathless again and again? How many cuts on her skin will she need to make life spring out? What if mum dies? Will I ever have my dad? Will I ever lose him?

Sexuality and identity

Here follows a session—among many—to describe a fruitful attempt at getting out of tricky imprisonment. It is about sexuality and identity, which is certainly at the heart of a possible development for this girl. It is about the use of the mind, which risks falling into a sort of spin and death by asphyxia, and about a possible way out. We are two years into the analysis, and well into Maria's adolescence.

Maria shows a certain state of anxiety. Quite soon, I recognise an emotional atmosphere in which it can be very difficult to speak, and also to listen. My perception is that Maria somehow puts forward some "surface" anxiety matters, which are quite intense, with the purpose of not getting to the point of actually saying what exactly the core thought is that is precisely worrying her at that specific moment.

Such "side" anxiety matters are intense and have, today as always, a considerable power to capture the other's attention, as if Maria wanted to take my attention and speech to something that matters but does not matter at the same time. When this happens, she can consequently complain about not being understood.

Such a condition is linked to a great difficulty in setting an internal scale of "values and sense". This is intertwined with the excitement and triumph of putting the object in the position of an almost inevitable mistake. Maria is not actually (completely) unaware of the point she would like to make. She knows what she wants to say, but she sidetracks.

As I seem to realise this element, which has been experienced many times in the sessions as a source of misunderstanding and complaints, I at first wait silently and then suggest that maybe something else is worrying her *more*. I am careful not to say that something else is worrying her *really*. If I said *really* instead of *more*, she would take it as if I were considering what she is saying as false and meaningless, which would allow her to complain about me, about my unwillingness to listen, and about my expectation to be told just what I like to hear and what I am interested in.

With a whining and sad tone of voice, Maria tells me she has had a fantasy lately, which she starts recalling with an obsessional thinking mode.

Her friends have boyfriends and she does not. So she has started to consider if she might be lesbian, and what having sexual intercourse with another girl might be like. Considering that she got scared about such a fantasy, in that the simple fact of thinking about being lesbian may turn her into an actual lesbian... or... the simple fact of thinking about being lesbian might mean she actually is... she decided to ask her mother if she (mum) thought she (Maria) was lesbian or not, and if she (mum) had ever had the same kind of fantasy. Her mother told her not to worry over it, that she did not think Maria was lesbian, and said that thoughts like this one often came to people's minds when they were Maria's age, although she (mum) said she had never had homosexual thoughts when she was an adolescent.

This search for "pedagogic" reassurance from the mother is well known and represents a non-reliable pseudo-solution, while the real purpose seems to be that of getting reciprocally aroused through each other's fantasy, according to a substantial position of voyeurism-exhibitionism, which is very similar to what usually happens between the two in their provocative and aggressive interactions.

Obviously, given these assumptions, this maternal reassurance did not work at all: Maria keeps being afraid that she is lesbian and she cannot get rid of this thought, which always comes to her mind in a way that is very disturbing and totally out of control.

On the other hand—she states with a sort of come-on look and a seductively lamenting tone—if it is "so" clear that she is scared of penetration, this must be the real reason why she thinks she is lesbian. By saying so, she makes me guess that if I tell her that her fantasy is linked to her fear of the penis, I already know that she knows it and consequently it is totally useless saying it. Psychoanalytic interpretations that might have been helpful in a certain context and had given rise to a positive development of knowledge, are subsequently stored and made meaningless. They can be used—as the come-on look reveals—as a tool to create emotional engagement with the interlocutor, on a register of *pseudity*, or to subtly try to penetrate and "know" what the other thinks and feels. This functioning can be understood as the reversal of a true self-knowledge founded upon the object's reverie.

Maria keeps repeating her thoughts in a crooked way and gives me the impression that she is not able to get out of or stop this circle of thoughts. I feel a well-known pressure to give useless reassurance, in the guise of her mother. I also realise that I have to pay great attention so as not to make statements that could be taken as "definitions", such as "you are lesbian/ you are not lesbian" … "you are such and such/you are not such and such." Maria would consider these sentences as "given facts", no longer modifiable, and suited to being immediately turned into acts and behaviour for which I would be considered totally responsible.

As usual, the main difficulty here is to keep the symbolic space alive, unsaturated, and sufficiently airy and expansive in order to allow the emergent mind to grow, in contrast to the occlusive immobility of obsessional brooding.

In the fatigue of contrasting the obsessional functioning, I also feel personally helped and deeply supported by the protected space of my theoretical
psychoanalytic background and by my model of the mind. Reverie responses
well based on theory. Due to the exquisitely separating function of theory, I am thus able to contrast the sterile, castrating, and occlusive obsessional procedure, which works according to a non-separating omnipotent
maternal code: the core problem of obsession is actually an unmanageable
separation anxiety, expressed through the register of the symptom. In this
sense, theory helps and supports healthy astuteness against obsessional
gambling, which is as hidden and dangerous as a minefield. This is one of the
tools I use in order to place myself sufficiently far away from and dodge the
cluster bombs of the analysand's mind.

Now I invite Maria to do some associative work on how she fantasises
having sexual intercourse with a girl. At the same time, I openly and assert-
ively say that for me the point is not to give her a "definition".

Maria's repetitive and blocked speech seems to progressively melt, and
gradually a clearer three-dimensionality and a truthful congruousness of
the affects come to the fore. Again, she speaks of her phobic fantasies about
the penis, but now with much more consistency and meaning. Step by step,
Maria's associations go in the direction of an idealisation of the female body,
and she progressively shows the fantasy of soft and rhythmic contact with
this body. The maternal quality of her fantasy becomes progressively clearer
when Maria talks in terms of non-separation, of endlessly hugging arms, of
her wish to be ideally understood without words. In this flow of thoughts,
the erotised component dramatically decreases and the dimension of an
infantile expectation for ideal containment becomes paramount.

I comment on how important it is that Maria can imagine a state of mind like
this, listening to a small child whose only wish is to stay in her mother's arms
as if in a kind of eternal paradise. I also say that even if this is very different
from what Maria thinks she experienced as a small child with her real mother,
and if it is also very different from the fatigue of her communication with
myself, that such a paradise that she can now imagine is, however, a sort of safe
ground of her mind she can now rely upon in her most difficult moments.

Considering that many aspects of the communication are probably quite
evident in this clinical vignette, as well as some obvious implications

of the analytic relation and of the state of the transference, I wish to limit myself to underlining that the change from the genital fantasy to the mother–infant one was crucial in order to gradually work through the matter of identity in this girl. Understanding the narcissistic ideal of the "heaven fantasy", certainly not as a developmental phase but as a state of mind that is necessary for the foundation of a sufficiently cohesive sense of self, is also definitively important. Working through primal narcissistic elements commonly reactivated during adolescence is obviously crucial for any healthy growth. In this frame, it is also worth remembering how Klein (1963) connects the fantasy of being understood without words to the sense of loneliness, where the capacity to feel "nostalgic" becomes essential. This is especially important in relation to overcoming separation anxieties, which are so relevant in the obsessional situation.

Further developments in sexuality

A turning point in Maria's development occurs when she is around nineteen. In the previous years, she had experienced what she called her "first love relationship" with a boy her own age, the relationship having developed almost exclusively through the internet. Although clearly defensive against the overwhelming anxiety of body contact and shared sexual arousal, this relationship was to a certain extent meaningful and important for Maria, in terms of a sort of preparation for a more "real" relationship. In some way—we may say in the way adolescents conceive *the virtual as real*, as *a peculiar form of reality among others*—Maria could experience emotions, passion, pain, joy, a certain attitude towards taking care of the couple, disillusionment, anger, jealousy, and a variety of feelings I would not call substantially different from what one could experience with a "flesh and blood" person.

Psychoanalytically speaking, we all know that the *reality of a real person* in the relationship is quite a complex concept, as it is interspersed with unconscious elements of the two people involved. The only significant difference from virtual relationships is constituted by the presence and closeness of the actual and fantasised bodies in mutual intimacy—with the complexity of their multi-layered languages—which cannot be substituted by any other tools or expressed and shared electronically. Such intimacy was surely the element Maria was unable to cope with, and—overcoming the risk of becoming fixated—the relationship with this guy eventually ended.

At the age of nineteen, Maria started a new relationship with a guy she got emotionally involved with, and she seemed very committed. For about one year, this guy was mentioned in the sessions through his nickname, Wild. Then I discovered his actual name was Francesco. Maria was slightly embarrassed to reveal this name, and looked at me with a sudden blush. Being quite an expert patient by now, and quite used to transference interpretations, she expected—I am totally sure—my comments on this person's name. Instead, I smiled slightly and sighed, without saying a word. She smiled back for a second, and carried on, visibly relieved.

Maria was at that time very mature for her age, having added to her natural intelligence a notable degree of introspection and sensitivity which she had developed over the years in her analysis. I was pleased for that, somehow glad for this daughter's growth, gently playing with Oedipus between the two of us. By now, and for many years, Maria had learned to use the analytic situation very constructively and her relationship with me was extremely solid at this time. Concomitantly, we decided to decrease the number of her weekly sessions from four to two. When she started university, she found a part-time job through which she could pay one of the two sessions, the second one continuing to be paid by her mother. This was an important step in Maria's emancipation and it boosted her sense of being grown up and "realistically" independent from her mother, and of being made responsible by a welcoming-and-weaning parent in the transference.

Maria was totally aware that starting a new relationship with this guy would be a challenge for her: she knew perfectly well she was about to confront herself with the issue of "real" sexuality, she knew it would be extremely difficult, but decided to go through with it all the same.

In the first months, Maria and her boyfriend were engaged in discovering each other's bodies. Wild/Francesco was very patient and sensitive with her, and kept being sexually attracted to her while she was coping with her sense of intense disgust for his penis and for his body hair, and had intense phobic reactions to his body fluids. She had severe dyspareunia and suffered intense pain at any attempt to be penetrated, which remained impossible for more than a year. As adolescents often are—notwithstanding their access to knowledge through the Web—they were both seemingly unaware of the most elementary notions in terms of the anatomy and functioning of the genitals. The vagina was imagined to have a kind of "perpendicular" orientation—as she said—and was supposed to be fitted to welcome the "whole" penis in quite an unrealistic way, not to mention that Maria had no secretions at all and—as a gynaecological check showed—she had a peculiar conformation of the hymen that made it particularly resistant. I had to advise Maria to consult a gynaecologist to get some basic information on sex toys and lubricants as well, just in case.

The first months of the relationship turned out to be very tough. Maria quite easily overcame her phobic reactions and started to allow some sexual contact, and basically became able to have active and passive oral sex. But, after many failed attempts to be penetrated, Maria adopted unconscious manoeuvres to avoid sexual encounters, and the relationship was at serious risk of deterioration. There was also a subtle tendency to keep her boyfriend bound to her in quite a frustrating and sadistic relation, in a sort of identification with her parents' way of controlling each other. Interpreting this element placed Maria in a deep conflict and created distress, and sessions—after many years—started to become quite difficult again.

During the summer break of that year, I received a phone call from Maria. She was in a very intense state of anxiety, saying that her obsessional symptoms had come up again after many years. She could not sleep and had started to fantasise again about knives and sexual assaults, and had the obsessive thought-impulse to kill people, including her mother and her boyfriend, and she was scared that the simple fact of fantasising meant that something would actually occur. She was desperate and said she was afraid of becoming ill again with no possible cure this time. She also said she refused medication and that she wanted to try to cope with the situation with her internal resources, and I said I would support this attempt. I reminded her that she was aware of the internal reasons of what was going on, and said that we had done a lot of work and that she could understand what was happening much better than eight years before. I said we would work on this on our return to the sessions two weeks later and that I was confident she could wait. And so was she. In about a month, this breakdown was solved, essentially through interpreting the revival of her persecutory fantasies about sexuality, which revealed a scared child inside her that always needed our attention and care, as if we were two parents taking care of a terrified young child.

In the following months after this episode:

Maria dreams of a little girl aged four or five, who has bruises on her body. The child suffers and has pain because of these bruises and accepts help from Maria and from an adult man who instructs her on how to deal with the child. At first, Maria spreads ointment on the child's skin, a peculiar ointment that can ease the pain and make a sort of massage. Then she takes the child on her lap and gives her food, some good and well-prepared pasta that the girl enjoys very much. Maria reports this dream with a lot of emotion. The ointment reminds her of some maternal care she has seen on TV about what African mothers do with their babies, but also of the lubricant she and her boyfriend use in their attempts to have penetration, and also of her boyfriend's sperm and body fluids that she had come to be acquainted with in the recent past. Regarding the pasta, Maria says she likes pasta very much, but she rarely eats it because she is always at risk of putting on weight, so she has to restrain herself. "Lucky her!" —meaning the child in the dream—"who can eat pasta and enjoy it without problems for her body!" she says.

I ask if she remembers what sort of pasta it was, and what the sauce was. Maria says it was Sicilian pasta, a sort of twisted macaroni dressed with tomato, aubergine, and salted dry ricotta. She says this is pasta that her boyfriend's mother prepares when she is occasionally with them for lunch on Sundays. His family is not Sicilian, but apparently his mother can prepare this dish very well and Maria loves it. "This is quite strange," she adds—"my mother hates aubergines and would get sick if she saw that dish, and as a child I hated aubergines too… well I always liked and disliked what my mother did… now I love aubergines and that pasta is absolutely fantastic!"

I interpret that the child with the bruises stands for what, on many occasions, we have named a Maria-child who felt beaten, violated, and attacked by all the people who were supposed to protect her, as well as by her violent thoughts. I say Maria is able to trust me again as the one who can tell her how to take care of this child, and this apparently works. The ointment and the body contact are not dangerous but soothing, and resemble the fatigue linked to penetration. I say that the child in the dream can "take in" something that comes from a "new mother", which is also Maria herself and myself, something that is beyond her identification with her actual mother.

> I say I think it is so important that something can be taken in and enjoyed by this child, with no sense of being damaged, the "allowed" new pleasure of the body being experienced instead.

Maria seemed very moved while listening to my words. Again, as in the previously mentioned session, working on the oral/maternal component in the transference proves to be effective in overcoming the sexual conundrum.

During the following session, she said she managed to have intercourse for the first time and that it was pain-free. Three months later, she had her first clitoral orgasm when penetrated.

Current developments: towards the end of analysis—jealousy and separation

Maria successfully finished her studies at university with excellent results and started practising to become a film-maker. Francesco/Wild is no longer in her life. She decided to end that relationship, after quite a hard working through of guilty feelings and anxieties regarding what this guy might revengefully say or do against her. The issue of separating from a loved object, the burden of acknowledging that love can end, the recognition that relationships can be unsatisfactory, notwithstanding her determination to make them good, all caused a further voyage through persecution and loss, as well as the interminable experience of my being imperfect in curing her pain.

A few months after separating from Francesco, a new guy comes onto the scene. Everything seems to go well, except for a disturbing sense of pervasive and slightly obsessional jealousy that captures her mind every now and then. Given that this guy does not give her actual motivations to be jealous, a reality she is capable of recognising, the issue ultimately concerns Maria's capacity to acknowledge that people cannot totally belong to her, and that loss is immanent and unavoidable. Loss includes mourning once again her fantasy of total and ultimate healing. Maria now knows she was not responsible for her father abandoning her, she knows that losses of every kind occur in our lives beyond our will and responsibility.

She knows I will not be with her forever. I told her explicitly that this is *the* issue—but have we worked on anything else over these thirteen years?—on which I am still here to work with her, for a limited period of time. Let us forget about symptoms or regressions of whatever nature, I am still here just for mourning. I am confident she can do without me, and after all, I say, if we remember her initial urge to go back to normality and not be called crazy, I think I kept my (supposed) promise, although normality has little in common with what she imagined thirteen years ago. She subtly shivers when I mention our separation, but she knows that I am not joking. And I am sure this is what she wants from me, once more.

So who is normal? Them or me? Concluding remarks

To conclude, Maria's and her parents' story—as well as Marco's—is quite a common one. Common in many respects, despite its harshness, which would make it look anomalous, strange, or at least peculiar, psychopathological. It is not so. Common is the sense that gets lost in doors that do not bind, lost in the carelessness of not providing shelter from the storms of fantasies, lost in the abuse of letting children be porous receptacles of the blind and deaf movements of adults. Lost in the invasive ideology of non-protection, which ferociously calls free and intimate what is actually abusive and thoughtless. Common is retreating into a paranoid solitude and barring the doors to defend from thinking, to attempt desperate isolation that turns into subtle and pervasive dementia.

It is common, also, for children to remain imprisoned and immobilised by all that, even if obsession is only one among the many possible forms of this paralysis. It is common to have no answers—apart from escape or consolation—to one's and someone else's death. It is common not to know how one can become a mother or a father. It is common to procreate with the burden of an unredeemed childhood. Without memory of a past devoid of the starting point of one's evil.

If we go back to Maria's dream of the zombies and reconsider all the matter regarding barred versus non-bounding doors, we come across a technical as well as an ethical problem. As in Maria's dream, it is very common that only the one who turns his back may look *normal*. Normal is only the one who places himself in the position of escaping, in the register of neglect and abandonment, which is essentially *anti-care*. Such a *depriving* position can only activate envious wishes of assault, a cynical search for power, reiterated abuse, generation by generation. Normalised. What is normal? Who is normal? Them or me?

CHAPTER SIX

Pharmaco-psychotherapy: the combined transference

Turn him to any cause of policy,
The Gordian Knot of it he will unloose,
Familiar as his garter.
—Shakespeare, *Henry V,* Act 1, Scene 1, 45–47

Tu es Petrus, et super hanc petram aedificabo ecclesiam meam.
—Matthew 16, 18–19

Introductory remarks

In this chapter, I wish to outline my guidelines when dealing with patients who require pharmacological treatment along with their psychoanalytic work. My reflection specifically regards those patients who are treated with a strict psychoanalytic or psychoanalytically oriented psychotherapy, where the analytic method is and remains the core of the treatment and pharmacology is just supportive to that, in a secondary although relevant or at times unavoidable role. The analytic setting and the centrality of containment and interpretation remain fundamental in my approach. Pharmacological treatment is intended to make the psychoanalytic work more effective in some specific circumstances and clinical conditions, as shall be described through the clinical material.

The issue of why and when a combined therapy is suggested to a patient is at risk of representing a mere countertransference enactment in response to a more or less subtle burnout and/or of being influenced by counter-identifications of the analyst with unprocessed or undetected elements in the transference.

On the other hand, no less relevant is the acknowledgement of the limits of the analytic method in a specific situation: the omnipotent denial of such limits can be no less harmful than the enactment of unprocessed transference elements or being contaminated by a subtle burnout syndrome.

More specifically, the acknowledgement of the limits of the analytic method in a specific situation may involve the following.

Internal factors

The severity of symptoms massively impinging on the patient's life and on the capacity to use the analytic situation to its full potential.

External factors

Economic, social, and/or cultural factors may diminish the capacity of the patient to work through internal conflicts in an exclusively analytic mode.

Technical skills

Dealing analytically with severely disturbed patients requires a great deal of clinical experience. Skills may not yet be fully developed in young analysts, despite their being appropriately supervised, or could be honestly and humbly acknowledged as insufficient also by expert analysts in specific circumstances.

Frequency of sessions

Patients and their contexts may not easily lend themselves to intensive analytic work, for whatever reasons. Working analytically inevitably involves, first, the living concept of the unconscious mind as a sedimentation of past experiences continuously causing effects in the present, as well as a source of new responses to the original patterns; second, the transference as the elective place for transformation; third, the intersection between chronological time and mythic time. Within this framework, we cannot but conclude that the frequency of sessions makes a remarkable difference. As a matter of fact, only when an analyst becomes really expert, which normally takes around three decades, can he or she work with one or two sessions per week with a similar effectiveness and depth to four or five sessions. This requires much effort and endurance on the part of the analyst, as well as a capacity of the patient to carry a much heavier burden, as things are obviously easier for patients if they are seen more frequently. All this cannot or should not be asked of young therapists who see severely disturbed patients. Young analytically oriented therapists should learn by seeing patients intensively, and should then treat patients less intensively if and when they become more expert.

Ethical issues

In principle, the supreme interest of patients prevails over any supposed purity of the method, whatever we may mean by this term. Consequently, it is the analyst's commitment to strictly adhere to the foundations of the analytic method, while making it flexible enough to cope with the internal and external reality of each patient. This task is far from easy, especially if we want to keep the method alive, without turning it into a sort of supportive, pedagogical, conversational, easygoing game. Keeping the method alive means adapting it to the polymorphous complexity of the patients' lives. Under no circumstances are patients supposed to simply comply with or to support the illusion of the method's self-sufficiency.

More specifically, and especially when dealing with children and adolescents, there is an issue that cannot be overlooked. For children and adolescents, going to school, feeling part of the community of their peers, feeling clearly equal to some and different from others, feeling able to learn, and feeling able to experience a sense of potency, are not options. These are essential elements, as vital as the air these individuals breathe. Faced with symptoms that cause deep impairments in these fundamental activities, we cannot afford to wait for symptoms to hypothetically decrease thanks to a pure analytic method, which in the specific case of severe obsessional symptoms, just to quote the topic of this book, is practically impossible. Time is precious at that age, and what is lost is lost. All child and adolescent patients described in this book expressed unquestionable pressure to go back to their everyday lives, to school and to their friends. This was a matter of life or death for them. No adult would exert the same pressure. Perhaps adults unconsciously develop what we call secondary advantages, or experience hidden erotised pleasure in remaining ill. Children and adolescents usually do not, with the exception of those who have prematurely and irremediably become cynical and icy criminals. In any case, subjective as well as reality factors have to be taken into account: under certain circumstances, the option of a pharmacological prescription is ethically a must.

Certainly, the pressure and the expectations, either conscious or implicit, from the context constitute a relevant factor that needs to be seriously taken into account. It is one thing to respond to the legitimate need of a young patient to go back to his or her normal life as soon as possible. Pressure from families and schools to simply normalise supposed abnormal behaviour without questioning the meaning and the profound implications of that clinical condition is quite another. Both patient and context may press to have medications for different reasons, intertwined with similar hidden motivations and collusions. The attitude of many families and contexts to simply fix the situation with no deeper questions and without challenging the equilibrium is a common fact, and the last thing psychoanalysis should do is work in favour of such demands of normalisation. This would be against its own nature, and no evolution of theory or technicality could support such a dehumanising goal.

However, and especially when working with children and adolescents, families and contexts must always be our allies. Young people cannot do without their families or their schools, and cannot be forced into an unmanageable conflict of loyalty. If they are placed in a conflict between the parents and the transference, they have a limited capacity to tolerate it, especially when they are very young. When families seek to interrupt the therapy, because their expectations of normalisation are not met, children cannot but choose the parents, sooner or later. This is usually an extremely painful situation for them, which may hamper their readiness to trust another therapist in the future. Consequently, the analyst has to be an open-minded mediator. Compromises cannot always reach the optimal level of dignity and decency, but similarly to what the ego does in mediating between different agencies within the individual, we try to operate in the service of making things reasonably good for the patient, with the aim of promoting personal growth in his or her real context.

Symptom, sense of self, and ego functions: aims of medication in psychoanalytically oriented therapy

The sense of self when facing symptoms severely impinging upon one's life must also be considered carefully, as it always implies coming to terms with shame. In principle, the vicarious function of the analyst via the transference supports the patient in working through symptoms as symbolically meaningful elements, and the inevitable sense of belittlement and shame that symptoms carry with them. This is an operation carried out by the ego in terms of cognition as well as the capacity to bear the contradictory and conflictual nature of fantasies and affects. The ego must be capable of such a complex task, which is not to be taken for granted at all, especially when symptoms themselves heavily impinge upon the complexity of ego functions.

In my practice, and throughout this book, I consider symptoms in the most classical Freudian view as the expression of psychic compromise between different internal agencies and between internal agencies and external reality. This is operated by the unconscious ego. As the ego implies different levels of consciousness and multiple interactive functions with both the internal and external worlds, symptoms cannot but impinge more or less severely upon its fundamental role. In this sense, working on the complexity of ego functions is a non-secondary task of the analytic method, which always involves challenging the symptoms.

The choice of implementing pharmacological treatment can be inspired by a classical medical model which privileges—broadly speaking—symptom control and behaviour normalisation. Or, it can be inspired by the psychoanalytic model with the aim of modulating the symptom and enhancing the plasticity of defences.

Therefore, the appropriate aims of medication in a psychoanalytically oriented treatment are *first*, to improve ego functions and increase the plasticity of defences in relation to internal and external reality;

and *second*, to make symptoms more available to analytic investigation and to the transference work.

Multiplicity of the transference

There are multiple levels of the patient's transference when medication is implemented that need to be considered carefully. They include:

- The transference onto the analyst/psychotherapist, including dis-illusionment, ambivalence, and the experience of the analyst's impotence.
- The transference onto the psychiatrist, including omnipotent expectations and/or persecution.
- Transference onto the medication itself, with relevant differences depending on the specific substance. In the case of obsessive–compulsive disorder, where an association of antidepressants and neuroleptics is prescribed, one should consider that the fantasies activated in relation to the two categories of substances are quite different and deserve specific attention and care. While antidepressants are more accepted, neuroleptics are more typically experienced as being linked to "madness" and activate a more powerful sense of shame and the fantasy of the illness being incurable. These fantasies need to be taken care of with great sensitivity, both on a reality level (by clearly explaining the difference in dosage when treating OCD compared to what is done with psychotic people, as well as aims and side effects), and especially in terms of the transference. Strict interpretations in the transference on every detail of what patients say and do with regard to the substance are absolutely essential.

The levels of the context's transference (mainly family, but also school in the case of children and adolescents) when medication is implemented, must also be taken into account with great care. These levels include:

- A more or less explicit devaluation of the psychotherapeutic work, especially if carried out by a non-medical professional. This more frequently occurs when the mentality of "quickly fixing the mal-functioning" is dominant in a family, and the psychotherapist is easily seen as the one who asks too many embarrassing questions and makes things too complicated. So it is a waste of time and money.

- Parallel to the devaluation of the psychotherapist, magical expectations are easily projected onto the psychiatrist, which are easily turned into persecution as soon as the psychiatrist reveals that he or she is not omnipotent.

- Overestimation or distortion of side effects, including manipulations and splitting. Side effects are always an enormous reservoir that is used to attack the cure, subtly creating an antagonism between psychotherapist and psychiatrist, which is commonly used by patient and family to boycott treatment. Such an antagonism needs to be kept under control on a reality level by the two professionals involved, and dealt with on the transference level with the patient and through appropriate interventions with the family. The task is to vigorously show all the actors involved in the scene that the therapeutic couple is similar to two parents working synergistically, and that these parents are too strong to be split and manipulated.

Given these elements, I consider it essential to work with colleagues whom I totally trust and with whom I have a well-established working relationship. Either when I have to work as a psychiatrist in cooperation with a psychoanalyst, or when I see a patient analytically and I require the help of a psychiatrist, I need to have a fully syntonic agreement with my colleague, a true sense of acting as one, that is, a sense of being a good parental couple at work.

If that does not occur, for whatever reason, and of course this has happened in a very limited number of cases, I prefer to play both roles myself with my patient. It is better to deal personally with the multiple facets of the transference in an ongoing state of complex impurity that needs to be continuously and strenuously worked through, rather than leave pieces of the transference unattended and dispersed in the magmatic confusion of two colleagues who are unable to properly talk to one another. Patients understandably have had enough of disturbed families and cannot be asked to put up with one more disturbed, confused, ambiguous, and weak parenthood.

Last but not least, in all the cases presented in this book, medication had always been proposed to the patients as something tentative and hopefully temporary. Without promising to be able to do this, I nevertheless do promise to do my humanly possible best to come to the point of decreasing the doses as much as possible, and to possibly do without the drugs some day, provided that the patients work hard in their analysis, which I always say is *the* treatment. This position is surely risky, but psychoanalysis deals with the risk of life and growth, and this has proved to be particularly important with children and adolescents. It gives them a strong motivation to work hard and cooperate with me to the best their minds can, at least the parts that are relatively free from repetition and cruelty.

In the present chapter, I shall describe the situation of an adolescent patient with whom I had the role of the psychiatrist, while he was seen three times a week by a psychoanalyst whom I have known very well for many years. The aim is to show the multiple levels of the transference, and how our solid therapeutic parenthood produced satisfactory results. In the previous chapter, I have described clinical situations where I played both roles with my analytic patients.

Immobile sounds, unheard voices: the story of Pietro

Pietro was sixteen years old when he was referred to me by the colleague who had been seeing him in psychoanalytic psychotherapy for some years. For a short period of time before puberty, the child had been in treatment with the same colleague for some significant difficulties at school that were becoming apparent. As soon as the problem was solved and things started to improve at school, the family decided to interrupt the therapy, despite the analyst's advice to continue in order to better understand and especially to prevent further problems in the forthcoming puberty.

Problems actually became severe around the age of fourteen, at the beginning of Italian secondary school, and seemed to quickly and dramatically reduce this boy's ability to perform at school and maintain good-enough relationships with his peers. His capacity to use his psychotherapy was also poor, notwithstanding the skilful and sensitive attitude of his experienced therapist. With the family's agreement and that of the patient himself, I was consulted for a possible pharmacological support, which was implemented shortly afterwards.

What the patient replicated with me in our initial meetings was apparently similar to what he commonly did at school: finding himself before any written test, he remained blocked and left the page blank; and when requested by teachers to answer questions or say what he was supposed to have studied, he would remain totally silent.

First session

After some minutes of silence, and after my cautious attempts and words of encouragement to try and make him speak, he says that his problem is that he cannot work at school. He says these few words with extreme fatigue, as if he had to move a heavy stone obstructing his path. It seems as if he is gasping. His face also depicts his extreme fatigue, he frowns, his gaze is fixed on the carpet. He sits with a rigid posture on the chair, and his hands clenched. His emotional state is immediately pervasive and creates an oppressive atmosphere in the room. I soon sense the contagion in the countertransference. I myself start to feel oppressed, time becomes infinite, I feel as if I were immersed in a gluey and dense fog, and I soon have the impression that this first session has already lasted for hours and will be interminable. I notice that I have a recurrent thought, a kind of question: "And now, what can I tell him? ... what can I tell him? ... what can I tell him ..." I feel I am unable get out of this imprisoning thought and my anxiety starts to increase. Two anxious people in the room. I eventually take a deep breath and say: "I guess you must feel very bad ... maybe there are disturbing thoughts that block you. Are you able to talk about that with your analyst?" "Not always," he says.

"You know I am here to see if I can be of any help," I say. He seems to melt a bit. "That is what I want. I'll do what is necessary," and he looks at me for a second before going back to gazing at the carpet. "OK, but I need to understand a bit better ... your therapist told me something, but I need to know your point of view."

He silently nods. ...

My obsessive question, "what can I tell him?" seems to me to be the core of this first encounter, a sort of diagnostic watershed. Its repetitiveness, the sense of imprisonment conveyed, the destruction of any awareness of chronological time, the sense that such an endless question in my mind was a disturbing element coming from *somewhere* and was aimed at boycotting our contact and not at helping it, were formal elements that all became meaningful to me. Furthermore, the picture of a primal container that is impotent while facing an incomprehensible baby, as well as a picture of an impotent baby while facing a deaf container, became vivid in my mind.

In the following sessions, with extreme fatigue, he let me understand that he gets lost in his thoughts. He does not really say what kind of thoughts they are, but I understand he is invaded by something he cannot control or get rid of. When I explicitly ask him if these thoughts are like unwanted invasions, something like a foreign element that takes possession of his mind, preventing him from doing what he wants or is supposed to do, he visibly nods and looks a little relieved.

However, the countertransference in many respects remained quite difficult to detect. There was certainly some tenderness in watching this clumsy six-foot-tall guy, his skin tortured by pimples that looked like vigorously suppressed bombs, who dressed like those adolescents who pretend to be classy but are extremely inhibited and so very scared and blocked. At the same time, it was like being in front of an alien, someone who comes from another planet, someone who cannot find a language to share with us humans. Someone who remains mute even when speaking, and substantially unheard. My disquietude regarding an unclear diagnosis of the real nature of his thinking disorder remained unsolved for several weeks. I was almost sure of the formal characteristics of his thinking processes, which sounded obsessional in terms of typical repetitiveness, invasiveness, and ego-dystonia.

But with regard to the contents of his ideation, and I am referring here to the conscious contents, not to unconscious phantasies, I found myself before a true mystery. Much of what he had in his mind seemed to be kept hidden and locked up. My suspicion of being in the presence of some obscure and possibly bizarre thoughts made me quite upset and uncertain with regard to a possible confusional, if not definitely psychotic, level of his ideation.

What I gradually came to learn from him and from my colleague over the following weeks was that his ruminations revolved around some grandiose fantasies of being a sort of genius in information technology and computer games, the one who would become some kind of superstar. That was seemingly accompanied by ruminative thoughts regarding the supposed inferiority and stupidity of his schoolmates. He fantasised he would learn everything without having to really work and study, and that he could have passed his tests brilliantly if he had only decided to do so. He substantially eliminated a great deal of his sense of frustration through a mechanism of isolation, thus making his failures and difficulties emotionally indifferent and neutralised. Such a mechanism, as I came to understand, was activated as a defence against a sense of devastating internal collapse, which became apparent when the illusion of being powerful and indifferent momentarily became shattered for some reason. It was a state of empty mindlessness, a vertigo of nullification, a numbing of the self, totally different, in my view, from the desperate plasticity, the deadly power, and the lively cruelty of true depression. Moreover, the repetitiveness of the patient's fantasies created a subtle state of arousal and pretended self-sufficiency. He practically lived continuously in a masturbatory state of mind, far away from everybody's world, at the periphery of himself. It was hard to say whether he really suffered or had contact with his nuclear pain, even occasionally. He surely felt oppressed by thoughts he could not avoid having and being overwhelmed by, he probably realised he was different from his peers, and he partly realised he made his parents frustrated, unhappy, and angry. But I would say he was not truly in contact with his despair and with his feeling profoundly unseen and unheard. The distance he kept with me and with his analyst was clearly defensive against being emotionally touched and having his wounds unveiled.

Sexuality was totally impossible to mention, immediately provoking extreme anxiety and phobic reaction. It is difficult to say if that was connected to the uncertainty and fluctuation of his orientation; or to the unconscious load of destructiveness; or whether the liveliness and possible beauty of erotised bodies was felt as being threatening. Erotised bodies happen to meet and sometimes dangerously melt with each other, and trigger the risk of an obscure uncertainty of love and hatred, and the pain of immanent loss. This was probably too much for him at that point in his life.

The main problem for him, however, was his performance at school, which was far from being easy to deal with. It was, I believe, a kind of Gordian Knot, the unsolvable core of any obsessional doubt. As I mentioned in the introduction to this chapter, his wish to be good at school (not so strong a wish, to be honest) could have been considered as a healthy desire, something to be supported and therapeutically helped via every possible means. The fact that the issue of his performance at school was not simply *the* preoccupation of his parents, but was also one of the clearest signs of their inability to understand him, made this desire very tricky. Whose desire was it? To what extent was his boycotting school a masochistic way of making his parents unhappy and breaking up their fantasies about him, given that he himself was partly identified with the same grandiose fantasies? Was there a less self-harming way to be rebellious to emotional deafness? Who would I really be helping should I make his symptoms weaker and make him a better student? His possible improvement, would it be in the service of his subjectivity or would it be captured by the flatness of numb adaptation that the family, and Pietro himself, seemed to seek?

It is good to ask myself these kinds of questions, and it is also good to acknowledge the potentially endless ruminative quality that they might have had in my own mind. But I was asked to act, to get things done, and possibly be of help. Help is like a precious stone, and you never know who takes it first. After all, all battles are to be fought on the same battlefield, and patients usually choose the weapons, at least initially. So the Gordian Knot had to be cut, and I made a prescription, following my general criteria and some specific guidelines that I shall describe further on. Before reaching this point, I would like to say something more about how the family and the context reacted to Pietro's symptoms.

At school

Teachers were particularly indulgent, in some way passive. I am talking about a normal public secondary school in town, and a normal class. Pietro did not have a special needs teacher: it was a deliberate choice not to officially certify his condition or implement a special programme at school, which would have created more complications. Teachers surely tried to understand the situation and the motivations of Pietro's difficulties; they knew he was in treatment and generously tried to help him as much as they could, with sensitivity and patience. But the other side of the coin was that they did not challenge him at all, thus increasing certain aspects of his grandiose defences and sense of superiority, and indirectly his anxiety and unconscious guilt.

As a general method, I always try to have direct contact with teachers. It is quite important that teachers feel supported by those who take care of the child professionally. Teachers typically want reassurance, and seek practical advice to know how to manage the situation. My approach is to try to increase their capacity to understand, which of course requires time and meeting them in person. This was not possible in this case, and contact with the school was mediated by the family, which made this aspect more difficult to manage. What could be done when Pietro started to improve was that they eventually started to be a little more demanding of him. I tried to let them know, via the parents, that Pietro was certainly to be understood and helped, but he was not Baby Jesus in the manger.

The family

The therapeutic project implied that I would see the parents monthly, along with my psychiatric individual sessions with Pietro, who was of course continuing his three-times-weekly psychotherapy with my colleague. The general attitude of the parents can be described in terms of what I usually define as the "fix-the-machinery syndrome". They are the kind of parents whose only preoccupation is with the normality of functioning and adaptation. Children are supposed not simply to comply with general and conventional rules of behaving well, but they are thought of as unquestionably set on pre-defined tracks: they have to be good at school, they must have clear ideas regarding their professional future (all the better if it is in some technical or economic area, because money counts, while humanism is dangerously vague), they have to have the right friends and socialise appropriately, find a partner of the opposite sex, get a driving licence, attend some prestigious university, spend some time abroad to study and learn foreign languages, find a good job, and eventually get married and have a suitable number of children. The tracks are rigid, but misleading enough to enable some slight variations to be called creativity. Adolescent turbulence, too, is usually well governed, some occasional excursion into alcohol or drugs, and sexual immoderation, is forgiven, especially if it supports the illusion of strength and power and legitimates the average belittlement of feelings.

All the sons and daughters of these parents' friends and relatives were apparently well established on these tracks, including Pietro's younger brother. So Pietro was substantially an alien. No question arose for the parents regarding the meaning of his state, not even a real awareness that he was suffering. To them, he was simply a piece of broken machinery. There was, however, another significant element in the group mind. Many years before, the father's sister had been diagnosed as affected by a severe form of chronic schizophrenia, and had spent all her life without any significant improvement in her condition. The anxiety in Pietro's parents, the father in particular, regarding a possible inherited psychotic disease was paramount, hardly but significantly neutralised through isolation and rationalisation mechanisms. The father talked about his suspicion that Pietro could become schizophrenic as if he were talking about one of his neighbours living down the street, and he tried to engage me in conversation about medication as if we were two colleagues who had to decide which neuroleptic or antidepressant was more appropriate for the patient. His demands of normalisation were particularly strong and rigid and heavily influenced Pietro. This father interpreted the son's difficulties as a direct attack on him. As if translating the vulgate of the Oedipus complex, he significantly used to say "he attacks the father"; he never said "he attacks me", which would at least have sounded somewhat more human.

As an example of my work with the parents, and particularly with the father on this particular point, I shall report a short note from a session.

> Father: [smiling, talking with his usual professional, patronising tone] He never takes a shower, like a homeless person, he stinks, he does that against the father [while saying so, he moves on his chair, turning towards me and slightly shaking his head as if wanting to tell me seductively "we know how it works"]
>
> Mother: [laughing, but doubtful, as if she were slightly conveying the sense that her husband is stupid] I don't know …
>
> Me: Perhaps by smelling he is telling you in the only way he knows that he feels like a piece of excrement, and he wants you to see that and maybe try to make him feel better.

Retrospectively, and with the certainty that Pietro is not schizophrenic, I can hypothesise that my initial doubt and disquietude regarding possible psychotic elements in Pietro's mind probably originally belonged to the father. Over time, the mother became more flexible, she came to terms with the crumbling of her idealisation, realised Pietro was far from being a genius, and she became more capable of understanding her son and diminishing her expectations and pressures, which I insisted upon with great determination; the father, instead, although with some improvement, seemed to remain more rigid and not very empathetic, and he apparently superficially adapted to what he took as being my behavioural prescriptions without being truly insightful.

The father's mental position remained over time the true limit of my intervention with these parents.

Managing the transferences

I will first of all distinguish the family's transference from the patient's. Second, I will consider the differences between the patient's transference onto me and the transference onto the prescribed drug itself, and will attempt to provide a description of these phenomena and the way I managed them.

The initial reaction of the family when I first came on to the scene was to idealise me and my intervention. As I was supposed to be the one who could fix the situation without all those silly psychological complications, I was expected to perform brilliantly in accordance with my public reputation and, once I had got rid of the oppressive fantasy of schizophrenia, I could give them back the ideal child they had in their minds. This position was immediately accompanied by the idea that psychotherapy was no longer necessary and could be stopped shortly afterwards. My response was unequivocal. I explicitly said that psychotherapy was the real core of the treatment, and that I was just a form of secondary support. I also literally said that my colleague and myself were "sold as one article", and that the two items could not be sold separately: if they wanted to take one, they had to take the other as well. I intentionally used this precise metaphor, which was close to the mentality and culture of the family, in some way countering their attack by using their own weapons. It is obvious that such a position can be maintained only if the communication and relationship between the two therapists is solid. Any element of unsolved competitiveness or ambivalence, any unrecognised transference between psychiatrist and psychoanalyst, works subtly unfavourably, and creates a dangerous breach through which attacks can reach the target. Effective parenthood is never easy, and requires unbounded trust and resilience.

Pietro himself made things more realistic in that first stage, which I took as an excellent sign of his determination and substantial cooperation. The first set of prescriptions was in fact totally a failure, he showed no sign of improvement and a number of side effects. This was very encouraging to my eyes, showing that, although formally compliant in terms of taking his pills regularly, he was not compliant with regard to the expectations of the family, or to what he fantasised as being mine. Although certainly boycotting the treatment on one level, asserting his position masochistically, his rejection of the first prescription of medication was nevertheless a sign that he could stand up and say no.

During a subsequent stage of our work, several months later, and parallel to the evolution of Pietro's transference, which I will shortly describe, the family's idealisation turned into persecution. A better set of drugs had been implemented by that time, and Pietro was starting to feel a little better, by that meaning that he was less blocked, but in some way he was suffering more overtly. That was actually the aim of the treatment, as I will explain further on, and he was also starting to make better use of his psychotherapy. But from the point of view of the family, this represented my total failure, and the betrayal of their expectations about me. So at this point, having strategically restored trust in the psychotherapist and her work with Pietro, they threatened to fire me—after all, was I any different from a plumber? —and find another psychiatrist, who might use, I quote them: "more up-to-date drugs and be in better contact with Pietro". The therapeutic couple, once again, resisted.

Mastering the split transference

After the failed response to the first set of drugs, the second choice worked better. I am not going to discuss this issue from a strict pharmacological standpoint. Rather, I wish to clarify its aims in the light of the principles described at the beginning of this chapter. Antidepressants (Clomipramine) in full doses were used in order to mobilise the patient, to the extent of making his anxiety more perceivable and in some way making his subjective suffering more evident for the psychoanalytic work, and less covered by the anaesthetic effect of his grandiose fantasies and omnipotent ruminations. As witnessed by the analyst, a formerly hidden level of subjective pain came to the surface, as well as a great deal of destructive and self-harming fantasies. The risk of suicidal conducts was strictly monitored by myself and by the analyst at that point, which was certainly a delicate stage in the treatment. In general, heavy anxiety entered the analytic room, and the analytic work could reach an intensity that had not been possible to achieve previously. The sense of trust that Pietro could experience in the analytic relationship was reinforced, even though he subjectively felt that he was suffering more, because he started to experience that he was able to use his mind in connection with another person, his analyst. The family, of course, had to be strictly contained, considering that this was totally different from what they had expected.

Atypical antipsychotics (Risperidone), used at low doses in association with antidepressants, were intended to break up the circularity of his thinking and decrease the intensity of his grandiose ideation. This contributed to a better circulation of complex and polymorphous emotions and thoughts, in synergy with the mobilisation of anxiety induced by antidepressants. Apart from mild sedation that might have reinforced certain aspects of the patient's passivity and numbness, and which he pretended was unsustainable after learning of the side effects on the internet, the assumption of antipsychotics risked increasing the persecutory fantasy of a latent psychotic state, which worried the father with regard to the clinical condition of his sister. While this treatment was being implemented, I saw Pietro more frequently for a few weeks in order to explain how the substances worked, and to clarify the nature and meaning of the side effects, distinguishing as carefully as I could which were real and which were not. At the same time, I tried to potentiate his positive transference to the drug, by underlining every favourable effect I could observe, and concomitantly I pushed him to discuss every meaningful element that emerged, including the deep implications of taking drugs, with his analyst and not with me.

In the following weeks, I progressively and intentionally stimulated a certain degree of negative transference onto me, and through a sort of dual split I tried to create a subtle compromise that could reinforce the transference to the drug, on the one hand, and improve the intensity of the analytic work, on the other. I am not saying I was operating such a split with the purpose of avoiding any work on the negative transference in the analytic situation, and my colleague is certainly not the kind of analyst who skips certain responsibilities. The negative transference had to take, however, a longer and more complex road for a certain period of time, which was necessary to potentiate the capacities of the patient's mind to face his internal pain. Every transference is a detour, and detours at times require more than one single interlocutor and split as a useful tool.

In practical terms, on certain occasions, I openly said to Pietro that I was not interested in understanding the meaning of what he said, that his emotions and feelings were not my business, and I would not make the slightest effort to do that. For this purpose, he had his analyst and not me. Placing myself paradoxically in the same position as his parents, who had not been experienced by Pietro as related to his *being*, but only to his *doing*, I said I was just interested in checking how his mind was working, the way he was functioning, and the results he had achieved. Nothing else. Of course, he knew I was listening very carefully to the subtlest hints of his emotions, he knew I am a psychoanalyst, and he was aware of my clear intention to be distancing and operational, knowing I could have been different. He knew it was not my character, it was my choice.

Parallel to this, my interventions were also aimed at challenging his obsessional defences as much as possible. This was done, for instance, by prompting meticulous self-descriptions, either of symptoms or any sort of states of mind, and by that means challenging the typical obsessional tendency to be general and evasive precisely about the elements that count, while getting lost in the fog of innumerable twisted trivialities and masturbatory ruminations. Beyond the aim of challenging the immobility of defences, I followed the principle that self-descriptions potentiate a sense of self-cohesion, especially if they can be expanded backwards in time through appropriate connections.

A short example of this way of working, several weeks after the therapy began:

> He talks about having left the test blank once again ... he says he just stared at the sheet of paper without being able to write ... he repeats these words several times ...

> Me: Can you tell me exactly what you had in mind at that moment?

> He is slightly irritated in response to my question, he snorts and actually repeats what he had said before with no variations.

> Me: I am sorry Pietro, I see you are snorting, but I really need to know. As you know, I am here just to check if my prescriptions work, or if I have to change something. So please. I cannot take things for granted ... so I must insist, please try to tell me ...

> I have to insist a couple more times, and eventually he gives a better description of his being captured in thoughts concerning his computer and a game he could not wait to play in the afternoon at home ...

Me: [intentionally critical] Well, it is quite an inappropriate thought when one has to translate from ancient Greek, is it not? ... So let us try to be honest ... if you tell me that you really would not be able to stop these thoughts, if you tell me they were as invasive as they were months ago, then I have to think of modifying the prescription. It is my job. Tell me then ...

P: [Blushing] Not really ...

Me: Ah OK! ... so it is your own business to understand the reasons of your indulging in fantasies, and the meaning of these fantasies. This is your and your analyst's business. It is enough for me to know that you had a choice at that moment, which is good. What you chose and why does not matter to me. So we do not need to change the tablets, they work properly: keep taking them regularly as usual.

He is visibly angry. I know that he knows that I notice this. He knows that I know that he would like me to comment and interpret his anger and frustration. I do not say a word ...

One more way of being challenging was to introduce a reality principle, confronting his grandiose fantasies of being a genius, but once again without entering the possible meaning of his grandiosity and his indulging in these fantasies. For instance, in a session one year after our first meeting:

P: [After some minutes of vague thoughts that I hardly follow, and after some prompting to encourage him to be more precise] Because—I say—I really cannot see what you mean ... and I am afraid that when the session is over, you are going to leave my office precisely the same as when you came in, which is now thirty minutes ago ... that would be a waste of time for both of us, would it not?

... he starts to tell about some thoughts concerning his schoolmates ... with a slight arrogant expression on his face, he says he considers them stupid ... and always thinks that one day, if he wanted to, he could do extraordinary things ...

Me: Well Pietro, I am sure you will discuss this issue with your analyst. It sounds as if it may be quite difficult, considering that you still have these thoughts after such a long time ... Allow me to remind you that so far you have not shown any signs of being a genius at all, and apparently your schoolmates can do better than you at school. I suggest you think of that in your analysis ... Given my role, if someone tells me the Earth is square, sooner or later I have to remind them that it is round.

The feelings and emotions I stimulated by challenging the defences, by breaking up the illusion of grandiosity, and most of all by frustrating his expectation to find a welcoming parental object in me (with the tantalising element of his awareness that I could have been so, but did not want to), were all placed back in the analytic situation. This happened in synergy with the effects of medication.

Of course, the negative transference onto me was attentively mastered and carefully taken care of, and was modulated by the experience of my attention and resilience, as well as by the tenacity of my alliance with his analyst, which was of paramount importance. When his family threatened to find another psychiatrist, Pietro had a big chance to get rid of me. But he did not.

Nowadays

At the time of writing, Pietro has finished secondary school, and obtained fair results. He did not fail any of the final tests, including the translation from ancient Greek. He has accepted, as his parents have, that he is not yet ready to go to university. He has even accepted the idea that he might never be able go to university, and that people can find their place in life even without a Masters degree or a PhD. His mother seems to have accepted this adjustment relatively well, while his father considers it a little more rigidly. So Pietro has decided to do a short course in computer technology, and then perhaps look for a temporary job, and see what happens next. He has got a driving licence and is able to plan trips with his friends. He has worked a lot in his analysis over these last three years that I have known him, although analytically speaking he still has a long way to go. Sexuality is still a minefield. But he knows that.

As a gift, he sent me the essay he wrote for his final exam at secondary school. The essay is a brief journey through the concept of boredom in philosophy, Latin, Greek, and contemporary Italian and British literature: Pietro was motivated in his choice by saying that he personally knows what boredom means. I said I am quite sure that he knows what it means, and that I would read it with much interest.

I take the liberty to quote one of the pieces of literature he uses in his essay. It is part of the well-known dialogue between Vladimir and Estragon, in Samuel Beckett's *Waiting for Godot* (1949/1953). My choice is certainly due to the fact that Beckett was one of my passions when I was his age, but this is of course irrelevant. Rather, the atmosphere of mental immobility and entrapment in the deadly circularity of non-finalised thoughts is masterfully depicted, so it is a pleasure to read it once again. Beckett's ability to penetrate this state of mind is peerless. It is the end of Act I:

VLADIMIR: We can still part, if you think it would be better.
ESTRAGON: It's not worthwhile now.
              Silence.
VLADIMIR: No, it's not worthwhile now.
              Silence.
ESTRAGON: Well, shall we go?
VLADIMIR: Yes, let's go.
              They do not move.

Beyond my passion for Beckett, as I am the one who tries to keep promises and I consider that in general we prefer it when things are done and not simply talked about, I told Pietro and his family that times are mature, after three years, to make an attempt to progressively decrease the drugs and possibly stop them altogether. I repeated that my promise was to try, not to succeed. My non-negotiable conditions to pursue this attempt are that I have to see him regularly, that I also have to regularly see his parents, that he continues his analysis with his three weekly sessions, and that I set the timetable of the whole process. Given the circumstances, democracy has to be temporarily suspended. I trust I will be forgiven for that.

CHAPTER SEVEN

Interlude: lie and obsession—variations on a *folie à deux*

Lia the liar

Lia was one of the daughters of the Second World War. She was just seventeen years old when the Allies, after interminable days of bombardments, invaded her native Sicily and forever disrupted her life as she had known it until then, and changed the future for her, for her family, and for the generations to come.

When she came to know that her father had likely died under the heaviest bombardment ever seen in that part of the world, decades of deaths coagulated in her eyes, giving them an indelible shade of rage that would never abandon her. She was to hate the Yankees forever. And without knowing it, she endlessly hated her father for letting them kill him. She had loved her father in a way he could not even expect to be loved, in a way he could not even imagine he deserved. His name was Turi, and he was a wounded son of the Great Earthquake. Carmelina was Lia's mother. This is their story.

*Messina, Sicily, 8th December 1908, 5.20 a.m.: the Great
Earthquake*

Salvatore, whom everyone called Turi, stubbornly refused to go to the
weekly parades of the Fascist Saturday, not exactly out of true political awareness or some intellectually sophisticated antagonism to the
regime, but because of an inherent oppositional attitude towards all
that was rule, norm, law. He rebelled against the fact that Giovanni, his
father, certainly not in an uncommon way for the nineteenth century
in Sicily, soon married another woman after his first wife, Rosalia, died
giving birth to Turi. Turi had never ceased to protest, not even when
the Great Earthquake had shaken his life for a second time—he was
twelve years old in the black and rainy dawn of that tragic December
in 1908—taking away his house but almost miraculously sparing his
father, his stepmother, and all his relatives. The earthquake, however,
could not but leave him some indelible and visible sign, the old bruises
of his soul not being enough.

A wall suddenly collapsed under the lashes of another violent
tremor, at the very moment in which he was escaping with his father,
stepmother, and stepsisters, and he was half covered in debris, a knee
badly fractured, leaving him crippled forever.

Giovanni was able to free him and carry him on his back, so deciding
for a second time—because, in his own way, he was a generous man—
that this son should live, even if mutilated. A male firstborn child
deserved to survive, in a world still imbued with rural culture, because
he was a resource for the future. Had he been a girl, maybe things
would have been different, but Turi was a boy. Therefore, he could
well be considered worthy to live, even if mutilated and born of a dead
mother, even if offended by a still immature body. A male could and
should expect—in perspective—some sexual and reproductive prowess and an ability to work in one way or another, while the integrity
of a body or its beauty were not necessary requisites. They were, so
to speak, irrelevant. The weirdness of the beauty and perfection of the
heroes of Ancient Greece had nothing to do with the lives of ordinary
people. Ancient Greece did not exist. Ordinary people, then, as it had
been for thousands of years, were well accustomed to deformity and
death. The survival of children was a luxury in itself, especially while
the earthquake was claiming, between sea and land, more than a hun-
dred thousand victims. If Turi had been a girl, he might have more

likely met death on that day, perhaps because of the negligence of the family, and probably without too much pain for Giovanni, and even less for his second wife and their two daughters born in the meantime. One less mouth to feed and one less daughter to provide a dowry for some day.

The only luck on that tragic morning was that of being a boy and not a girl, and in principle having the right to stay in the world. So Giovanni picked him up and rescued him from the debris, as in the same way that he had decided to keep him, the moment he left the womb of his dead mother, who had not even had time to look at him or hug him, not even once. Rosalia had died without seeing him alive.

No one could know, while the town crumbled, while fires broke out in every corner and criminal gangs did not wait to rob whatever they could, and while the big wave devoured the few who had searched for shelter along the coast, which destiny would have awaited Turi if he had not broken his knee. Life had chosen him through the hands of his father, his mutilation would save him from the fate of many others of his age, to be one of the soldiers of the Great War, *the guys of '96*, to die in some icy trench among fellow soldiers he did not even understand in some weird dialect they spoke.

Death would have to wait another war to catch him, through the hands of a bomb of the Liberators. More than thirty years later, they would recognise his corpse because of the mutilation of his knee. His mutilation always marked his identity.

In the meantime, at twelve, he was still alive. A survivor. His father, the only person who mattered to him, was alive. The one who had wanted him. Messina, his town, his world, was dying. Like his mother.

By pure chance, Giovanni met a friend who was escaping from the deadly earthquake on a cart pulled by an old mule, headed to the countryside. That was the only reason why Giovanni did not search for shelter on the coast, where thousands met their death shortly after. Sicily was poor, but the land was generous and could feed many, as it had done for centuries, every time the quake, or the volcano decided to intercede wars or epidemics in order to cut the number of the living. Many had died on that morning in December, and so there was enough food for the survivors. The dark clouds of the dead city did not reach the countryside, and the lashing rain on the day of the earthquake soon gave way to the consolation of a warm sun, and to the blessing of the colours of Sicily. The winter was soon over.

While Turi was screaming because of what the butcher was doing to his knee in order to fix it up as best he could, and then surviving days of fever and delirium, a girl only two years younger than him, Carmelina, showed her mettle by surviving the catastrophe. Carmelina was strong, as hard as a rock, and at just ten she was already as stubborn as a mule. They said of her that she was good to have children and to work hard. And they were right. They had let her stay at school until the age of nine, because a daughter who can read, write, and count can find a better husband, yet she is a slave, almost like a beast, though she can be sold with dignity. The family of Carmelina was the poor branch of a wealthy family, and this daughter could always work as a servant for the wealthier relatives who frequented the noble and the wise. If she could read and write, the wealthier relatives would treat her with more respect, and who knows, they may even be able to find her a good husband.

And on top of it all, Carmelina was blonde and pretty, and had light green eyes. As an anonymous descendant of the Normans, she had something more than the average dark girls of her age. Her younger sister, Giacomina, was much weaker and darker than her, and many years later would find a husband who abused her for a lifetime. Not so for Carmelina. She was more beautiful and stronger, knew how to defend herself, and learned to survive endless disasters for many years to come.

Everybody thought, not without reason, that she would die one day in her bed, beloved by children and grandchildren, admired for her strength that made her survive the earthquake, poverty, two world wars, and various diseases, never feeling humiliated or defeated. On the day of the earthquake, Carmelina took her weak and scared sister Giacomina by the hand, and her old grandmother upon her back. Without losing sight of her mother and father while the house was crumbling, she managed to escape. Along with their rich relatives, who had become just a little less wealthy that day, they took refuge in the countryside, in the same village where Turi and his family were living. There they met. And never left each other, until death separated them.

There in the village where they lived for a few years before some quarters of their hometown were rebuilt, Carmelina occasionally watched that skinny guy, with that black hair and those dark, deep eyes, so bright, so strangely melancholic. She certainly could not know why, nor could she imagine, that the veil of melancholy had appeared in the look of Turi the moment he was born, when he had looked for the body and skin of Rosalia, following as all puppies do, a smell and a sound, and had found a dead body, immediately smelling of death and forever silent and motionless. That melancholy strangely attracted Carmelina, perhaps because it was mixed with an unusual delicacy of his features—almost feminine—perhaps because his lameness made him different from all the other guys, and did not allow him to do the most tiring activities, or even the usual games males played during rare moments of leisure. Turi was naturally kind, although everybody said he had a bad temper. He never submitted to impositions and discussed everything and seemed to enjoy being argumentative towards the elders, first of all towards his father. To mothers, he showed a certain touch of subtle arrogance, as if wanting to assert his position beyond their unwritten laws. As if he could never show that he needed them. Evidently he believed that needing a mother was too big a risk to take. He proclaimed his masculinity, and this appealed to Carmelina, but in a way that was certainly different from the usual drab of the other males of his age.

With his slender body and that injured leg, he could not flaunt any prowess, he could not fight or run, climb walls or trees. But he could nevertheless use a secret confidence, almost a silent certainty, to have his own cards to play, and with females—when circumstances would have decided so—he would perform the task that biology, as well as the social role, had assigned him. When he looked in the mirror, in the shade of the house during a sunny afternoon, the nude image of his slender body told him of a mysterious force that he would not be able to describe but which nonetheless fascinated him. Only he was not able, in those circumstances, to look at himself, fearing perhaps to intercept ancient shadows that he would find unbearable, the wide and glassy eyes of his mother.

Carmelina liked to watch, without being seen, that guy who was so different from the others, so insolent with fathers and so conspicuously superior to mothers, always ready to speak out, so capable of making himself respected by the other guys, so smart at telling jokes. But what especially attracted her, without even realising it, was his melancholic look, that kind of closeness to death she felt he had. Carmelina knew that she could never rebel or be as bold as Turi, nor did she even happen to feel she had any reasons for that. What she did and what she was, was simply fine and naturally so, she had no grounds for conflict.

She traded implicitly on the strength of her body, on her stubbornness and tenacity, and on what everyone said she was, that she was a strong female, good for work and having children, and that she would surely have prevailed over adversities. She would not have been able to say all this, or think it, as a matter of fact. She just knew how things were. It was so, so very obvious and unchangeable. She considered it a privilege to have stayed at school until she was nine, she, a poor unexceptional daughter. Her wealthy relatives belonged to another world and, in a sense, were themselves an indirect privilege for her.

As it was pre-destined, she occasionally worked for them, which was enough to make her feel that she had a place in the world that was by far better than that of many other females. Without even knowing it, she was already feeling very intrigued by Turi, showing through this curiosity a propensity not to fully adapt to the usual and the obvious. But certainly, if anyone had asked her, she would not have said so, and she would not have been able to even think it. It was just so. Certainly, she liked the fact that Turi went to school, because Giovanni had decided that this son, this eldest son wounded by the earthquake, was to be cultured. Giovanni then broke his back in the fields in order to pay Turi's school fees. He respected his silly second wife—but he had never forgotten Rosalia in the secret of his heart—and the two daughters whom he did not love. Turi could not work the land, so he had to work with paper and pen. This was what Giovanni decided, and Turi did not rebel this time.

The great lie

Ten years later, Turi and Carmelina were married, and lived in a decent home in the part of their town that had been reconstructed. They saw the sea from their bedroom window, the same sea that had killed so many when they were children and had miraculously spared their lives.

There had been another Lia before our Lia, the liar. A Lia who died of pneumonia at three months of age, just as many children did. At that time, the death of a child was not unexpected. Although it was painful, it was accepted as a sort of natural event that was part of everybody's everyday experience, whatever cause was implied, either flu or war, earthquake or typhoid fever, a tempest on the sea or a difficult pregnancy. People simply died, and destiny or God were unquestionably responsible.

Turi accepted the death of that first daughter with some sort of resignation. He already knew that mothers die, he knew that girls could die more easily than boys, as his father had shown him beyond any reasonable doubt. Nobody would have been desperate over the death of a little girl. The first Lia was not mourned, not as much as she would have been if she had been a boy.

Carmelina was more upset, and cried for this daughter. For the first time in her life, she thought that her strength was not enough; maybe those who thought she would always overcome all difficulties were not totally right. She was determined to prove that she was the one everybody, including herself, had thought she was.

Lia the liar was born nine months later. She was as beautiful as her mother. Blonde hair and green eyes. And Carmelina again felt she had a place in the world. Regarding Turi, for the second time in his life, he realised he loved a female. The first was Carmelina. The second was Lia.

On an ordinary day, some fifteen years later, Turi refused as usual to go to the Fascist Saturday parade, even on the special Saturday when Mussolini was visiting his town. Everybody was acclaiming the *Duce* who was once again haranguing the crowds by promising to conclude the reconstruction of the city, more than twenty-five years after the earthquake. Nobody truly believed him, but everybody applauded. Turi had trusted his father, who twice had saved his life. That was enough. He did not need to trust the Dictator. Turi had never worn the *black shirt*, and was determined never to do so. He thought he would see Mussolini hanging from a rope somewhere in a square, some day. History would show he was right, although he died two years before his antagonist, killed by the Liberators' bomb.

Rather than attending the parade, and considering that he was undisciplined by nature, he preferred to walk on the main street of his town, hand in hand with Lia, and enjoy the magic light and the coolness of a summer sunset. Lia was a beautiful fifteen-year-old girl, and Turi was a forty-four-year-old handsome man, looking much younger than he was, and proud of his ability to raise such a stunning daughter. And Lia loved him like nobody else had done before, nobody, not even Carmelina had loved him with that special kind of devotion. Lia had his same character, his same tendency to oppose and be an antagonist, to turn facts to her advantage, was as strong as her mother, and thought she would be good not only at bearing children or surviving adversities, but at much more. Since she was born, Turi had thought she would go to school and become—who knows—a teacher or a nurse. He thought she would not be as weak as her dead sister, the first Lia. Nor as weak as his mother. Turi thought Lia would never die. And Lia thought the same of him.

Lia was good at school, and she was proud to fiercely reject the courting of many ordinary guys. She was willing to somehow accept the discreet courting of a young doctor, more than ten years older than her, just because this made her father proud.

The Liberators, however, had different plans, something that did not match her expectations and attitudes. Freedom had to be obtained, regardless of what Lia might wish. Regardless of her walks hand in hand with her father at sunset. Regardless of the dazzling light of the sun on the stone of her renowned town, and the sweetness of blossoms.

The bomb did not simply kill her father. It killed an illusion. It was a betrayal of what she had thought her destiny was to be. The Great Earthquake had not changed the destiny of her mother, it had made it factual. The bomb turned Lia's destiny upside down.

Secretly, she started to hate her father, for the unforeseen fact of letting the bomb kill him. He was himself a betrayer. He had not kept his promise to love her and make her a strong and forever loved woman. He had not kept his promise to be her forever beloved father. Stubborn Turi no longer existed.

He was a liar.

She still had her mother, a sister, and a brother. But the bombs of the Allies had destroyed their house, their everyday lives. Nothing was left. Nothing had survived. As refugees, they reached the North, where their wealthy relatives lived. They helped Carmelina and her children once again. And Carmelina proved to be strong and determined to live, once again. But one bomb, the one that killed Turi, unexpectedly brought the lie into Lia's mind. Forever. About that, there was nothing Carmelina could do. And her daughter was lost.

Ten years later: men have to be punished

As often occurs to women who have an interminable controversy with life, Lia fell in love with the worst possible man. He was already married and had a family he did not want to leave, in the Catholic Italy of the 1950s, and when Lia got pregnant, he declared he would never take responsibility for the situation and substantially left her and their son to their destiny. But as cruelty is rarely linear, he never completely or clearly left her. He cruelly kept her in his orbit, somehow letting her cultivate her illusion to have him some day. She in turn never let him go, and kept her control over him through sexuality, and subtly blackmailing, threatening to disrupt his career by revealing he had an illegitimate child.

In the meanwhile, Lia had developed a peculiar attitude of continuously lying to people, and of bragging to be who and what she was not. She pretended to be wealthy, belonging to high society, and to have had important men courting her. She had a special disposition to seduce men whom she despised, whom she rejected sexually after teasing them. She was proud to keep her power with such great tenacity. But she could not stand not seducing someone, and compulsively needed to have at least one man at hand. To each of them she told a different version of the story of her life. Every version included different details of her pretended belonging to exclusive clubs or frequenting people in high places. The few who knew her better and knew the truth, including her mother and siblings, were too scared to contradict her. They did not fully realise what she did. They did not know who she really was.

She could not but call her son the original name of her father, Salvatore. In every respect, Salvatore had to become the substitute for a non-betraying father, someone who had to totally belong to her, someone who had to become an integral part of her lying system. As a child, he was engaged in controlling the family of his natural father, whom he saw occasionally and had contact with. Salvatore had to support and comply with a series of lies that Lia told when she wanted to blackmail this man, his wife, and his daughters, with an uncommon ability to make all feel subtly persecuted and invaded, but without doing anything that would allow them to call her a stalker. She did not show the gross possessiveness of stalkers, and was too smart to be rough. As a major weapon she had her seductiveness, which most people found irresistible, and her capacity to play the role of the victim was equal to the performance of the greatest theatre actress. Her lies had become more and more sophisticated; it was enough to place them here and there, like the rarest ingredients in the tastiest recipe of a master chef. She had learned to never exaggerate in her tones or behaviours, it was enough to pretend to be a victim or strategically perform some imaginary physical disease, and everybody was at her feet. All women hated her, except for her mother, because Carmelina could not even conceive the idea that a daughter or a son could be hated. Men were regularly dazed.

Salvatore soon became one of her tools, the most precious one. He had to obey with no insubordination, controlled through the pervasive sweetness of her gestures, through the subtle message that Mum had suffered enough and could not stand any more hardships, and through the idea that all men, and principally his father, had been betrayers. Men are by nature treacherous, she told him. All but one.

Things did not change substantially when Lia decided to marry a man much older than her, much wealthier, who remained in her life for five years before dying of a neurological disease. She did not love him and did not hesitate to get rid of him the moment he got ill. This man of course was not a problem for Salvatore, who had always been used to having a privileged relationship with his mother with no rivals. The presence of this man just meant that for five years he could not sleep in his mother's bedroom as he had always done, and as he resumed doing after this dull stepfather was gone.

Such a temporary waiver did not mean at all that he had stepped down. Lia continued to use him as her privileged ally with his biological father, and continued to take care of him as if he were a baby. Although he was by then an adolescent, she rubbed his back in the bathtub, or hugged him in bed, or cut his toenails, or gave him a massage when he was ill.

So for Salvatore, there was nothing to complain about. The transitory stepfather was a matter of money, just a step in the plan. His temporary transit in the marital bed had to be accepted. After all, his mother's marriage was one of the many lies. Nothing more than that. He just had to show a certain degree of formal respect and compliance, and his icy attitude of distancing this man would have been taken as a normal manifestation of an average adolescent.

Everything seemed to be stable. Nobody would expect any change in the system. Things could have gone on indefinitely with no change. This was what everybody thought.

Until one day, when a new unexpected bomb exploded in Lia's life.

The second bomb and the attempted liberation

He was a thin blond guy, as slender as his grandfather Turi, and moved with a strange sort of attitude. He seemed somewhat arrogant and patronising, pretending to be the one who did not need anybody, ostentatiously proclaiming he was not interested in treatment, and was in front of a doctor just to comply with his mother's decision. At the same time, he looked paralysed and scared, as if he were imperceptibly trembling like a war child, or the survivor of an earthquake.

During the months before *that morning*, as he called it, he had felt progressively strange, he was no longer interested in school and friends. He felt he had lost himself, and no longer recognised the meaning of things he had done for years since he was a child. Given that he felt he had always been very powerful, as his mother had deceived him into thinking so, he decided he had to take his life into his own hands. His way of providing for himself was classifying everything, and finishing what he had left incomplete over the years. In his opinion, this would lead to an *honest completion* of his personality, a sort of cleaning and ultimate restructuring of his life. So if he had stored volumes of his collection of comics, and realised he had not adequately or fully read every page, he had to complete the reading. If he had left a book unread or unfinished on the bookshelf, he had to read it. If he had missed studying something at school, especially if it was linked to cheating the teacher and to having got a good mark undeservedly, then he had to learn precisely what he had missed, word for word. This also included music: he had to listen to his stored music in order to be sure that, for instance, all the soundtracks of an album had been listened to the same number of times. So he had to establish how many times he had listened to each track in the past, and then calculate how many times he had to listen to the others to even the score. He had hundreds of records at home, so the task was huge. Things had become more and more complicated over time, because reading books and comics, studying, or listening to music was, after all, relatively easy, unless the doubts about what he had done or missed, or about how appropriately he had operated, were not excessively torturing.

Much less easy were the tasks of classifying thoughts, ideas, moral beliefs, religious or political orientations, sexual fantasies, judgements about people, and feelings towards his mother and father. These fields were much harder to master, details much more difficult to remember, conflicts more demanding, nuances more insidious and at times impossible to stifle. On top of it all, contrary to what he expected, the more he proceeded with his effort to remedy and classify, the more he felt anxious and progressively overwhelmed by a process which, instead of making things simpler and manageable, turned his life into a labyrinth of uncontrollable thoughts and manoeuvres.

One morning, he woke up at dawn, covered in sweat. His mind was paralysed, he could no longer put thoughts one after the other, no more words crossed his mind, no more swinging back and forth, no more contradictions and doubts. His mind was still. His body could not move. He could not choose to make the slightest change to his position. Intentionality was dead. Just a subtle shiver of his body was present, to testify he was still alive, had anybody watched him from the outside. Yet, he was unable to know if he was alive.

There was no more subject. Just still life.

Lia was sleeping beside him, as usual. She did not realise what was happening until she woke up. It was only the sweating, and the subtle trembling of that thin body that made her think her son was still alive. She caressed his long blond hair, the only sign of normality in that body, in the years when young people listened to rock music, dreamed of a better world, and had long hair, the only trait that made Salvatore similar to the other guys of his age. She screamed, as she had done years before when they found the bones of his father, the wounded knee being the only clear sign it was him. Everything else had vanished. She had said *it's him*, that day in the morgue. Then she let her deep scream pour out of her mouth, like uncontainable blood. She heard herself screaming in the same way for the second time, that morning in front of her son. The one she thought was invulnerably hers.

There was a tradition of psychoanalysis in the city where they lived, and it was thought to be the best possible cure. At least for rich and upper-class people.

Salvatore was helped to recognise how frequently he lied to his analyst, hiding relevant details of his symptoms, manipulating the truth, and always assuming to be able to provide for himself. The psychiatrist who took care of his medication, which was rudimentary but nonetheless effective, was treated in the same way, and the drugs were often misused or abused. Salvatore forced the analyst to obey his will, and made him feel impotent all the time. He did so intentionally, with a sense of triumph and contempt. He could not admit that his attempts to remedy and classify everything had not worked. This was something that made him furious, as he had always thought he could achieve all possible goals. As his mother had always said.

Gradually, he was helped to recognise that there was something definitely crucial in his wish to be *honest*, and to make things *right*. He was surprised to hear that maybe the *how* was inappropriate and unnatural, as it was founded on the delusional idea that a human being can do everything by himself. He was astonished to hear that human beings are biologically interdependent, that they are naturally a *group* in a relation of supportive mutuality. His honesty regarded a wish to clean his life of the manipulation and confusion in which his mother had entrapped him, that is, ultimately to clean his internal world of his mother's past. Around his name much work was done, with regard to the incumbent image of his grandfather, as well as on the story of his family, about which he became very curious and which he tried to discover and understand with the greatest precision and passion. He learned to trust his analyst and to gradually consider his lying part as an antagonist. Talking about his grandparents, Turi and Carmelina, helped him to realise that their strength was different from what he thought strength was. He discovered that both were able to help and be helped by other people, that their stubbornness was not equivalent to self-sufficiency, that they were able to endure and to receive support. He especially learned that there was some difference between who Turi actually was, and the Turi that his mother had in her mind. It was the latter who had contaminated his life.

He moved some steps in the direction of partial independence and separation from his mother. She tolerated that he stopped sleeping in the same bed as her, unexpectedly claiming his own room. She even tolerated that he found a part-time job, a job that he was very proud of. He had failed to go to university, as his capacity to use his mind was still limited, and the idea of learning something from someone else was still very conflictual. Therefore, being able to go to work and to have some contact with a reality that did not consider him as special as his mother did was something that he was very proud of. He surprisingly found in himself a wish to live, and he proclaimed this with strength, even though at times this sounded like a lie to his analyst.

His analyst thought that his coriaceous difficulty in learning at school was the result of his drive not to become fully independent. His sexuality remained for a long time confined to fantasising violent and pornographic scenes, and in reality he usually kept girls at a safe distance. This was also seen as a sign of the weakness of his will to grow and separate from his mother. Parallel to this, Lia tolerated his partial developments. She was smart. She accepted that he no longer played the usual game with his father, and that he slept alone and went to work almost every day. She tolerated, although with great suspicion, the presence of the analyst, the first male antagonist in her life.

The analyst thought that this kind of partial improvement was a sort of lie, something similar to a state of probation, an illusion of freedom that did not truly question the fundamentals. Salvatore was allowed to have some free space, but he was still in prison. The analyst had to be deceived into thinking he was doing the right job, with a patient who pretended to cooperate and a diffident but tolerant parent, the real secret horizon being very narrow.

Things never happen by chance. Laura was a teenager, the daughter of a businessman who moved to a different country every six months. She was used to having boyfriends without getting too involved. She was rebellious and free, and did not care about love. Her contraceptive pills freed her mind from the only risk she did not want to run.

What made her feel attracted to Salvatore remained a mystery. Maybe the fact that he was so subtly arrogant, or that he was vaguely scared and had a strange light in his eyes that usually kept girls at a distance. But Laura was attracted by what people found scary. Months before meeting Salvatore, she had an affair with a boy who all of a sudden disappeared and was discovered a year later to be a member of a terrorist organisation. So Laura apparently had a sixth sense in finding unconventional partners.

But also Carmelina had found Turi, who was quite unconventional, so there is not much of a surprise.

Unexpectedly, Salvatore had no difficulties in having sex with Laura, and the two had a lot of fun. She treated him as she had always done with all the other guys, without getting involved, which possibly matched the secret arrangement of a limited freedom that Salvatore had in his mind. The fact that she would be moving to another country within months was a further guarantee.

But this was not enough. Salvatore did feel attached to Laura, and progressively felt something he could not at first define: that sort of desire to see the other person, to share every moment of the day, to spend time together, a strange sense of longing to be with her when she was away, and a painful sense of bewilderment when she ostentatiously declared she did not care about him and that they had no future. He realised this was different from the simple enjoyment of having sex. He eventually realised this was what people usually call love.

Something totally alien, which made him feel disoriented, the moment he understood that freedom is essentially freedom to love.

This was too much for Lia. She started to have a series of physical symptoms that confined her to bed for many days, and she required total assistance that only Salvatore could provide, or so it seemed. She became more and more demanding, and Salvatore, who at first had tried to withhold his help, was progressively pulled back to her. Until he made his choice.

A few weeks later, he was again overwhelmed by his symptoms. He became obsessed with cleaning, and spent hours every day in the shower. He had to wash his hands countless times, making his skin worn and pale, transparent like wax. He could not eat, because every morsel of food required minutes of rituals and compulsive manoeuvres, and he considerably lost weight. He missed one session after another, and when his analyst did manage to see him, Salvatore looked desperate and impenetrable. He seemed to want to keep a weak link with the analyst and begged not to be sent to hospital; his mother instead wanting him to be admitted. He knew what his symptoms meant and like someone sinking in quicksand, he was trying to ask for help one last time. But he was weaker than Turi, weaker than Carmelina, and unfortunately weaker than Lia.

Lia the liar felt immediately better when her son fell ill, and her symptoms disappeared. She stated that Salvatore was a chronic patient, and that she as a mother had to take care of him. She promised her endless abnegation, and said she would take care of her son until the end of her life. She took him to hospital and after that she refused all kinds of therapies for Salvatore, except for an appointment twice a year to check his medication. She did not allow any further therapeutic relationship. Her baby was back. As far as we know, forever.

Liberators continued to be persecutors. Liberators had to fail.

PART III

THE ANAL CONUNDRUM

Introduction to Part III

The two cases presented in this section show a close connection between death and the organisation of anal fantasies. The anal element has been meaningfully central to the psychoanalytic elaboration on obsessional neurosis since Freud's seminal studies, as already described in Chapter Two.

As a core problem, the equation between baby and faeces, described by Freud in the case of Little Hans (1909b), is symbolically relevant with regard to the fantasy of possessing the object, and consequently to the issue of defending against the threatened irreparable loss of the object. Absolute possession, mirrored by the sense of absolute loss, implies that the other person can be neither conceived as separate from the self, nor as sufficiently independent to determine his presence or absence, or to be regarded as a free person. The idea of denigration and decay is objectively implicit in the fantasy of absolute possession. A totally and omnipotently possessed object may be defensively idealised, but it can never be truly appreciated in its intrinsic nature, it can never be respected and given the freedom to love us, or leave us, or hate us. Metaphorically speaking, to possess another human being, we need to somehow turn him into an excrement. Excrements can be kept or disposed of with no concern. Sadistic and absolute power, private as well as collective, is founded upon such mechanisms. Related to that is the evacuation of anxiety, as well as love and dependency, into the object, where these feelings are eventually attacked and devalued.

Before showing how these elements are at work in my clinical cases, I shall describe some outstanding contributions made by the Italian film-maker, poet, and political commentator Pier Paolo Pasolini.

CHAPTER EIGHT

The arrogance of power: Pasolini's *Salò*

The arrogance of power: possession, obsession, mercilessness

Salò, or the 120 Days of Sodom is a well-known film written and directed in 1975 by Pier Paolo Pasolini. It is based on the novel *The 120 Days of Sodom*, by the Marquis de Sade (1785). The film was released posthumously, Pasolini having been tragically murdered just before the film came out.

The story is set in the Republic of Salò, founded in northern Italy after the fall of Benito Mussolini and the armistice of July 1943, when the Italian Fascists were allied to the occupying Nazi forces. That was the beginning of a tragic period of civil war in Italy that lasted until the end of the Second World War in 1945. The partisans in northern Italy, together with what remained of the Italian army in the rest of the country, ruled by a provisional government supporting the Allies, strenuously fought against the Nazi-Fascists. Those were two years of terror and deep suffering for the Italian population.

The story in the film is divided into four segments, inspired by Dante's *Divine Comedy*: Antinferno (the Vestibule), the Circle of Manias, the Circle of Shit, and the Circle of Blood; it is a tragic metaphor of the abuse perpetrated by perverted Nazi-Fascist political power, and in Pasolini's vision it was a pictorial representation of *inevitably abusive* power in general.

The film is meaningfully an endless repetition of the number four. Four Lords, the libertines, representatives of all the Powers, gather in a villa along with four Hags, and a group of captured young people, the children of partisans and ordinary people, who are subject to four months of extreme violence, sadism, and sexual and mental torture. The young people, males and females alike, are divided into four groups: the victims, the soldiers, the collaborators, and the servants.

After Antinferno, in which the Lords sign their hellish pact, the three mentioned Circles follow: Manias, Shit, and Blood. In each of them, one of the Hags plays a narrative that aims to incite the Lords' physical and sexual violence and to instruct the young victims.

Although the core scene of coprophagia, at the climax of the Circle of Shit, where the victims are forced to eat their excrement served as if it were a luxury dinner, is certainly the most brutal with regard to the impact on the viewer, the stories told by Signora Maggi, one of the Hags, centre on a series of absolutely crucial issues.

Let me mention one technical element before considering the stories: Pasolini never left anything to chance. Sophisticated literary and pictorial influences permeate all of his films. Well known was his philological accuracy as well as the precision with which he worked on every detail of words and images.

The Salò, a huge fresco on the anarchy of power and the loss of memory, differs from a technical point of view from most of Pasolini's films. He was known for chosing non-professional actors, and even when he used professional actors, he asked them not to play as professionals. He would shoot a large number of sequences, and only at a later stage, as in sculpture, would he extract from the mass of raw images the crucial moments that he found expressed what he really meant.

This was not so, however, in Salò: as he himself said in several interviews, the film was edited while being shot, and this required an almost obsessive precision in the shooting of several scenes. Therefore, the actors, whether professionals or not, had to perform very skilfully. Many scenes were filmed countless times, until exasperation, and this provoked moments of open rebellion among the actors—especially the young ones—when facing some of the hardest moments of the script, which is hardly surprising.

Four dreams from the Circle of Shit

I have taken the liberty of paraphrasing some crucial passages of the script and narratively proposing them as if they were dreams. In accordance with the structure of the film, I have chosen four scenes. As these sequences certainly speak for themselves, I prefer not to comment on them extensively. They shall simply serve as an introduction to the clinical stories that follow, also concerning control and feared loss, feelings that have been turned into excrement, and young lives that have been threatened with death, but most of all, the experience of being in essence excrement in the mother's mind.

Dream one: Signora Maggi's memory

I reached the home of my client, who wanted to be swaddled like a baby. Shortly after I had terrible cramps in my abdomen. The man rejoiced and forced me to expel under his very eyes. So, babbling like a baby, he forced me to pick up some of my droppings with my fingertips, and make him suck them. My man, swallowing everything, cried like a baby and ejaculated in his bands.

The erotised subversion of the mother–baby relationship is iconically described through the replacement of maternal milk with faeces.

Dream two: Signora Maggi killing her mother

My interest in that perverted client was huge, but my mother that night was more intransigent than usual. She was weeping and pleading not to go, to change my life and … I could not resist the temptation and I killed her. After all, it was the only thing to do. And it is foolish to suppose we should be grateful to mothers for whatever reason.

Gratitude, as an expression of nourishing dependency, is nullified. The paternal law in the mother is murdered; no restriction to desire, especially if motivated by love, is tolerable. The power of desire is absolute.

Dream three: Blangis, the Gentleman, and Renata, the Victim

Blangis recalls the moment of arousal when he killed his mother. Renata cries at this point, remembering her own mother who was killed when trying to protect her. Renata's cry provokes extreme excitement in Blangis and in the other Gentlemen. Renata implores him to kill her soon, but Blangis says he wants to enjoy her suffering for a long time. He then defaecates on the floor, and forces Renata to eat his faeces. Retching and crying, Renata eats. Signora Maggi says she cannot understand why the silly girl is not appreciative of such delicacies.

The appearance of mental pain related to mourning is not tolerated by the sadistic Lord, rather it stimulates his triumphant violence. Cruelty and denigration become *the* means for opposing mourning. Renata's pain does not liberate her, she cannot but be tortured as a consequence of her pain. There is no escape. There is no other food than the jailer's stool.

Dream four: Signora Maggi and the death sentence

That Gentleman could only experience sexual arousal with women who had been sentenced to death. The more they were close to death, the more he paid, and given that he was a member of high society, he could always have what he wanted. He made these women defaecate in front of him, because he assumed that no excrement was smellier and tastier than that of a woman who was about to die.

The conjunctions between faeces, sexual arousal, denigration, and death are carried here to the extreme, as a sort of Last Rite. The tragically grotesque representation of mother and baby in the first dream pairs with the image of the death sentence and the last terrible rite, as in a dramatic closing of the circle of life under the dominance of cruelty.

CHAPTER NINE

Encopresis, obsessional control, and the development of sexual promiscuity

Introduction to the case

Paolo was referred to me at the age of twenty-two, just after being diagnosed HIV-positive. In general, young people like Paolo often show massive denial and are totally unaware of virus transmission and prevention. They do not usually have periodic checks done of their serological condition, and are commonly diagnosed HIV-positive only if they are partnered with an HIV-positive person who declares his or her state after unsafe sexual intercourse, or—as was the case with my patient— for clinical conditions that require non-routine investigation, being found resistant to common therapies. When he was twenty-two, Paolo had severe pneumonia that was resistant to common antibiotics, and he was eventually tested for HIV.

Paolo had unsafe promiscuous sex since the age of sixteen, occasionally as a prostitute. He kept having promiscuous sex, often unsafe, for some years after being diagnosed and when he was already in analysis, which created relevant problems within the transference–countertransference interplay. Sexually, he could interchangeably play the roles of top and bottom, which was, as it became clear during his analysis, linked to massive projective identification either with his mother apparently having

169

intercourse with several men, or alternatively massive projective identification with these men having sex with his mother.

Identification is one element, the other being rivalry. The erotised other represents the internal child of the mother, which mother and child see as the "essential child", as Bollas puts it (1992, p. 156). Such an internal child of the mother is a rival and a double as well, and is killed and re-created in the arena. It is important to note that during latency and at puberty, Paolo had an imaginary twin who had a perfect body with superpowers and was sexually attractive, while he himself always felt clumsy and devalued. The imaginary twin comforted and supported him as a best friend would have done, and we may say that they spent a lot of time together.

When Paolo was at home, his mother sometimes locked him up in the bedroom (which was the marital room, as Paolo slept with his mother) while she received her lovers. This increased Paolo's claustrophobic reactions, as he would feel entrapped in a paradoxical/psychotic situation where he was at the same time segregated and excluded. Such a state of affairs was also expressed in his main symptom throughout his childhood, which was encopresis. Faeces explicitly stood for penises, and the anus was equated to an omnipotent vagina, able to take control over the penis. Paolo frequently and overtly fantasised about giving birth, faeces being his baby. He imagined he would be seen as a marvel and be in newspapers and on TV for that. He imagined he was a sort of boy-girl, a boy with a womb, which made him special. At the age of twelve, he apparently had a depersonalisation episode when playing this game, stimulated by the actual pregnancy of an aunt, with whom he massively identified.

He also developed compulsions during his childhood, which went unnoticed, and that were partly connected to his mother's obsession with cleaning and order: he had to place books and toys on the shelves in a precise order, and to read the succession of letters on the back covers of various volumes of an alphabetical encyclopaedia before being able to go to school or in connection with going to the toilet. The activity of secretly soiling and washing his underwear was also ritualised and replicated in exactly the same way countless times during the years of his childhood.

This is how Paolo himself describes his ritualised game with his faeces:

> I crouched down and pushed my left heel against my anus. I then released my
> muscles and the sphincter as if I had to defaecate, making my heel prevent

the stool from getting out. Everything was perfectly synchronised, I always recognised the special pleasure I felt when releasing the muscles and the anus, sensing the poop pushing but being able to keep it inside at the same time. I perfectly knew the outcome: one option was that the stimulus ended after a while, and the pleasure ended as well, and my pants were clean. That was subtly unsatisfactory, like an orgasm after disappointing sexual intercourse, and I felt slightly depressed. The second option was that I soiled my underwear. Although this was a kind of failure, pleasure continued in some way. I felt subtly excited in smelling and sensing my shit in my pants against my skin, and kept it as long as I could, and would secretly go to the bathroom to wash myself and my pants, pretending my mother would not know what I was doing. This game lasted many years throughout my childhood, with the same precise sequence. It was my private game, it made me feel safe, as a kind of ritual to face all sorts of difficulties.

Being perfectly instructed by his mother, he used to clean his room in a very sophisticated way and was a perfectionist; at the age of seven, he was already well able to mop the floor, clean the windows, and dust whatever he had in his room. Being a solitary child, he had a passion for Lego constructions and spent hours making complicated buildings that he always had to destroy before dinnertime because, as mother prescribed, everything had to be in order by that time. Upon special permission, he could keep some of these constructions for a few days, but only if there was appropriate space on the shelves and provided that he would dust them regularly. Before going to sleep, he would perfectly fold his used clothes, put them in the laundry basket, and prepare his clean clothes for the following morning. In the morning, however, he only pretended to wash himself. He actually made the water run from the taps, and wetted the tiles and towels so as to make his mother think he had washed himself, which in actual fact he had not. This ritual lasted for years, with the only exception of a bath taken weekly which was also very long and ritualised in terms of precise manoeuvres of rubbing and using shampoo and lotions.

After puberty, he usually masturbated in the tub and contemplated his sperm floating in the water, excited by letting some residues of it dry out on his skin. Similarly, when he masturbated in bed before going to sleep, he let his sperm dry on his skin under his pyjamas and felt somehow enveloped in the tactile and olfactory sensuousness. At school, he was quite a good student, although he had some difficulties linked to the fact that he got lost in his fantasies, and his capacity to stay focused on his work was very discontinuous. But he was very clever at going unnoticed in being absorbed in fantasies and rituals, and usually he obtained good results.

> I used to spend an indefinite period of time at school as well as at home fantasising that I was a special boy, someone with special powers, including being able to learn or even reading a book or listening to the teacher without any effort. But what was especially peculiar was my total belief that I was invisible, nobody would ever see my rituals and my thoughts, or my body. Myself and my invisible friend could have lived forever alone without needing other people.

Since his childhood, he would spend hours at home secretly watching male nudes in art books and fantasising about the uncertain role of males in sexuality, experiencing a subtle excitement that he never felt when he watched female nudes. Female bodies had always been connected to a sort of slight disquietude, and male bodies to a confused sense of admiration and envy that was connected to a dimension of a never-reached peace and quietness. This is the element Paolo stressed when he said he thought of himself as always having been gay.

The mother

Paolo's mother was described as an overtly abusive beautiful woman. She used to sexually tease him in a very sadistic way, provoking and rejecting him at the same time by exposing him to her nudity while telling him not to watch her, or by saying he was her beautiful boy but not masculine enough, just like his father. She explicitly threatened to expel and abandon him, and was extremely controlling over him. She emotionally blackmailed him through her pseudo-physical symptoms and was tyrannical and rigid in her rules, while at the same time idealising him as the only important person in her life. She created a symbiotic alliance with Paolo, who was an only child, against her husband, whom she openly despised, thus preventing Paolo from developing any positive bond or identification with his father. She abusively put her own representation of her husband into Paolo, saying he was identical to his father in terms of a non-masculine body. At the same time, she ambiguously told Paolo he had to be respectful towards his father. She concurrently said she had always wished to have a daughter, as daughters were, in her opinion, more naturally devoted to their mothers. What she seemingly meant was that daughters are their mother's exclusive property. The quality of the transference retrospectively clarified many aspects of this mother as an introjected object, particularly the subtle seductive quality of Paolo's way of talking to me, always trying to increase the level of arousal of our interaction and be rejecting at the same time. Paolo always tried to create confusion, ambiguity, and a peculiar sense of being trapped in situations with no escape, where everything was wrong whatever you chose to do.

Besides what he actually said and did in the session, one element of the countertransference I frequently took note of regarded my sense of having to deal with an unmanageable baby in a sort of panicky state, which could be linked to some memories of what his mother used to tell Paolo about breast-feeding. His mother had suffered from mastitis which meant that breast-feeding had to be interrupted when Paolo was one month old. He recalled breast-feeding as extremely painful and somehow linked to a peculiar lamenting and theatrical voice of his mother which felt like "bits of sharp glass on his skin". His mother did not refrain from repeatedly saying that she fantasised that Paolo, who had cried a lot, would be neurologically injured and mentally retarded. It is relevant that several years ago, this woman had a psychotic breakdown with delusional ideation and depersonalisation, which had a deep emotional impact on Paolo, allowing him to come to terms with the "madness he had eaten", in his words, ever since his birth.

The father

When analysing infant and young child observation material, I usually consider threefold representations and functions of the father: first, the actual father, meaning both his maternal and paternal identifications and functions; second, the father as an internal function of the mother (her capacity for healthy castration and sense of separateness); and third, the mental representation of the actual father in the mother's mind (which relevantly introduces and mediates the father principle to the child, as well as the relationship with the actual father in the oedipal constellation). The three levels were all deeply disturbed in Paolo: the actual father was in fact dangerously detached and, as Paolo put it, "silent". The mother showed a controlling, incestuously intrusive, and erotised attitude to Paolo, but rejected him at the same time. She was essentially psychotic, with no sense of boundaries, and did in fact function according to the confusion/expulsion paradigm. Finally, the mother's representation of the actual father was that of a castrated and disgusting body: she forced this representation into Paolo ambiguously, saying he was similar to his father but was her beloved beautiful boy at the same time; or she would convey a sense of contempt for the father but proclaim that Paolo had to respect him, and then create an alliance with Paolo against him.

Ambiguity, more than ambivalence, was the core of the internal position of this mother regarding the father and the paternal principle. Such a condition made it impossible for Paolo to choose and distinguish between any elements whatsoever with a sufficient degree of clarity. The creation of obsessional symptoms and structures cogently expresses this impossibility to choose, this being at the same time a powerful defence against psychotic anxieties of a confusional nature.

Childhood and puberty: narrative 1

I took the liberty of summing up in the form of a narrative a number of memories and reflections provided over the years by Paolo regarding his childhood, selecting them among those which were somehow made substantial through the transference. Similarly to dream work, I lend representation, condensation, symbolisation, and secondary elaboration, as it were, to the patient's material as it unfolds over the years. The process of creating this narrative includes the countertransference. Considering that much of the reverie work we do as analysts is not substantially different from dream work, especially in terms of re-dreaming the moment-by-moment material together with the analysand, I do not think that my mental operation in presenting the material in narrative form can be considered a methodological abuse. In fact, there are some interesting descriptions regarding the sense of living in the other's mind, or according to the other's desire or representation of oneself.

All things considered, I don't think I ever was truly free. I think I've always lived inside the idea or exactly according to the idea that somebody else had of me. Maybe my mother or my father, but I'm still not sure to be honest. I don't like talking about my mother and father. After a while, the thought of them both riles me. And then it takes me forever to calm down.

It's as if I've got something stuck to me inside, something that's hard for me to bear, a dark, heavy lead ball or something, where your heart is. It's a feeling I've had since I was a child, when my mum would threaten to send me away from home—if I wasn't the way she wanted me to be. And she'd make those wicked eyes. Or when my dad would turn dead quiet. I've never understood why dad's silence hurt me so much. Anyhow, I don't like talking about those two. Thank goodness my analyst was patient and didn't make me speak about them too early on. I'd have just left. It's hard for me even now to speak about all that.

Anyway, I know that they used to tell me I was a lovely child. And so I'd become a lovely child. Or that I was good at school. And I'd become good at school. Or that I was a bit dumb and not as smart as the other boys. And that's how I'd become. Or that I couldn't move well. And I wouldn't be able to move well. Or that I had a high-pitched voice. And I'd have a high-pitched voice. Or that I had a girl's bum. And I'd feel that I had a girl's bum. And that I wasn't allowed to tell anyone about my mum's friends who'd be about the house now and again. They were younger than dad. More handsome than he was. More lively. And so I didn't say a word to anyone.

I'd always played with my bum. I'd keep my plop in my belly for ages until I couldn't hold it any longer. I'd push it back in when it would start to come out, crouching in some strange way that I wouldn't even know how to describe. I'd play like that for hours, while I built things or played with my soft toys, or while I did my homework for school. I'd often soil myself. And, even if everyone knew, I'd go and secretly wash my underwear. Or else I'd sit on the toilet and have a plop that by that stage had become as hard as stone. I practically had to take it out with my hands, it was so hard and big. It was sore but I liked it. Is that what women did? Is that what they did when they were giving birth? Is that what mum did with her men friends?

Each time my plop came out it was a bit of a relief. My belly would stop hurting. My backside could rest a little. I liked it. I'd wait for days so that I'd have lots of plop in my belly to start my game all over again. I loved waiting. I'd feel a sort of mild excitement about my belly filling up again. And feeling that pressure again from inside on my bottom. I also liked getting my mother to check, almost every evening before going to sleep, if my bottom was clean. I'd bend down in front of her and open my buttocks with my hands to let her see my bum. Am I a dirty or a clean boy? Mum, tell me what

I ought to be. Let me into your thoughts about me. That way I can become the boy you want me to be. Is this OK, mum? This is what you do with your friends, isn't it? Shall I do it, too?

The only times I didn't like playing with my plop and my bottom was when—and perhaps I'd carried things too far—I couldn't go for days and I ended up with a temperature. So they needed to give me an enema. I felt ashamed, because everyone would talk about my plop. It wasn't a secret any more. Everyone said I was a child who had problems with his plop. And I'd become a child who had problems with his plop. And they also said I'd have felt ashamed had they informed my school. And so I felt ashamed. As if they'd told my school. Because I'd always become what others thought of me.

The last time I played with my plop, that I played with it in that childish way, was when I was twelve. One of my aunts was expecting a baby. I thought I'd children in my belly, too. My plop was my baby. Or lots of babies. I'd imagine, no, I was sure, that one day I'd have given birth and the whole world would have talked about me as if I were some sort of marvel. And all the while, mum kept on seeing her friends, down there in her room. And I couldn't say anything. I got scared and stopped this plop game shortly after that. Maybe because when I believed I had babies in my belly and that everyone would have said what a marvel I was, I ended up not knowing any more who I was. I'd get all nervous and lose track of things. I didn't know who I was any more. I didn't know what I was. And I was too scared so I stopped playing that game. Since then, I've been plopping normally. I gave the game up because it scared me. And also because my pubic hair started growing and so did my penis. When I was little, my mum called my penis by a strange name, maybe it was some sort of pet name of hers. I can't remember very well. It was chi-chi-tah or something similar. Did it mean something like "little chubby"? Why did my mum use a feminine noun for it? And why did that strange name send shivers down my spine?

Sexual compulsion, playing with death: narrative 2

The sexual compulsive activity was carried out in a mental state where in general terms Paolo's identity was suspended. As Bollas describes such a condition, personal identity is turned into an "impersonal third person singular" (1992, p. 148), an "it", a "transitional sexual self", and the contacts are it-to-it encounters where participants replicate a sense of self-erasure and death, while at the same time searching for a love object—love being at the same time uncanny and terrifying—in "an effort to arise out of the ashes of it-to-it erasure into love, mutual knowing, and possession of identity" (1992, p. 150). The arena can be a place for embodiment for those who have lived, especially as children, as disembodied selves: a place for recovery, while being a place for replicating depersonalisation and death. The experience of the arena is in many respects trance-like, which re-creates (but is also an attempt to gain control of) the experience of the cumulative moments where the patient feels "erased by the mother's usage of him as her 'it' within her own fantasy world" (1992, p. 153), even if he empowers her authority by projective identification. The child does not know who he is to the mother, and consequently loses his sense of who the mother is. She becomes an intimate stranger. This is connected with Paolo's continuous sense of living inside the other's mind and becoming identical to the other's representation of him. As a child, he had fantasies (or delusions) of being a boy-with-a-womb, he occasionally played transvestism games, wearing superhero costumes or the mother's kitchen aprons.

It is interesting to note how the level of anal fantasies, the issue of passivity versus activity, the mechanisms of control, the obsessional doubt, and the sense of identity dispersion and of being dead underwent transformation before puberty through to adolescence and then to young adulthood. The kind of situation in which the patient was likely to have become infected with HIV is described in the following narrative, with all the complexity of emotional layers and re-enactments that were played out. The description sounds not so different from Pasolini's Salò. Paolo literally took me to see his hell, and all I could do was stay there with him, with him in his hell.

> When I stopped playing with my plop, I also stopped having a chi-chi-tah. I'd grown up. It was as if I now had a "dick". And it was great. A friend from the swimming pool told me that it was big, and so I had a big one. And another friend and another again said it was big. And so I had a big one. And it was great. My friend from the swimming pool would want to get changed with me so that he could look at it. His was small and mine was big. But he was stronger than me and he made me do it. He told me mine was big, and so I felt I had a big one. But he was stronger than me and he subjected me to it, and sometimes he seemed violent and I didn't know what to do. But I'd look for him to watch him and be subjected to him. It excited and humiliated me. It humiliated me and made me excited. I was still that little boy everybody said was dumb and weaker than the other boys. And so I was dumb

and weak. Really. Because everybody said so. My friend from the swimming pool did, too. Even if I had a big dick. Because I always become what others think of me.

He really made me excited. It was thinking of him that I ejaculated for the first time. Thinking of his little dick, a little boy's, and his round girlish bum, like mine. And also his strength. Were mum's friends like that, too? I was afraid when I saw that white, dense stuff come out of me. I didn't expect it to. I knew nothing about all that. Because I was dumb, as everyone said I was. I thought I was ill and that something inside me had burst. It was that first time that I connected that white substance to being ill. Was I going to die? All of you tell me if I'm going to live or die? I can't tell by myself. I knew I couldn't show my mother that stuff. I couldn't do as I'd done with my bum years before that. I knew she wouldn't have wanted me to. I didn't think of asking dad, it didn't even cross my mind.

Was I going to live or die? That white stuff that came out of me, that was so different from my plop that I'd been used to, and that I controlled so well—OK, I'd soil my underwear and every now and then I'd get a temperature, but I could control my plop well, almost always—this white stuff that slipped away, that had no outline, that became transparent and trickled and dried out and stuck to me. Would I live or would it kill me? By keeping it in my pyjamas all night, letting it dry on my skin and on the fabric, it covering me with its rancid smell in the morning, by doing that would I live? Would it keep me warm? Or would it kill me? And if I drank it … would I live or would it kill me? Why wouldn't anyone tell me? If they had told me, I'd have become what they told me to. I'd have lived or died. I've come millions of times since that first time, and I still haven't had an answer.

I've come millions of times, wildly. Thinking about my friend. Not the one from the swimming pool. Another one. He was a bit cruel, too. He knew I liked him. He'd tease me just so that he could reject me. He'd humiliate me by showing me his dick and talking to me about girls, or football or tennis. And, of course, I was lousy at football and tennis. That's what everybody said. And so I was lousy. And girls, let's not even go there. At least not in the way my friend talked about them. I felt I loved him. Or that I really wanted to be with him. Yes, I really wanted to be with him. I'd masturbate thinking about him. Now and again, I'd imagine the two of us going to America, together, when we were older. That he'd have preferred me to everyone else, even to girls. That he'd have kissed me. But at the back of my mind, I knew it would never happen. Perhaps I liked the cruelty of focusing on something that would never happen. Maybe I liked wishing for something that I believed could really be my own. Not someone else's wish, but mine. At long last, not copying anyone. Being the master of my wishes. Just as I'd been with my plop when I was a boy. Or so it seemed. It was my wish. An impossible wish. But it was mine, even if it would never come true. And then everyone said that gays aren't truly able to love one another, that all they have in mind is sex. And that all they want to do is have lots of it with lots of people, never twice with the same person. That's what they said. That's what they thought I'd become. And I always become what others think of me.

I thought of becoming a thing. I don't know if it was out of disappointment or euphoria. If it was to dull a pain or to stop me from feeling joy. I thought everyone could be things, with their pieces of body and their wild desires. This aroused me and it still does. Removing the wish from its meaning. Making it become a silent wish, mute. With no identity and no name. Just a desire, without knowing why. One that's ignorant but never ignored. Inserted into pieces of me from one moment to the next. In my dick or in my hands, in my backside and in my nipples, in my mouth and in my piss, in my feet and in my shit. And in everyone else's. Just because. Without knowing anything about it. Without knowing any names.

All I could do was rush into things, as I didn't know what my wishes were. My wish knew me. After all the toilets and bushes and streets, there's no age limit there, I was told about cruising places. I waited until I was eighteen. I waited to be able to give my name—I was scared—so that I could be connected to that ring of clubs. It's odd. The law makes you leave your name and identity in order to be part of places where identity is wiped out. Shut-off places, hidden orgies. Ignored by the world, that knows but doesn't see. Identity is needed to shut yourself off and then lose it.

I chose one of those places, the one that seemed the most exciting. It was called after a prison, The Black Door. Prison cell bars were drawn on the wall. There was a sign. Naked Party, from 11.00 p.m.

I walked around the streets for a couple of hours or maybe more before going in. I had a slight anxious feeling. I thought it was because it was the first time. I soon found out that wasn't why. It became routine, too. I learned only through time that the only thing you needed to avoid was going to that sort of place when you were feeling sad, weak, and needing some warmth and affection. You get slaughtered. You need to go there when you feel you want to win, you want to conquer as many pieces of bodies as possible, to triumph over weakness and death. The initial anxiety is acceptable, as something that goes along with the euphoria. Nothing more.

As soon as I went in, a guy who had that air of knowing what's what—he can't have been much older than me—gave me a couple of plastic bags. He realised immediately it was my first time. He could have put me to shame, and I couldn't but feel ashamed. As usual. Instead, he told me short and sweet what to do, put my clothes inside the bags and give them back to him. He was almost kind. At least he showed some pity for my unease. He didn't treat me like a loser. Maybe he understood that I could learn quickly from others and from experience. The changing room was dark and narrow. Bars cordoned it off from another part of the club. Some men were looking. Others were getting undressed with me. Their eyes to the ground. Perhaps everyone had that initial feeling of anxiety. Was there a bag for that, too?

I gave everything to the guy at the entrance, who put a wristband on me with a number printed on it. He disappeared with the bags and I went into the nearby room. Naked, like all the others. At the party, like all the others.

A hazy and euphoric feeling came over me, a sort of daze and a physical feeling of infinite power that acted as a plastic bag for the initial anxiety, when I felt that everyone's eyes were on me. Well, not exactly on me. Certain looks were on my dick, the big dick that everyone had told me I had. Others were on my round backside, that everyone had said was girlish. Others were on my nipples, or on my mouth. Others on my feet, or on my hands. The looks took me to pieces. Each piece made the anxiety disappear and the feeling of power increase. I too began to do the same to them. One piece, then another piece. While walking around the dark maze. They took me and used my pieces, I took and used pieces. Dicks and backsides, hands and mouths. Walking around, back and forth. In almost total darkness. Your eyes got used to the dark and you could see faces and body pieces, looks that took my pieces, that used them and let them go. I did the same. Being careful not to come, everyone was careful not to come. It was too early. The night was still young. There were only a few of us at that point. The party was just beginning. Time went by just wandering around. Other people kept arriving. The space filled up. We were sweating. We walked around and took each other. One with another. One piece with another piece. Two with me. I with three. Pieces with pieces. But it was just the beginning. I learned some tricks. The older ones stayed in the dark corners. They sought out and mingled with each other. They kept out of sight. Now and again, they would find some piece of young, sweaty flesh which they captured as best they could. Someone like me. Who finds pleasure in being sought by the older ones and giving them some pleasure. And perhaps leaving them before they had too much. Not everyone liked my kind. Because I didn't have enough body hair and muscles, maybe. Or maybe in the dark you could still see too much of that dumb, weak boy, the boy who had wanted to go to America. Even if I tried to kill him each time I went round, each dick I sucked, each mouth that took me. But I'm a quick learner. I did as the expert ones did. Those with more muscles and body hair. Like mum's friends.

I was sweating just like the others. There were lots of us now. There was no air left. I couldn't even take a step without someone's body pieces mixing with mine. I walked round and round. Like everybody else. An exciting haze gripped every last corner of me. I forgot my name. I remembered nothing about myself, where I came from, and what I did outside when I wasn't feeling that way. But was there a time when I didn't feel that way? I didn't even know why I was there. I didn't have my desires any more. They had me.

Then, the game toughened up. You could hear screams. The guy who had been lying on the sling, waiting with his thighs wide open had finally found someone to fist him. A hand, then a wrist, and then almost a whole forearm inside that backside, back and forth. A couple of dicks in his mouth. Suffocating the screams. He was the evening's first that I saw and heard coming, in the middle of the smell of his shit, that covered the smell of his sweat and blood, after some of that game.

He got up, the others kept wandering around. I followed him to the toilet. Heaps of toilet paper. He cleaned then washed himself in a big washbasin. The toilet was the only corner that was slightly lit up, except for the room with the bar, several metres further down. He saw me looking at him. He looked at me. I looked at him as he was removing the pieces of shit that had run down his thighs. And I recognised him. He didn't know I knew that game. And had done for some time. My looking at him made him excited. And, having got what I was after, I left the toilet and went back to wandering around.

More screams could be heard. And hitting. Sounds of flesh being hit, smacked, whipped. I couldn't see well, there were too many taking part, doing, taking, enjoying hitting and being hit. Wandering around, I found a guy I'd already come across, in pieces, an hour or two beforehand ... but I'd no idea how much time had passed. He avoided me, I avoided him. Never with the same person twice. It would go against the code. It's a risk you can't run. Only the older ones, in the darkest corners, grouped together and looked for the same guys they'd been with an hour beforehand, two hours beforehand, or all the time. Only the older ones, in their dark corners, showed their suffering and laid bare their need for contact. It seemed as if they couldn't do without it, the older ones. That wasn't our case. We were playing, pretending to kill our need for someone. We were playing to defeat our impotence, to triumph over being alone and weak, unseen and unsought-after, and to defeat our being shit to the other. We were experiencing being a body. As we took it to pieces.

There was one guy who was as big as a mountain, a muscle man covered in leather studded belts. Now there was someone with a big one. They had lied to me when they told me mine was big. His was really big. I wanted him and I touched him. But I got it wrong. I was too delicate. And after that, I thought that he was interested in my backside or in my mouth. But he wasn't. I wanted him. I wanted to take that big thing that seemed like a drawing on some railway station toilet wall. He didn't want me. I kept my distance. It was a failure that needed remedying. Immediately. It wasn't difficult. I walked past the bars, the ones in front of the changing room. I stood beside a guy who had his between the bars, there was another guy on the other side, still half-dressed, who was sucking it. I did the same and stuck mine between the bars. Soon someone was there, doing what I had wanted to do to the big, studded guy. I came in his mouth. I couldn't even count any more how many times it had happened that night. How many times I'd come and inside what. I wasn't aware of how much time had passed. I went to the bar to get something to drink, it was almost morning. But I hadn't had enough. The bar was full of tired loners, drinking and watching porn films on the screens. I went back inside as I needed to go for a piss. I saw the big guy from before, sitting on the ground in a corner, his legs apart. There was another guy, wearing boots, who was hitting him on the balls, rhythmically. The big guy was enjoying it, and he came on his studded belts. I understood where I'd gone wrong with him. I hadn't understood what he wanted. And I didn't have boots.

A bit further on there were two guys talking to each other, perhaps they were hugging. Perhaps they were kissing. That wasn't expected. No, it wasn't. I couldn't look at them. Could you get off with someone? Could you meet someone? Could you speak and fall in love with someone? In this place? I couldn't look at them. Me, who had wanted to go to America. I couldn't look at them. No, I couldn't.

The loo was a sort of trough attached to the wall. There was a guy lying in it. He was waiting for people to come and piss so that he'd be pissed on. I stopped in my tracks. Why did I hesitate? He looked at me as if to ask if I was going to do it or not? I was dying to go. At first I couldn't. He looked at me. Are you going to or not? I pissed. He drank it. And he wet his chest, spreading my piss over it with his hand.

Drink … drink … I wanted to drink, too. Ever since I was twelve. Would I live or would it kill me? I asked myself. They had told me about the virus, but I didn't think I could have got it. And then, maybe it was enough to wash yourself well, just as they'd told me to do. One guy—they told me—gave himself enemas with seawater, which disinfects. Another guy, they told me, washed himself with bleach. Maybe it's a stronger disinfectant. And then, I couldn't have got the virus anyway. Or could I? I couldn't tell by myself. Would I live or die? What the heck, I wanted to drink and be full up. A big guy with muscles, all shaved, arrived. I could see him clearly, as we were in the toilet and there was some light. I took it in my mouth and he went back and forth. I liked it. It was mine. He didn't stop. I widened my buttocks. Just like days gone by, when I was a boy. Some guy arrived and stuck his inside me. He didn't stop either. Right till the end. Both inside me. It was my strength. Until I was full up and I had drunk. It was warm and dense. But I already knew this. Back and forth. There, in the toilet.

That was enough for tonight. I got my clothes, and with the smell of that place on me I headed back to my hotel. It was dawn by this stage. My friends would be in bed. Maybe they'd been out wenching. They'd tell me the next day. And I didn't really know what I'd tell them. Perhaps they'd laugh. I didn't know. I walked through the streets with a feeling of victory and emptiness. Of power and of nothingness. Tell me if I'll live or die. Tell me. I can't tell by myself.

I took a long, a very long, boiling hot shower. Before falling into an endless sleep. Without breathing. Until the next time, the next endless times.

Concluding notes

If I had to highlight what the main therapeutic factor allowing some meaningful development was, I think it would be my determination to respect and see the patient's individuality and dignity in the darkness of the blood, despair, shit, and denigration that he violently showed me. Pasolini would have defined his life as a *scandal*, by that meaning the disruptive impact on knowledge and normality, the scandal of contradicting oneself, of being with the other and against the other at the same time, with the other in light, against the other in the darkness of the bowels. In search of oneself. He could have been like many others, simply living his life as a mute repetition of acts. The virus imposed some awareness, but he could have ignored it, and simply continued to kill and be killed. Or simply cure a body and make it normal, with no scandal. Something, instead, made him choose to seek radical answers and be a scandal to himself. Nobody, including myself, would have bet a single penny he would have remained in analysis for about nine years. His expectation to find responses was still there. Alive. This is the true scandal.

Given the therapies for HIV, there is no surprise he has been in perfect physical shape. He went back to university and found a good job. He left the arena, having had enough of wounding himself. He found a boyfriend, but it didn't work. Then another one, which seemed to work better. Perhaps this guy will never take him to America, but for sure he has kissed him a lot, with the scandal of the simplest everyday love.

CHAPTER TEN

Anal stench: Alex and the gas of solitude

Introduction

The psychoanalytic work with Alex, aged fourteen, lasted for nearly five years, with some good results. He had been forced to come to me after several previous therapeutic attempts had failed due to the convergence of his tough oppositional attitude, the heavily collusive ambivalence of the mother, who took him to therapy and then removed him abruptly, and the father being strongly against the psychoanalytic method.

The parents divorced many years before but kept fighting with each other, there being no apparent solution to their conflict. Alex, who lived with his mother, learned to incestuously take sides with each parent alternatively, according to the consolidated pattern of two allies against the third, the third being easily interchangeable. Since his childhood, Alex, who was markedly overweight, had shown great difficulties in relationships with his peers, and was very isolated. He related to people through the character armour he put up, with a sense of grandiosity and arrogance, as well as with suspiciousness and fear. This seemed to have derived, in a kind of imitative incorporation, from a certain attitude his father had that I soon learned to cope with.

Since his early childhood, he had developed intense obsessive rituals, in particular having to compulsively accumulate objects, showing deep anxiety when somebody tried to clean his room. As a child, he had also suffered severe constipation, which at times required enemas and intrusive manoeuvres through his anus to break up the impacted stool.

Throughout the five years of my work with Alex, the father continually refused to meet me, and I managed to talk to him by phone only a couple of times. On these occasions, he was extremely arrogant almost to the point of insulting me, and would speak to me with a peculiar tone of voice that was artificial, metallic, and sharp, as if he were a killer robot.

The mother was a very rude and superegoish woman, and only with great effort on my part did she manage not to collude again with her son's attempts to interrupt the therapy. Professionally, she was somehow related to death and the dead, which I always considered a non-secondary element in Alex's mental suffering. She was a mother who dispensed food and rules, but her son was a kind of faecal object in her mind.

Her concern was completely centred on school performance, and she seemed totally unaware of, and unwilling to hypothesise the existence of, other levels of suffering. She asked me, as if the diagnosis could relieve her, if Alex was schizophrenic. The diagnosis of OCD, already established in the past, was not enough for her. When I dared to say that psychiatric diagnoses for her son's age group are by definition uncertain and fluid, and that things could vary even dramatically in a short period of time, depending on a number of factors, she reacted very negatively and insisted on having a stable diagnosis, preferably the worst, as she implicitly led me to understand. On several occasions, she openly told me that this son was not wanted, that she never felt like being close to him when he was born, and on several occasions over the years she had even thought of getting rid of him—and she really meant it. She called him, chillingly, "the beast".

She occasionally phoned me, pouring out all her anger and complaining about his school performance, clearly implying that for her also my performance was very poor. But I persevered for five years, seeing her periodically, and she gradually developed—alongside some improvement in Alex—a non-marginal awareness of his suffering and even a few moments of empathy and tenderness that Alex received over time with the greatest surprise. Naturally, she strongly refused to go to therapy herself, and the only reason she accepted coming to me periodically was that she could control me and complain about Alex. Being at first totally illiterate regarding affects, she nevertheless learned something and progressively developed some ideas regarding the fact that at times human beings, including her son, may suffer and need comprehension and help.

First stages of the analytic work

Here, I shall give an account of some elements as they presented themselves in the course of the first year of the therapeutic work, conducted on the basis of two weekly sessions, with emphasis on the anal issue in particular.

At the time Alex was referred to me, he had major difficulties at school, on a relational level as well as in connection to the learning process. He lived in an almost constant state of isolation, indulging in masturbatory omnipotent and repetitive fantasies, a world of weird characters and superheroes, some taken from Japanese comics or characters of certain role-playing games he partly created by himself. As far as it could be reconstructed years later, genital masturbation was not accompanied by clearly sexual images and fantasies. Rather, he usually rubbed his genitals against his pillow until he ejaculated, taking more pleasure in keeping his sperm on his skin without cleaning it and enjoying the smell when it dried out. Anal masturbation had always been present, constipation being his main symptom during early childhood and latency. Around puberty, hoarding seemed to have partly substituted constipation as a prevalent symptom. He became an obsessive collector of comics and gadgets, and could not get rid of any single object. Rituals had become progressively more invasive, and he spent hours checking if the position of his objects was perfectly correct, without being able to leave the room if a single detail looked imperfect.

He spent much of his time in his room surrounded by music and smells—he almost never washed himself—and eating and reading comics. Regarding music, which I always try to understand and learn about when I work with adolescents, I came to know that his favourite genre was Death Metal and one of the bands he liked was a Polish band called Anal Stench. Just out of curiosity, among the tracks in this band's album *Stench Like Six Demons* (2003), we can find "Anal blast", "Stripped, raped, and strangled", and "Koprofuck997", among others.

Sounds and musicality were also important on another level, that of his voice and prosody. He spoke partly like his father and partly like his mother, in a kind of imitative oscillation between the two modes, which included hardness and arrogance, contempt and persecution, and bizarre ruminations and cutting sentences, as if he were invaded by objects that precluded any vital identification.

In the first sessions, with his bizarre and arrogant voice, he declared that he had no intention of cooperating and contemptuously affirmed that—as his father also said—one must not talk about private issues with strangers. Then he spent the entire first year of his therapy replaying this sequence again and again: he would come running into the room, throw himself heavily on the couch, stay prone, and fall asleep right away. Before entering, he would set the alarm of his watch in order to wake up just thirty seconds before the end of the session, then he would get up and go away triumphantly. Either at the beginning or at the end, he would sometimes deign to tell me a few contemptuous sentences about my uselessness.

The duration of the session, for the first year, was therefore occupied by Alex's sleeping. He snored loudly and continuously farted, thus filling the room with his intestinal gas. This gas had a peculiar heavy smell, rancid and pestilential, infernal I would say. It even seemed to have a tactile texture, a thick plasticity, seeming to invade the room, myself, my clothes, my skin, my interior, like a kind of dense, muddy, and oily glaze.

Apart from the effects on thinking, these smells remained in the room, on me, and on the fabric of the couch for several hours after he had gone, and opening the windows had little effect. I could not use the room for another patient immediately after Alex. And usually I would have loved to take a shower.

Alex is on time today. I open the door and I see him with his usual gloomy expression on his face. His mother, behind him, seems particularly angry, she looks at me for a second and goes away. Alex is looking at his phone and grunts while entering my office. I realise he has set the alarm as usual. Sarcastically, he says that this is one whole waste of time. I say: "Maybe not". He laughs mockingly. His voice is metallic. Immediately, I have a sense of despair, and some stomach-ache. He seems to stink today, even more then he usually does. He runs to the couch. As usual he lets his bulky and stinky body plunge into the couch. He turns his back on me, as usual. In less than a minute, he is sleeping and snoring. I remain alone, left with my "maybe not".

It seems relevant that Alex, who proclaims total hostility towards me—which he does not fail to underline when he arrives or when he leaves, or through the words of his mother—comes into my office almost running, impetuous, and literally throws himself headlong on the couch. I understand this attitude as a concrete expression of his desire to find an object to penetrate and be contained in, with understandable aggression, but certainly with the desire of exclusive and total possession. Aggression and hostility are all too easy to recognise here, as is despair, and my sense of frustration and loneliness connected to the patient's response to my saying "maybe not" is certainly descriptive of his being neglected in his right to be seen and contained. But the bodily attitude in his penetrating the couch tells of an urge to experience the illusion of total possession of the mother's body, and especially of having a joyful mother exclusively and lovingly devoted to her baby. Such an illusion needs to be lived, in order that disillusionment can play its fundamental role for development. In this light, we can also say that, notwithstanding deprivation and a lack of containment that he has continuously experienced since the beginning of his life, to say nothing of the explicit contempt on the part of his mother, Alex shows that he still imperiously wishes to find a container. In other words, his preconception, or archetypal expectation, of a container has not been totally killed. He still has the representation of a soft place to violently penetrate and occupy, and in which he can somehow fall asleep. This is theoretically and technically relevant to consider, such a preconception being of use to transference work. The "maybe not" is the rudimentary expression of this. The self and the container are both toxic at the same time, full of the excrements of a failed encounter. Stench is our shared music.

I would also stress that fact that Alex always falls asleep prone with his back to me. Apart from the fact that in this way he can more easily shoot his anal bullets, I guess that by taking up this posture, he must somehow trust me. By contrast to the paranoid features of his father, which Alex has incorporated, I consider that no prey or gregarious animal would take up such a position in front of a predator. If submissive or wanting to placate the enemy, any mammal would choose to show its belly; if wanting to fight, it would stand well awake in front of the predator and show its teeth.

I also understood the pervasive quality of Alex's smells as an expression of his tenacious need to remain stuck to me and control my mind. Smelling was in this sense totally coherent to his obsessional functioning. I think this was a way of countering the sense of falling into the void, linked to his being *the beast* in the mother's mind, an abortive, disgusting, and non-humanised object.

Yet, I cannot exclude that such mephitic gas was also—in the inner world of the mother—a dead and putrefied object (perhaps indirectly at the origin of her professional interests for the dead), evacuated and installed in her son's mind. Parallel to this, the overt paranoid attitude of the father may have conveyed the experience of something poison-ous that was always threatening to invade the mind, the threat being even more poisonous than the supposed persecutory object itself. Obsessional symptoms and rituals, especially hoarding as a develop-ment of constipation, had likely worked defensively in this patient on a dual level: first, to take the feared loss of the object under control, thus avoiding depression; and second, to master persecution. The two components show one of the essential features of obsessive–compulsive structures, which is to avoid passivity and be tentatively active in mas-tering the internal world.

Similarly, being bulky, somehow wrapped up in his fat and his smells, was certainly a sign of his being full of foreign bodies, but it served principally to restrain and master his rage and sense of misery, which had the quality of an impenetrable shelter.

Given that Alex substantially slept through his sessions almost entirely for the first year of his analysis, with very few exceptions, it is quite clear that much of the work was done on the countertransference with a high risk of arbitrariness. Generally, despite my giving much value to the countertransference, I am suspicious regarding easy trans-lations of the analyst's fantasies and emotions, and quite doubtful with regard to the efficacy of self-disclosures. Usually, I verify the counter-transference by comparing it to the smallest details of what the patient actually expresses, verbally or non-verbally. Working with patients who, for whatever reason, do not speak maximises the risk of construct-ing a delusional picture of the patient in the analyst's mind, giving rise to a massively inconsistent repertoire of interpretations, a risk that was extremely high with Alex, who was not simply silent but asleep, thus eliminating plenty of the elements of non-verbal communication we might see in wakefulness.

Moreover, there were the mother's communications intruding into my mental field. That was unavoidable, considering that I had to see and listen to her periodically to contain her and to prevent her from disrupting the therapy. The work of differentiating the maternal from the patient's fantasies and acts, their transference and the impact on the countertransference, which is actually far from being easy in normal conditions, was in this case even more complicated because Alex had no explicit voice and, as it were, no primacy with me. Many voices came first to my mental ears. There was a high risk of my relating to the "Alex in the mother", to my fantasies on the mother, to my fantasies on Alex, and to my fantasies on the father, considering that I had no communication with Alex as an awake person.

Certainly, when he was asleep, my experience with autistic children supported me, where words are not available for years, or pseudo-words interfere with proper understanding. Additionally, reference to the mental position of the observer in the infant observation setting was certainly helpful, especially when, as observers, we happen to stay close to small sleeping babies for the whole hour, trying to remain focused on the baby and not to be distracted by external stimuli, and to take note of every detail in the baby's movements, the slight sucking motion of the lips, a finger that points, a fist rhythmically opening and closing, a slight sigh, a burp, or an imperceptible shiver. The difference is that in the observational setting, we remain quiet; while with patients like Alex, I talk. I used my voice as a melody, paying particular attention to the prosody and intonation, and to the kaleidoscope of my emotional and physical responses activated by Alex's slightest movements, and by his smell. My words were mainly descriptive, but when I happened to understand something, at least in terms of a reasonable hypothesis, I put my thoughts into words. Of course, the potentially delusional nature of my fantasy being heard and understood had to be taken into account very carefully. I tried to avoid becoming delusional in this respect, getting lost in magical thinking, but on the other hand, I was, as I always am, scientifically aware that mothers understand and speak to their babies, or sing lullabies, even when they are asleep, and are able to reach them even though babies cannot understand cognitively, as it were, what mothers are saying. So I trusted the most archaic form of communication, including the sense of despair that mothers experience when babies are felt as if they are dying or totally unreachable, but stay alive.

I tried to give shape to the tenderness I felt at times, as well as to my disgust and my wish to take that horrible bulky body and free myself from its stinky presence. The sound of the mocking and contemptuous voice of his mother calling him a beast and the cutting arrogance of his father many times invaded my ears like terrorists blasting themselves into my mind, kidnapping my humanity. The smell was almost unbearable; I frequently found myself fantasising about what the stench of the dormitories of Auschwitz must have been like. The smell of reviled and blasphemed humanity.

A brief example of this:

Alex has been sleeping for ten minutes now. I have managed to calm down and work through my fury, and try to watch him more benevolently ... He has farted more than once so far, the stench is getting more and more suffocating ... His head is turned towards me, and I can see his lips moving as if he were sucking rhythmically. I think it is strange to feel something tender for him, but I do, to my surprise. I say: "You are dreaming of being a baby sucking your mum's milk, which feels very good, mum is all yours." I repeat this a few times, until he stops the movement. I think he has finished dreaming now. He slightly changes his position on the couch, as if wanting to be more comfortable. I say: "You want to be comfortable here, like a baby in a cot." In the meanwhile, time seems interminable, the smell is unbearable. I am tempted to wake him up and say this session is over, I cannot stand him any longer. It has been like this for months. A sudden thought comes to my mind, it is the memory of a lullaby I sang to my first child, when she could not sleep because of some disturbing intestinal gas and I took her in my arms and walked around the room. I know I am desperate, colleagues would call me a fool, but I cannot but start singing loudly in front of Alex. Am I singing to myself, or to him? Am I trying to keep my loved objects alive in myself, and rescue them from mass destruction? Could some of this reach Alex? Or should I let him die? Singing takes me back to some tranquillity. The beep of Alex's watch announces the end of the session. He gets up quickly and goes to the door. I say: "You have slept peacefully today, something bad seems to have gone. See you next time Alex." He growls, and says, "Goodbye," with his usual distancing and metallic voice. I am relieved when I can open the window and breathe.

Concluding remarks

The following four years of Alex's therapy, when he eventually let himself stay awake and talk to me, allowed us to clarify many of the structural elements described above. His sense of primary deprivation was very intense and the defensive function of hoarding and obsessional control against depression and abandonment was made progressively clear. I cannot say it became easy to work with him, but the vicissitudes of the transference took more common paths. He became an average patient. Nobody could ever say to what extent my talking to him when he was sleeping and my surviving his poisonous gas had worked. *Something* had worked, however. And in any case, mothers do not need to explain to children what they have done. To everybody's surprise, including mine, and although remaining a bit bizarre, he had a better development than one may have foreseen for him. He became one of the many freaky nerds in town, thus finding a sort of community of peers. His musical passions evolved to less deadly tastes, despite remaining expressive of some tough and dark aggressiveness that was not so different from what I had listened to when I was his age.

To everybody's relief, he started taking a shower every now and then, he did not become a flower garden, but he was acceptable. Sexual issues remained taboo, although he at least allowed himself to conceive that people at times did those strange things called sex and love. School was not bad, he even got occasional satisfaction from discovering that he was not so awful in certain subjects.

Around the age of sixteen, he admitted that, having put up with him for so long in the first year, I must be tough. "You've got balls", he said, to which I silently nodded. When he was close to his nineteenth birthday, he told me he thought he could go on by himself, and asked if we could finish the therapy, although his mother was quite against that. He could have stayed for ten more years, I realised. But I trusted him and agreed. Two years later, I happened to see him in a bar in the city centre, and I observed him for a few minutes without being seen. He had a long beard, and was having fun with some bearded friends in front of a good pint of beer. I secretly wished him good luck and silently left the bar.

PART IV

THE DEPRESSIVE THRESHOLD

Introduction to Part IV

The clinical cases recounted in this section explore that kind of psychopathological situation already described a century ago by Abraham (1924) in his studies on depression and obsessional neurosis, as described in Chapter Two. I refer in particular to the intermediate condition whereby obsessive and compulsive symptoms are in a state of partial remission even after suspending medication, and the patient lives in between a proper obsessive personality disorder and an overt obsessive–compulsive disorder, with which a more or less severe state of depression is intertwined. If we imagine a spectrum with severe symptomatic OCD at one end, and severe depression at the other—both requiring medication, if not hospitalisation—such an intermediate state obtains great advantage from psychoanalytic treatment, especially if it is carried out with a high frequency of sessions and with intense work in the transference. Synthetically, the main issue in such a clinical condition revolves around the structures of oral and anal sadism in relation to mourning and to the fear of irremediably losing the object, such fear being kept under control through obsessional mechanisms.

The case of a young woman seen in a four-times-weekly analysis who was exposed to her parents' sexual intercourse during adolescence is discussed in this part of the book, with the aim of highlighting the features of sadism in determining a mental structure where depression and obsessional ideation are intertwined with each other.

I then give an account of a long-term analysis, conducted on the basis of five-times-weekly sessions, of a man in his early thirties who suffered the amputation of his lower left leg at the age of eighteen as a consequence of a car accident. In his twenties, this young man developed severe obsessional ideation—mainly centred on the fantasy to rape and kill young women, which had actually been covertly present since his childhood—and he had some sort of psychiatric treatment and medication before requesting analysis with me.

The role of the amputation in relation to what the patient felt as his right to be furious, including being furious with his parents for giving birth to his younger sister, are discussed in connection with the transference–countertransference interplay.

CHAPTER ELEVEN

Sonia: the king-size coffin— Imprisonment 1

Sonia, a woman in her mid-thirties, was in analysis with me on the basis of four weekly sessions. She had concluded a psychotherapy almost one year before starting her analysis with me. During the assessment sessions, she looked moderately depressed, talking about her having eventually separated from her partner, described as a depressed man, after being stuck to him for years, and vaguely saying something about feeling bad after leaving her previous therapist some months before. She said it was typical of her functioning to take a lot of time to make up her mind and decide something, and to separate from something or someone. She looked evasive, and I had the impression of a more severely disturbed person than what she pretended to be, in terms of obsessional functioning and a depressive and sadomasochistic structure. Sonia apparently had chosen me as an analyst after listening to a public lecture of mine on sexual abuse in children. She also talked a lot about her mother as "negative" and intrusive, in a way that made me think that her previous psychotherapeutic work had not enabled her to consider the mother as an internal object, and I noticed that she was still very projective.

Months before seeing her in the assessment sessions, I had met her previous therapist during a professional meeting. She told me Sonia would contact me for analysis, saying Sonia was quite a difficult patient with supposed autistic nuclei that she (the therapist) had been unable to reach and work through; given that I was fantasised as being an expert in autism, this colleague was glad Sonia had decided to consult me for analysis. I refrained from making any comments to this colleague, but I felt somewhat uncomfortable receiving this quite ambivalent communication, and had the impression that the colleague was not unhappy to have eventually finished her work with this patient, and to challenge my supposed ability to deal with so-called difficult patients. I certainly took note that this analysis would start under the auspices of ambivalence. Over the years of her analysis, I never felt the unquestionably evident states of withdrawal of this patient as being autistic in nature, although on many occasions she looked mindless and emotionally flat. She also looked impenetrable and with a sort of subtle and pervasive sensuousness that could deceptively resemble autistic children every now and then. However, I have always understood these states of mind as tri-dimensional and therefore as being quite different from the flat and adhesive bi-dimensionality we observe in the mindless autistic conditions. Through projective identification, the patient seemed to aggressively get into psychic enclaves, filled with endlessly repetitive erotised-incestuous fantasies, and she would poisonously engage the external object as a part of her internal scenarios, which is not autistic at all.

When I eventually started my work with Sonia a few months after the consultation sessions, which had taken place some time before the summer break, she looked severely depressed and entrapped by her ruminations, as if she had suffered a true breakdown. She had become progressively unable to work, and complained about being stuck in unsolvable situations at work and in her everyday life, where she felt constantly kept on a sort of tightrope without being able to find a direction. Concurrently, Sonia looked trapped in severe obsessional brooding, a sort of yes-or-no perpetual questioning of everything. She was continuously moaning and grumbling, saying "a man" was missing in her life, having occasional encounters with men she got sexually involved with, and immediately developing a sort of avidity which made them fly away after a while. She looked totally unable to think and elaborate on her state, as if nothing of her previous analytic work had survived, and seemed to have no tools to cope with her condition. She had totally destroyed her analytic work with my colleague, and she continuously destroyed all my work for her, session by session, too. This state of affairs actually lasted for more than two years. Sonia firmly refused to be medicated with antidepressants, saying she would manage the situation with her own resources, but in saying so she also sadistically triumphed over my supposed potency as an analyst. She definitely preferred to continue to suffer and remain blocked, and make me be blocked with her, in what I perceived and depicted in my mind as a king-size marital coffin, where we could possibly remain forever buried until the end of time. Here is a short example of this, taken from my notes after a session, not unlike countless similar sessions. This is the third session of the week, on Wednesday.

Sonia had angrily rejected one of my comments on Monday regarding the repetitiveness of the way she played out her conflicts with her mother, and how she and her mother seemed to be mutually involved in attacking and devaluing each other. Sonia had kept rigidly silent throughout the entire session on Tuesday, with no response to my comments regarding how she was apparently refusing to allow me to intervene in the close relationship between herself and her mother, as if I had to be kept out of that couple's business. During the Tuesday session, I had also commented on how she seemed to block the two of us in a way that was similar to what occurred with her mother. This produced no effect on her, and she remained silent throughout the session. Today, I notice that Sonia, on her way to the couch, has a slightly triumphant expression on her face. I also notice she is very elegant as usual, not a single detail is wrong in her outfit, the colours and accessories are perfectly coordinated, which is remarkable for a person who is pretending to be deeply depressed. Like the previous day, she remains silent for minutes. In the general and initially confused turmoil of my fantasies at that moment, I progressively distinguish a sense of rage, mixed with a sort of sadistic arousal, as if I wanted to physically assault the patient. Were I to act out my fantasies, I think, I would spit and hit her violently on her face, and kick her belly. This is mixed up with the idea that the full repertoire of my comments would not work, and that only my professional responsibility and the analytic setting are preventing me from assaulting the patient, but my capacity to help is nullified. Impotence is mixed with rage, and I feel imprisoned. The image of a rat running in a spinning box comes to my mind. I realise Sonia could potentially remain silent for days or weeks, maybe forever. I realise how people can become suicidal, as a chance to somehow be set free.

I say that this silence seems to be potentially endless, and that I wonder if she is telling me about something very cruel, cruel and imprisoning, with no way out.

She sighs. I have a sense of relief when I notice she starts talking, after a minute. I realise I feel like a child who hears his mother talking to him again after a punishing and endless silence. My relief is immediately frustrated when I hear Sonia speak with a lamenting and subtly provocative voice and say that she feels she is not able to think. When I try to investigate more, she says she cannot make up her mind with regard to recruiting a new accountant for her father's company. I take this as a total dismissal of any meaning concerning herself and the transference, and as an ostentatious way of keeping me at a distance. I explicitly comment on this, and she replies that in any case it wouldn't work. I notice she subtly smiles mockingly.

Session ends.

The countertransference here is quite descriptive of the level of murderous interaction with the mother as a primary object, and especially of the deep sense of frustration the child feels when expecting the mother to finally talk to her, but the moment she talks, she is concomitantly neglecting the child. Children cannot but love mothers, and cannot but feel bound. They cannot escape, whatever the quality of the bind is. This is an example of how hatred and frustration can be the glue that keeps people tightly bound to each other. No movement or development is allowed, immobility being the guarantee for possessing the object. The void of an incommensurable depressive state is avoided through sadistic control and paralysis. Finalistic thinking as a function that distinguishes and separates is not possible, and is substituted by imprisoning endless ruminations. In switching from a passive to an active position, anxiety is turned into arousal, because whips must always be held in hand.

After one and a half years of treatment, Sonia resolved to quit her freelance profession, which had to do with childcare. Since then, she has worked in the family business. Although the fact of quitting something could somehow sound like progress, the process of abandoning her profession was accompanied by torturous anger, and in the transference I was held responsible for not being able to heal her as I was expected to do, with the fantasy that I was keeping the privilege of an ideal profession for myself and expelling her from my perfect world. The concomitant fantasy of being excluded from taking care of children was also linked to the idea of not being able to get pregnant. Two years later, she met a man, almost eight years younger than her, who was jobless at that time and whom I suspected was planning some sort of parasitic relationship with this wealthy woman and her upper-class family, in his role of providing a good sexual/sensual function and the guarantee that he would never leave her. It is not necessary to retrace the anal symbolism to understand that money, the dung of the devil, binds people like nothing else. So the combination of obsessional control and financial parasitism potentially made this couple indestructible. Any attempt to investigate the nature of this relationship in analysis caused deep hostility in the patient and long silences that Sonia was able to keep for entire sessions over many weeks.

The quality of the transference during the first years was characterised by a tendency to provoke frustration and anger, as if she subtly tried to constantly increase the level of arousal in the session and be triumphant over my misunderstandings or failures. She smiled sarcastically when I made mistakes or did not understand, and looked quite determined to make me fail. Each session where she seemed to take in something of my contribution was immediately followed by a number of sessions in which she became hostile and distant again, with the proportion of one to ten. Silence was particularly torturing. Her triumphant attitude was apparently connected to the maternal element: the mother was described as extremely controlling and contemptuous, always criticising and devaluing everybody, always mocking people, including Sonia when she was a child. The father was also significantly involved in the transference. He was described as the one who had always devalued Sonia's wish to be a freelance professional, and particularly her interest in children, by saying this was stupid and useless because it did not make enough money. The state of the transference told me that there was something heavily true and real in what the patient said about her parents, especially when she talked about their contempt, their inability to understand, and their roughness in considering psychological care useless and stupid. What I actually thought was that they were emotionally illiterate.

Although historically true and even more true in the transference, what Sonia repeatedly said about her parents were rationalised and repetitive statements that did not push our work and understanding forward. I soon realised that we could have used these explanations virtually for years in a masturbatory and totally useless way. As I showed in the quoted session, I frequently felt stuck in a sort of paralysed and over-aroused sadomasochistic condition, which I have already defined as the *king-size coffin*, often tempted to attack the patient and talk to her with a harsh tone of voice, and easily captured by devaluing fantasies regarding her cruelty, her stupidity, and her previous therapist's foolishness. I suffered the inability to move and the extreme sense of frustration in feeling continuously driven back to the starting point and being called useless, as if no elaboration were possible, and no creation, no fecundity, allowed. Staying with this patient implied the constant difficulty of distinguishing between resilient containment and endless masochistic imprisonment.

A core memory

The ongoing interpretation of these transference–countertransference elements over time led to the emergence around the third year of analysis of a significant memory of an episode (or sequence of episodes) that occurred when the patient was thirteen or fourteen years old. Sonia remembered being with her parents during the summer holidays in a house near the sea. Quite frequently during the night, she heard her parents having sexual intercourse, particularly her mother panting and being aroused. Her parents did not seemingly care about being heard or seen, to the extent that they actually became abusive because of their crude insensitivity. Sonia remembered she was embarrassed on one level but very excited on the other, and started to masturbate. This situation seemed to occur frequently, and over time Sonia would pretend to be asleep and intentionally wait for her parents to have intercourse, so as to masturbate. In this way, she turned the passive experience of being abusively overwhelmed by the sensory experience of the parents' intercourse into feeling actively participating. The shift from passive to active is one of the well-known fundamental defence mechanisms in obsessive disorder. That made her enter a sort of dreamy-hallucinatory state, where she felt as if she were concretely taking part in the parental intercourse. Moreover, I found it remarkable that this experience had not been discussed during her previous psychotherapy and had not emerged until more than two years into her analysis with me. It was not that Sonia did not remember these episodes; rather, they had been made emotionally indifferent in her mind and gone unseen and unprocessed over many years of analytic work. The specific defence mechanisms of isolation and undoing were powerfully at work with regard to this particular mental experience, in the sense that the cohort of emotional-affective elements was kept separate from the representational components, and detached from the time sequence: thus memories were not repressed but made substantially irrelevant.

Now, however, memories were turned into being affectively meaningful as a result of the working through in the transference–countertransference. Memory apparently contains elements of incest/confusion, the dimension of imprisonment/immobility, and the aggressive fantasy of infertility, which were all massively present in the transference and countertransference, as I have described. With a striking resemblance to what Freud described in the case of the Wolf Man (1918b), this series of experiences occurred at puberty, and may be regarded as traumatic in the strict Freudian sense of the *après-coup*. In many respects, this experience became a core element in the subsequent analytic work, both in terms of understanding the past and as a point of reference in the comprehension of the here and now of the transference on many occasions. This is shown in the following example, which regards the interpretation of a dream that was in turn considered as a cornerstone in the following years of analysis, and was remembered and reconsidered on many occasions.

A core dream

In fact, the dream that comes onto the scene here represents a meaningful change in the situation of this patient. We are many years into treatment, and the general state of the transference is much more plastic and vivid, even though moments of block and rumination are still present every now and then. This session is the third of that week, on a Wednesday, a few days before the Christmas break.

> Sonia remains silent for a couple of minutes, which is not much compared to other sessions. I nevertheless feel quite on alert and slightly nervous as the Christmas break is approaching … meanwhile I think it is good that I see Sonia around 1 p.m. after a break following some morning patients, as I always feel one needs to be in a good state to cope with her.

Quite surprisingly, Sonia says she has a dream to tell.

I arrive on a beach. A lot of people are there. Fish jumping in the water. While talking to a person, a whale appears, it is black, as a killer whale is, but it is shaped like a normal whale. With its tail it makes a huge wave. Everybody escapes, but I stay there. The beach is like a high dune, I decide to climb to the top ... but how can I do it? I think ... maybe from here I can swim ... finally I find some stairs leading to a small restaurant at the top ... the waves end and nothing has happened ... I try to go out by walking through the restaurant ... and I wake up.

Sonia says she has dreamt these waves several times before [I do not remember that ... possibly she has not told me those dreams in the past]. This time, there was a killer whale provoking the wave, but the wave was not as big as it was in the other dreams.

[I realise I feel tempted to prematurely use a "dictionary of symbols" to interpret the whale, without considering the transference. And I get immediately suspicious of the risk of intellectualisation.]

"It seems that I can face it this time. I think I can face the killer whale this time ... I remember you saying once that there is a killer in me."

"It seems as if you can start thinking that the killer is not so overwhelmingly powerful and unavoidable ... maybe you have a different/higher perspective from which you can look at yourself, and there is also a restaurant/analysis which is not flooded and destroyed."

"Yes ... it can be like that .... Although I still find myself tearing everything to small pieces ... well ... not really everything ..."

"Maybe this is the reason why you had this dream, to remind yourself that you can avoid tearing everything to small pieces, also here between the two of us. The small restaurant may stand for myself and our work as a shelter and nourishment."

"Many people in the dream took shelter in the restaurant and had lunch. I thought I could stay there too. When I have my thoughts [meaning her ruminations], I think I cannot make it. I think I can come here and talk about that, but when I am actually here, I cannot do it ... it's all in bits and pieces ... but ..."

"But ...?"

"I think I can come and speak to you ... yes ... my idea is that I can come and tell you ..."

"This dream may sound reassuring to you, but it also claims some responsibilities. When you know you have resources, you are called upon to use them. There is not only the killer whale, there is also the ability to position yourself differently. In some way you have the freedom to choose which side you want to stay on, what you want to use in yourself, especially when I am away for the Christmas break—will you choose to kill everything or keep the restaurant/analysis as a resource?"

(Silence)

"I was thinking of the killer whale, and the wave ... I think ... that will happen again ... will it exist forever or not ...? Or will I be more capable of coping with it ...? Anyway, I am happy to see that I have some chances ... I need time to improve and learn to use my resources ... it is true that it is always me ..."

"Of course it is you ... and you could also ask yourself why you provoke the wave. Is it a way to replicate a sort of sexual intercourse?" "That" intercourse?

[getting clearly emotional] ... "yes, it might be ... the whale and the wave ... as it were ... as if I must expect the wave and pine ...".

"Expect and pine are quite different verbs ... meaningful."

"Maybe 'pine' because I think I am forced to show this side of myself. For me it is evident that I have to do it in *that* way ... it is natural ..."

"What do you mean by natural? ... is natural a way of saying unavoidable and therefore something you cannot but passively suffer, or could it be that there is something you are able to expect ... foresee ... explain ... and possibly prevent ...?"

The capacity to think is enormously developed here, compared to dozens of previous and of course also subsequent sessions. It seems that the dream work has constructed the possibility to differentiate between different levels of functioning and representation, and especially the positioning of ego functions as capable of *choosing*. Considering that choosing is precisely opposite to the never-choose immobility of obsessional functioning, nothing could be more relevant for a patient like this.

Among my associations to this dream that came up in the following sessions, I remember having thought of the beautiful scene of Jane Campion's film *The Piano* (1993) where the *mute* protagonist is sinking into the sea with the rope that tightens her piano to her ankle. In the silence of the sea, just moments before almost drowning, her voice says that surprisingly *her will has chosen life* and she manages to loosen the rope and re-emerge. Many times I communicated this association to Sonia, always stressing that the dream says *she* can choose life. I preferred—as I do in the quoted session—to use the personal pronoun *you* rather than *your will* to better involve her sense of being in charge, and in some way also the ethical responsibility to determine her destiny through her *freedom to choose*. What is remarkable in the dream is the fact that the dreamer could choose to be killed by the whale or to try and escape. Sonia has two options here, she is free, and choosing one option implies *separating from* the second option. In some way, she has found a solution to the threat of depression, and to the need for the immobility of obsession as a failed remedy for the total loss of the object. She is out of the coffin.

Further developments

Coffins are nevertheless always seductive, the propaganda of a psychic dimension where one is never threatened by expulsion being quite intriguing. We may idealise wombs and our pre-natal paradise, but we all know that sooner or later, we have to leave it, and we actually had to. Coffins instead are the only home where we stay eternally, the only object that never betrays or abandons us. Making coffins real when we are still alive is more than a temptation. Sonia dreams of something in this area, but again she finds solutions.

> I'm on a train with my husband. We have to get off at a station but the car where we are is standing still in a tunnel. How do I get off? My partner is sleeping, and other people get off the train. I try a different door but it is barred.

The train starts moving backwards. I wake my partner up, and I think we will manage to get off at another station. We then find ourselves in a patisserie. Lots of cakes all around.

The sleeping partner stands for a part of herself that sleeps when faced with separations, and it traces back to the position I had been sentenced to remain in in the transference for many years of the analysis. The train stuck in the tunnel resembles the immobility of the masturbatory dangling of her obsessions, but once again Sonia *decides* that she has to find solutions, and she is determined to get off. It is better to go back rather than remain entrapped, and she awakes the deadly sleeping partner in herself. At this point, I have become a patisserie which is worth a visit.

Months later, Sonia manages to get pregnant, just in time to overcome the limitations of her biological clock. She copes with the average anxieties of every pregnant mother, regarding her ability to carry her pregnancy through or regarding the health of her baby. Nothing out of the ordinary, in this respect. She is quite aware that she may find it difficult to separate from her child, and struggles with the fantasy of not being able to consider her child as a separate person. The only remarkable moment during the pregnancy in terms of the recurring obsessional position regards the choice of the *name* to be given to the child. Nothing is more separating than giving a name, the name being the essence of one's separate identity. Sonia remains blocked for weeks, she has several names in her mind but she cannot come to a decision, nor can she accept her husband's proposals. The situation is eventually unblocked when I remind her that *she* had been given a name by our ten years of work together, so she might allow her daughter to have hers. And the given name is *Allegra*—cheerfulness now has some right to exist.

CHAPTER TWELVE

Fabio: the right to be furious— Imprisonment 2

Introduction

Fabio was in his early thirties when he consulted me, having decided to face his problems with the help of psychoanalysis after being in treatment with a psychiatrist for almost ten years throughout his twenties. Severe and increasingly intrusive obsessive symptoms—at first, slightly interspersed with asymptomatic depressive mood—had become apparent almost one and a half years after a dramatic motorbike accident he had at the age of eighteen, as a consequence of which Fabio suffered the amputation of his lower left leg. Fabio has a prosthesis, which was implemented one year after the accident and currently has a good degree of motor autonomy: he can drive and walk, he has a special prosthesis for swimming, he can go dancing and carry out most everyday activities in much the same way as a non-disabled person.

Over the decade after the accident, he had been medicated with antidepressants, and had undergone a few months of cognitive-behaviour therapy, having been diagnosed as obsessive–compulsive. The outcome of these treatments was considered poor by the patient, although on a reality level his life quality was acceptable and symptoms sufficiently controlled. I have been seeing him five times a week for a number of years, and he was able to stop his medication after one and a half years into treatment.

As far as I could reconstruct, at the onset of symptoms in his early twenties, Fabio had likely shown one main feature of OCD: the sudden uncontrollable appearance of ego-dystonic thoughts of hitting, wounding, assaulting, or killing his girlfriend, or any woman he happened to be emotionally involved with, especially when the woman somehow resembled his younger sister; or at times of hurting children, particularly, but not exclusively, girls. These thoughts were accompanied by a great amount of anxiety and guilt, in the shape of ruminative self-accusation thoughts and the fear of acting out his murderous fantasies by losing control over them, and they were defended against through essentially phobic mechanisms like distancing, detachment, and avoidance.

As for what I could understand of the decade before I met Fabio, ruminations had never been massive, possibly due to continuous medication over the years, and at least in some areas of life, had never prevented Fabio from mentally operating on reality in a finalised and proper way. Fabio in fact managed to get his Masters degree, he was able to learn foreign languages, read and study books, and function properly at work. On the other hand, Fabio had built his identity as a handicapped person, in terms of indulging in hidden thoughts of self-denigration and unsolvable rage for not being like all the other guys of his age; at the same time, however, as a reaction formation, he would pretend to deny any difference between himself and other people or any specific difficulty linked to his handicap. That a girl could not feel sexually attracted to him because of his handicap was totally denied.

Uncontrollable obsessions mainly regarded the world of relations and affects. He felt he could kill women whom he was physically and emotionally involved with. At times, he experienced women as if they were lovely little girls who reminded him of his sister, but in that case he could not have any erotic investment: his incestuous fantasies to live with his sister, and his extreme jealousy when she met boyfriends, came to the fore and had to be kept under control with various compulsive manoeuvres. He happened to suddenly wish to hurt and kill these desexualised women, and consequently had to keep a distance. However, distance was never clearly and truly separating. He continued to keep women in the loop: the sexualised ones, by seeing them for occasional sex, with no investment on his behalf but with deep jealousy and rage when they revengefully treated him in the same manner; and the sister-like ones, by sadistically deceiving and substantially humiliating them, and never letting them go free and live without him. He basically treated women as faecal objects, that he retained and released with a sort of endless masturbatory movement—metaphorically speaking—through an omnipotent mental sphincter.

Rationalisation defensively intervened by overestimating his family's and friends' expectations of social normality, both in terms of being sexually potent and of getting married—as he fantasised—like all men of his age in the world. His attitude towards women was defensively turned into its opposite by pretending to show kindness and respect, to the limits of being passive and submissive, and—in a sort of self-punishment—by remaining stuck to all situations in which women took revenge on him and treated him as a devalued object. He was particularly skilled in unconsciously creating situations in which male friends were more successful with women, and he could consequently feel like a perpetual loser and humiliated by everybody. Furious rage, rivalry, and jealousy towards men was interspersed with self-denigration and accusations towards the entire world, which was evil, tantalising, and unreachable. The circle of these thoughts was presented as apparently unsolvable, with strict pseudo-logical arguments, each supporting the immobility of the other.

Reconstruction of personality traits and meaningful elements before the amputation

Fabio's younger sister was born when he was just fifteen months old. As far as we could understand, the birth of this little sister was likely experienced as a deep wound, not simply for his being dethroned too early from his idealised position of the "one and only child", but also because it raised deep aggressive and clearly murderous feelings. In fact, the first appearance of murderous obsessive thoughts dates back to Fabio's early childhood, when Fabio was overtly captured by sudden thoughts of throwing his sister out of the window or drowning her in the sea, or killing her with a knife. Such thoughts, which he could not talk to his parents or anybody else about, were immediately compensated and tentatively controlled by overprotective attitudes towards the sister, whom Fabio took care of as if she were a fragile doll that was totally dependent on him for her safety and survival.

Seemingly, such an omnipotent position was potentiated by the family's pedagogic attitude, which encouraged Fabio to behave and take care of his little sister without allowing any open manifestation of aggressiveness, and most likely overloading him with unsuitable responsibilities. The patient could realise, in the course of his analysis, that the parents' expectations to behave and be responsible for the sister's safety were not as heavy as he had fantasised and did not exceed the demands of an average family. Overt incestuous fantasises progressively came to the fore, in terms of pervasive sensuousness and fantasies of fusion with his sister, who apparently was the substitute for an idealised mother he wished to possess exclusively. Remarkably, the tone of his voice and the prosody of his speech when he reported to me his sensuous feelings and sensations regarding his sister conveyed a subtle but strong sense of asserting an unquestionable right, in the guise of a king talking about his kingdom. As I mentioned, when Fabio gets involved with women who in some way remind him of his sister—basically, if they are healthily vital and positive, as she apparently is, but also delicate and possibly fragile—he gets more frequently captured by his obsessive-like murderous thoughts, intermingled with a sense of pseudo-tenderness which defensively causes his total loss of sexual desire.

The relevance of the sister/parent problem has also been made clear and consistent through the vicissitudes of the transference. Fabio usually behaves and pretends to look very calm and submissive, I should say icy on many occasions, by using conventional jargon and pseudo-psychological terms and explanations, or by being compliant with what he thinks I am expecting from him. While doing so, I perceive him as very aggressive in a subtle way. Typically, through projective identification, he is able to make me feel loaded with fury while he is speaking with the iciest calmness, regardless of what he is talking about. Second, he commonly cuts and tears what I say to pieces and then turns its meaning upside down—basically turning it into some persecution I am supposed to perpetrate or into some supposed pedagogic prescription. This state of the transference has to do, on the one hand, with the "pedagogic parents" (in terms of the sadistic over-demanding ego-ideal), with the correlate of murderous rage evacuated into me via projective identification, and on the other hand, with the fantasy of the parents blamed and expressly considered as guilty for giving birth to his sister.

The latter element has taken on a peculiar shape in the internal world of this patient, with a quasi-delusional concreteness. Fabio was dogmatically convinced that, by giving birth to his sister, his parents had actually abandoned him and committed a true crime against him. In his view, this is true guilt, it is an actual crime, and not at all a fantasy or a simple subjective experience. Consequently, he assumes to have the right to be furious and revengeful. Being legitimated through the analytic relationship to feel angry in some way perversely reinforced his delusional tendency to consider that, as a victim of true abuse, he was actually legitimated in his being cruel to other people, including myself. Given his ability to be icy and emotionally frozen, as well as his ability to use projective identification to evacuate heat, passion, and rage into the object and attack them once located there, his rage would at times resemble the cold determination of certain criminal minds. Defrosting him was not an easy task and raised persecution, often potentiating expulsive phenomena.

During a certain period of our work, Fabio thought I had viciously planned to make him be addictively dependent on me, in a sort of imprisonment. To him, I had cruelly shown how bad, envious, and evil he was; I had shown him how he used women for his perverse purposes, and in so doing I had forced him not to get involved with women and with people in general, and so I had caused him to be more isolated and lonely. I was a kind of sadistic jailer. He declared he could not go away and get rid of me at that point, somehow challenging me to solve the problems I had caused, which, needless to say, was considered impossible. Consequently, he also felt justified in his being phobic and angry because of me. In general, phobic elements (some social phobia, or phobia of travelling alone, or in general his common choice to eschew emotionally loaded relationships) were in the service of keeping a sort of retreat from which he could continue to blame and envy other people, feeling like a victim justified in being angry and poisonous.

The role of amputation

In general, it is not difficult to consider how devastating a trauma like the one Fabio suffered can be for a teenager, who is reaching the age of being more independent from his parents and sexually more mature.

There was certainly a healthily hypo-manic reaction to the event, on a certain level, by developing a sense of self-sufficiency and potency. On another level, amputation reinforced the depressive elements in Fabio's mind, and made rage omnipotently felt as non-processable. Concreteness, impossibility of recovery, and persecution became paramount. Concrete castration made symbolic castration more difficult, including the awareness of having limits, of not being the only child, and not being able to control feelings and people omnipotently. This element worked synergistically with phobia, both preventing full access to castration and to healthy ambivalence. The lost leg was the representative of an irremediable lost primary object, which he tried to keep alive and controlled by developing obsessional symptoms shortly after the amputation when the illusory function of his transitory manic reaction lost its effects.

Pain

Projective identification has always been a privileged means of communication for Fabio. This has been the case regarding rage and persecution, but it is also the case when the element at play is pain. In the countertransference, a big effort has always been to live hand in hand with frustration, rage, icy violence, and distortion of meaning. That was like a sky blackened with thick clouds. The appearance of bare pain every now and then, with all its warmth, was something I welcomed, like the sun through the clouds, but it was no less difficult to cope with, for its overwhelming intensity. This made me understand that the level of psychic pain in this young man was huge, and made comprehensible to my mind why he had to freeze and operate in an obsessional way in order to survive. As I will show in the following clinical vignettes, the main risk with this patient was to increase persecution and detachment through a repertoire of distancing interpretations as well as through the enacted musicality of a sadistically sharpened voice. No less difficult was the work of coping with pain, and of promoting the depressive position together with it. My general style of working always implies naming and reinforcing the container as much as possible, in terms of underlining the expectation that the object is able to welcome, stand, understand, give meaning to, and so forth. This is also my way of defining the archetype as the potential each individual has to name and give meaning to emotional experience within the relationship with the object. Naming the expectation of a container for rage, hatred, and persecution is hard, but relatively easy. Naming the expectation of a container for supposedly unbearable pain—being more strictly connected to love and loss—is much harder, often at the limits of an analyst's personal capacity. Flying back to persecution sounds reassuring in some way, for both parties.

Given that mere obsessional functioning decreased over the years, I wish to attempt to show my work with the patient's rage, provocations, and psychic pain. The vignettes quoted below regard a well-developed stage of the analysis, despite the fact that the patient still seems rigid and defensive. Having at my disposal a huge amount of material, I have chosen to consider the meaningful presence of the father as an object of love and hatred, with patent reverberations on the transference. The meaningfulness of the father as a lost—or nostalgically longed for—object seems to be at the core of this patient's internal pain. Without overlooking the importance of the mother, it seems that the father either primarily or by displacement plays a fundamental role in the movement from the dimension of an irremediably lost object (depression), through to a tentatively controlled object (obsession), and on to the healthy and painful apperception of the mourned object.

On a Monday

Fabio: [Speaking in a rather confused way] Last time I was talking about my rage towards my parents .... You told me that I am not able to understand this issue ... that I consider this story as a "tale" (*una favola*) and not as something real ... [meaning "something not to be taken seriously"]: It is not true ... I do not consider that as a "*favola*" ... I just find it hard to work on that ....

[In the countertransference, I feel immediately challenged, I am sure I did not say anything that could sound that way ... but I am also puzzled by the subtle confusion ... I think I might risk misunderstanding him ... who is misunderstanding? who is being misunderstood?] I ask Fabio to tell me what he means when he says that I told him he does not understand or that he does not take this issue seriously ... and what exactly it is that is hard ...

Fabio: [now speaking a little more clearly, to my relief] When facing this issue of my rage towards my parents, I never know what to say ... I can't understand how to cope with that ... It seems to me that the *simple* [stressing this word] fact of having raised the issue ... has helped me to consider more realistically that my mother is a loving and caring mother, attached to her children [I am particularly struck by his using the plural, I could swear it is the first time] ... maybe not always capable of understanding my feelings but ... a caring mother who is afraid of giving more to one child than to the other ... and tries to compensate if she feels she has given more to one of the two ...

Me: What you say, the issue of your rage ... has not been easy at all along your analysis over the years ... it has not been a *favola* at all ... nothing was simple ... this has been a *fil rouge* over the years, it was something you had mentioned right from the beginning and what you say today is the result of hard work ...

[I pause ... and he speaks ... in what I perceive as a good rhythmical sequence]

Fabio: Yes, but at the beginning I did not fully recognise that I was angry ... and how and why I was angry.

[I clearly have the impression in my countertransference that Fabio has spoken in a highly integrated way, being able at this moment to acknowledge the differences his subjective emotional perception has undergone over time, as well as to acknowledge "the space for three": mother and two children, and not the usual paradigm "mother-with-sister/Fabio-rejected"]

Me: I think you are recognising the difference between your feelings when you were a child ... when you felt rejected by a mother you called guilty for having made a little sister with daddy ... a real crime against you .... and the reality of a caring mother who could take care of two children, not just one. There was enough mother for two. I would say this difference is quite important ... and has been very hard for you to acknowledge ...

Long silence.

Me: Do you not think so?

Fabio: Yes, I think it is important .... At least I realise that thinking this way makes me feel better ... it's strange ... I don't feel angry if I think this way.

Me: Well ... it is quite relevant that you do not feel angry now ... I think that this is linked to it being possible to recognise the difference between facts and feelings. It is a fact that you lost a leg; it was a feeling—when you were a small child—that you were abandoned. Feelings may have huge impacts on our lives, as they have on yours, but, as you may see, they can be changed. That is what we have done here, it would seem. I will never be able to make your leg grow back, but your feelings have changed.

Fabio: [With a slight polemical tone, as if wanting to accuse me] But you tell me that there is still something in myself that works against the good, and that I am still angry with my parents and don't accept my sister ... and this has to do with my difficulties with women ... you tell me I haven't changed ...

Me: Am I saying this right now?

Fabio: [embarrassed] Well ... maybe ... not really.

Me: It is quite meaningful that it seems so difficult to fully take in what I am saying now, which regards the appreciation of what you have done with me over the years ... instead you seem to underline something supposedly negative that I am supposed to have said ... on many occasions, I have spoken of what you quote, and apparently it worked, considering that your point of view of yourself has changed so much ... But it seems that misunderstanding is always lurking ...

[What I really feel at this precise moment in the countertransference is that I cannot be off guard for a single second with this man ... it is always like being at war ... or guerrilla warfare ... and I consider how affective misunderstanding must have been a primary pattern between him as a baby and his mother.]

Fabio: I have to admit that analysis has made me see things from different perspectives ... it is true that since the beginning of the analysis I have said I felt angry with my parents and felt rejected by them, but I could not initially see the extension and implications of my anger ... which were much bigger than I thought ... and I couldn't see the connections with the birth of my sister ... and with my problems with women ... [pause] ... ah ... when I recently visited my family I noticed how nice and loving my parents are with my little nephew ... I wondered if they had changed over these forty years ... if that's how they were with me and my sister ... I don't think my mother has changed ... I imagine she was the same with us forty years ago ... not my father maybe ... I think he has recently become more capable of affection and closeness ... I remember him always being so distant ... he was always away on business, and when at home he was always in his room ... or in the country house ...

(time is up)

Me: This is something which you may feel like speaking about again ...

[Fabio's last words activate a sense of pain in the countertransference ... a kind of nostalgic mood ... about someone/something longed for and deeply missed.]

Session ends.

On this occasion, and although interspersed with control and provocation, the patient shows a good capacity to acknowledge the legitimacy of the parental intercourse and to overcome the persecutory dimension linked to the primal scene. In relation to this, he shows he is able to partly recognise a space for plural relationships, basically a mother with a father, a mother with each child and with the two of them. The dual dimension of idealistically being-at-one-with as opposed to being-against-an-enemy in a persecutory way is replaced here by the democracy of complex relationships and feelings. This process seems to imply that the mother as a primary object is represented here as a fairly good object, *present* in her capacity to attune to children. Contrary to this, the father is represented as *absent*, if not overtly rejecting. The issue of the lost object, with all its implications, seems to revolve around the father image. And psychic pain seems to emerge with great intensity.

In fact, a week later:

[Quite rigid, with a flat tone of voice .... hesitant ... immediately giving me the impression that he does not feel like being here or talking to me ... using a language that would be more suitable for a business meeting, and also slightly implying that I was demanding something, expecting him to talk again about his father ...]

"At the moment I don't think I have much more to add to what I said yesterday regarding my father (he had been particularly in touch with the issue the day before ... with memories of his father emotionally detached and irritated by his supposedly annoying presence) ... if something comes to my mind in the future, I'll tell you ..."

"You seem to suggest that it is me who wants you to talk about your father ... as if I were a father you had to please ..."

"No ... it has been the issue of these last sessions ....Yesterday I did not add anything meaningful ... so for now, I'm going to drop it ...".

[I am quite struck by his saying that he had nothing meaningful to say yesterday ... I myself having the exact opposite impression ... it evidently sounds like a denial ... which is mixed in with my impression that he does not feel like being here ... but I decide to leave this element pending, and see what further elements come up, so for the time being I do not comment.]

"Other than that, I was thinking of my relationship with some people ... in a group ... some Neapolitans ... occasionally if they organise something I happen to participate [his tone is slightly patronising, underlining his contemptuous view of them as Neapolitans ... kind of "His Majesty graciously sharing his time with the commoners ... and what commoners!"]. So two weeks ago, we went to the Blue Note [a very well-known club in town, for live jazz/blues music, with a restaurant, which is considered a place for sophisticated people, and I notice he takes it for granted that I know the place] ... a woman of my age, who was very friendly towards me... I am not interested in her at all .... Because she is a moaner and depressive.... She asked me if I wanted to take her out some evening for dinner and to the cinema afterwards .... Just the two of us ... I don't know why I accepted ... I was kind, I smiled ... I was gentle .... And she approached me with some messages as if asking for a friendship that I don't want ... my feelings are negative ... I don't like her ... why did I allow myself to get stuck in that ... maybe not to feel lonely ... but I was kind because I wanted to respect her and so kept a distance ... the same thing happened with a friend ... we went out for a beer ... just to go out but my feelings were cold ..."

"I realise you touch on the issue of using people and respect ... this is important of course, but also it seems to be in an area which is very familiar between us ... a repertoire ... But I cannot but notice that quite clearly today you don't feel like being here ... that you are here because you want to be kind, and you want to be kind and compliant, but you are keeping me at a safe distance ... as if now you have, as it were, become the father you were talking about yesterday ... but it seems important to me that you do not pretend we are here together to truly talk, when in fact we are actually distant ..."

[He suddenly turns emotional ... and gets quite confused ...]

"I don't know if what I say about my father is a fantasy. I have true feelings towards some friends ... but if he doesn't want me under his feet ... Is he frustrated ...? ... I also happen to feel like having nobody around ... but this does not mean that I don't have feelings ..." [with quite a heartfelt voice]

"Of course you want me to recognise that you are capable of having feelings for people and for me as well. Your voice now is making that very clear ... but I was trying to understand your being distant earlier, your pretending to talk politely while being cold ... I did not mean that was an absence of feelings; rather I meant that feelings were hidden and put somewhere ... and I noticed your behaviour seemed to be exactly as you describe your father's behaviour to be ... meaningful ... don't you think?"

"All right" ("Va bene" with resigned "patience"): "... I am sadistic in distancing ..." [his voice is now lamenting/passive, while using a repertoire of interpretations]

"I don't understand ....That "va bene" sounds like ... the child is ready to be scolded and spanked ..."

[Suddenly insightful]:"Being distant and cold allows me to keep things under control, with the idea that I am the one who decides the when and how ... and I know I am able to make the other person feel my coldness and my distance ... I know the ways to make other people realise I'm being cold and suffer my coldness and distance ..."

"If we imagine you as a child with your father, and your feeling his distancing you, or even his 'repulsion', as you said yesterday ... I can well imagine you have learned to hold the whip hand, as we have seen so many times ... the side effect being your sense of loneliness ... if you are the flogger, links are cut ... but I also wonder why yesterday you could 'speak' about this, whereas today for most of the session all this has become so 'enacted' again as it has on so many occasions ... could it be that next week you are 'really' going to miss your Thursday session which I have cancelled, so I am again 'the father who prefers doing something else rather than staying with such an annoying child' ... and in response to that you hold the whip hand, you have the upper hand ...?"

[To my surprise] "Yes ... I realise that the simple thought of your private business automatically activates my reaction of being icy and distant."

"And quite contemptuous ... I agree you are totally able to make the other person sense your distance, coldness, and I would add, contempt, which is what you felt coming from your father as a child and which hurt you so much ... you have shown me that ability innumerable times over these years ... It is important to underline that this kind of becoming identical to your father, holding the whip hand ... may give you the illusion of power; but it makes you feel lonely ... more and more lonely ... and scared, as you were before, that people, including myself, may think that you are a monster, a person with no feelings at all, unable to love ... I am sure that is not your intention ...

He remains silent for the three remaining minutes of the session. Silence is intense. I notice the intensity of his breath.

Session ends.

This session, it seems to me, speaks for itself: we see the invitation in the countertransference into retaliatory irritation at the garbling of the previous session and by the implicit contempt, the attempt to cast me into the persecuting superego; the attempt to evacuate the feared inferiority of the Neapolitan "hicks", in fact the "hick" analyst, and to distance me with coldness in a subtle way, or the girl more crudely. By confronting him, I allowed the patient to become emotionally real, so that he could then start to think about his actual relationship with his father. There is then a reprise of the attempt to cast me into the superego father, which allows me to show him how he identifies with his father's perceived distancing (*"holding the whip hand"*) and then make the crucial link to the real transference issue, that is, Fabio's sense of hurt rejection at the prospect of the forthcoming cancelled session, crucially consistent with his uncontained sense of vulnerability.

I think this can be an example of how I have to tactfully confront a patient who is prickly and paranoid on account of his vulnerability; but as well as tactfully, also in a way that circumvents his capacity for intellectualisation and distortion, which requires timing and a gradual build-up to the transference interpretations. All of this means that I need to negotiate and assess the patient's capacity to attune with me, this being a capacity that varies from session to session, I would even say moment by moment.

Occasionally, over the years, Fabio has shown me directly or indirectly that his life improves, that he is more capable of coping with his and other people's limitations more realistically, that he loves being with people, and that he is at least "interested" in solving his affective problems with women. As if I were a longed-for father, he nourishes my will to take care of him, which he does not take for granted, as he appeared to do in a distorted way when I was supposed to be his sadistic jailer. So he gratifies me at times by saying that our work partially works. Not too much of course, because gratitude is dangerous—just enough to keep things going.

REFERENCES

Abraham, K. (1924). A short study of the development of the libido viewed in the light of mental disorders. In: *Selected Papers of Karl Abraham* (pp. 419–501). London: Karnac, 1988.

Abramowitz, J. (2006). The psychological treatment of obsessive–compulsive disorder. *The Canadian Journal of Psychiatry, 51*: 407–416.

Abramowitz, J., Taylor, S., & McKay, D. (2009). Obsessive–compulsive disorder. *The Lancet, 374*: 491–499.

Abramowitz, J., Taylor, S., & McKay, D. (2011). Exposure-based treatment for obsessive–compulsive disorder. In: G. Steketee (Ed.), *The Oxford Handbook of Obsessive Compulsive and Spectrum Disorders* (pp. 322–344). New York: Oxford University Press.

American Psychiatric Association (2013). *Diagnostic and Statistical Manual of Mental Disorders*. Fifth Edition. Washington, DC: American Psychiatric Publishing.

Anal Stench (2003). *Stench Like Six Demons*. Poland: Metal Mind Productions.

Beckett, S. (1949). *Waiting for Godot: A Tragicomedy in Two Acts*. New York: Grove Press, 2010.

Bion, W. R. (1962). *Learning from Experience*. London: Karnac, 1984.

Bion, W. R. (1965). *Transformations*. London: Karnac, 1984.

Bollas, C. (1992). *Being a Character: Psychoanalysis and Self Experience*. Hove: Routledge, 2006.

Cambray, J. (2006). Towards the feeling of emergence. *The Journal of Analytical Psychology, 51*: 1–20.

Cambray, J. (2009). *Synchronicity: Nature and Psyche in an Interconnected Universe.* College Station, TX: A & M University Press.

Cambray, J. (2011). Moments of complexity and enigmatic action: a Jungian view of the therapeutic field. *The Journal of Analytical Psychology, 56*: 296–309.

Campion, J. (1993). *The Piano.*

De Sade, M. (1785). *The 120 Days of Sodom.* London: Penguin, 2016.

Dougherty, D., Rauch, S., & Greenberg, B. (2010). Pathophysiology of obsessive–compulsive disorders. In: D. J. Stein, E. Hollander, & B. O. Rothbaum (Eds.), *Textbook of Anxiety Disorders* (2nd edn., pp. 287–309). Washington, DC: American Psychiatric Publishing.

Esman, A. (2001). Obsessive–compulsive disorder: current views. *Psychoanalytic Enquiry, 21*: 145–156.

Fordham, M. (1985). *Explorations into the Self.* London: Karnac, 2002.

Franklin, M., Abramowitz, J., Foa, E., Kozak, M., & Levitt, J. (2000). Effectiveness of exposure and ritual prevention for obsessive–compulsive disorder: randomized compared with nonrandomized samples. *Journal of Consulting and Clinical Psychology, 68*: 594–602.

Freud, S. (1894a). The neuro-psychoses of defence. *S.E., 3*: 43–61. London: Hogarth.

Freud, S. (1895/1950a). Project for a scientific psychology. *S.E., 1*: 283–397. London: Hogarth.

Freud, S. (1900a). *The Interpretation of Dreams. S.E., 4–5.* London: Hogarth.

Freud, S. (1905d). *Three Essays on the Theory of Sexuality. S.E., 7*: 125–245. London: Hogarth.

Freud, S. (1906a). My views on the part played by sexuality in the aetiology of the neuroses. *S.E., 7*: 269–280. London: Hogarth.

Freud, S. (1908b). Character and anal erotism. *S.E., 9*: 169–175. London: Hogarth.

Freud, S. (1909b). Analysis of a phobia of a five-year-old boy. *S.E., 10*: 1–150. London: Hogarth.

Freud, S. (1909d). Notes upon a case of obsessional neurosis. *S.E., 10*: 153–249. London: Hogarth.

Freud, S. (1911c). Psycho-analytic notes on an autobiographical account of a case of paranoia. *S.E., 12*: 1–84. London: Hogarth.

Freud, S. (1913i). The disposition to obsessional neurosis. *S.E., 12*: 311–326. London: Hogarth.

Freud, S. (1914c). On narcissism: an introduction. *S.E., 14*: 67–104. London: Hogarth.

Freud, S. (1915e). The unconscious. *S.E., 14*: 159–216. London: Hogarth.

Freud, S. (1917d). A metapsychological supplement to the theory of dreams. *S.E., 14*: 217–236. London: Hogarth.

Freud, S. (1918b). From the history of an infantile neurosis. *S.E., 17*: 1–122. London: Hogarth.

Freud, S. (1919h). The "uncanny". *S.E., 17*: 217–252. London: Hogarth.

Freud, S. (1920g). *Beyond the Pleasure Principle. S.E., 18*: 7–64. London: Hogarth.

Freud, S. (1923c). The infantile genital organisation: an interpolation into the theory of sexuality. *S.E., 19*: 141–148. London: Hogarth.

Freud, S. (1926d). *Inhibitions, Symptoms and Anxiety. S.E., 20*: 77–174. London: Hogarth.

Gabbard, G. (1994). *Psychodynamic Psychiatry in Clinical Practice* (2nd edn.). Washington, DC: American Psychiatric Press.

Gabbard, G. (2001). Psychoanalytically informed approaches to the treatment of obsessive–compulsive disorder. *Psychoanalytic Inquiry, 21*: 208–221.

Goodman, W., Price, L., Rasmussen, S., Mazure, C., Delgado, P., Heninger, G., & Charney, D. (1989). The Yale–Brown obsessive–compulsive 87 scale: validity. *Archives of General Psychiatry, 46*: 1012–1016.

Goodwyn, E. (2010). Approaching archetypes: reconsidering innateness. *The Journal of Analytical Psychology, 55*: 502–521.

Hales, R., Yudofsky, S., & Weiss Roberts, L. (Eds.) (2014). *The American Psychiatric Publishing Textbook of Psychiatry* (6th edn.) Washington, DC: American Psychiatric Publishing.

Hettema, J., Neale, M., & Kendler, K. (2001). A review and meta-analysis of the genetic epidemiology of anxiety disorders. *American Journal of Psychiatry, 158*: 1568–1578.

Heyman, I., Mataix-Cols, D., & Fineberg, N. (2006). Obsessive–compulsive disorder. *British Medical Journal, 333*: 424.

Hogenson, G. (2009). Archetypes as action patterns. *The Journal of Analytical Psychology, 54*: 325–338.

Jung, C. G. (1912). *Psychology and Alchemy. C.W. 12*. London: Routledge and Kegan Paul.

Jung, C. G. (1938). *Psychology and Religion. C.W. 11*. London: Routledge and Kegan Paul.

Jung, C. G. (1959). *The Archetypes and the Collective Unconscious. C.W. 9/1*. London: Routledge and Kegan Paul.

Kaës, R. (2007). *Linking, Alliances, and Shared Space: Groups and the Psychoanalyst*. London: IPA Publications.

Klein, M. (1963). On the sense of loneliness. In: *Envy and Gratitude and Other Works 1946–1963*. London: Karnac, 1993.

Knox, J. (2003). *Archetype, Attachment, Analysis: Jungian Psychology and the Emergent Mind*. London and New York: Brunner-Routledge.

Knox, J. (2009). Mirror neurons and embodied simulation in the development of archetypes and self-agency. *The Journal of Analytical Psychology, 54*: 307–324.

Knox, J., Merchant, J., & Hogenson, G. (2010). Responses to Erik Goodwyn's "Approaching archetypes: reconsidering innateness". *The Journal of Analytical Psychology, 55*: 522–549.

Meltzer, D., Bremner, J., Hoxter, S., Weddell, D., & Wittenberg, I. (1975). *Explorations in Autism*. London: Karnac, 2008.

Murray, C. & Lopez, A. (1996). *The Global Burden of Disease*. Boston: Harvard University Press.

National Institute for Health and Care Excellence (NICE) (2005). Obsessive–compulsive disorder: core interventions in the treatment of obsessive–compulsive disorder and body dysmorphic disorder. *National Clinical Practice Guideline Number 31*. The British Psychological Society and the Royal College of Psychiatrists.

National Institute for Health and Care Excellence (NICE) (2013). Obsessive–compulsive disorder. *Evidence Update 47*. The British Psychological Society and the Royal College of Psychiatrists.

Ogden, T. (2003). On not being able to dream. *The International Journal of Psychoanalysis, 84* (March, Part 1): 17–30.

Pasolini, P. (1975). *Salò, or The 120 Days of Sodom*. British Film Institute: Retrieved 4 April 2016.

Poincaré, H. (1908). *Science and Method*. New York: Cosimo, 2010.

Sinigaglia, C., & Sparaci, L. (2010). Emotions in action through the looking glass. *The Journal of Analytical Psychology, 55*: 3–29.

Urban, E. (2005). Fordham, Jung and the self: a re-examination of Fordham's contribution to Jung's conceptualization of the self. *The Journal of Analytical Psychology, 50*: 571–594.

Vajda, L. (1954). *Marcelino pan y vino (Miracle of Marcelino)*.

Van Grootheest, D., Cath, D., Beekman, A., & Boosma, D. (2005). Twin studies on obsessive–compulsive disorder: a review. *Twin Research and Human Genetics, 8*: 450–458.

Veale, D., & Roberts, A. (2014). Obsessive–compulsive disorder. *British Medical Journal, 348*: g2183.

Vezzoli, C. (2009). Introduction to papers from the conference on "Neuroscience and analytical psychology: archetypes, intentionality, actions and symbols". *The Journal of Analytical Psychology, 54*: 303–306.

Wilkinson, M. (2006). *Coming into Mind: The Mind–Brain Relationship— A Jungian Clinical Perspective*. London: Routledge.

INDEX

229